An Englishman in the Seminole War

A Memoir Based Upon the Letters of John Bemrose

Randal J. Agostini

An Englishman in the Seminole War
A Memoir Based Upon the Letters of John Bemrose

ISBN: 978-1-949810-09-7

The Florida Historical Society Press
435 Brevard Avenue
Cocoa, FL 32922
http://myfloridahistory.org/fhspress

Cover image: Detail from the painting "...DO YOUR BEST!"
The last hour of Dade's Battle, December 28, 1835
by Jackson Walker

Dedicated to the
World-Wide Progeny
of John Bemrose

Table of Contents

Foreword

Between November 1863 and May 1866, John Bemrose wrote a series of sixty letters to his eldest son, Weightman. These letters were then transcribed for all his children, who included William Scofield Bemrose, my great-grandfather. The Scofield letters were found by my great-aunt Beatrice under William's bed in his London apartment during a clean-up after her parents departed for retirement in Wales. They then passed into the hands of George Lee, my grandfather and husband of Beatrice's younger sister, Dorothy.

When I was a boy attending boarding school in England, my two sisters and I lived with George and Dorothy Lee, our maternal grandparents. I recall on several occasions my grandfather referring to some letters and a book that he was having made for our grandmother. I thought no more about it until my grandfather presented the completed book to my grandmother as a birthday gift in 1957.

Following Dorothy's demise in 1966, George gave the book to his eldest daughter, Betty, my mother. The book lay forgotten up to the time my mother moved to the United States, when she asked me to make copies for her four sisters. As the book was an amalgamation of typed pages that were produced on an old-style typewriter, the copies were of poor quality and difficult to read.

In 1995, when I was working on my mother's biography, she gave me the original copy of The Bemrose Book. By the time my own mother died in 2006, I had completed a computerized work that I called *The Life and Adventures of John Bemrose*. That work was essentially the conversion of what was a typed manuscript of the original letters into a computer PDF document, that could be widely read by extended members of our family.

John Bemrose had his own style of writing, which was sometimes confusing but probably fairly common during the time he lived. A more immediate problem was the amount of words that were misspelled by the typist who wrote the book, which sometimes changed the meaning in a sentence. There were no corrections on any page, so I assume that the errors I found went unnoticed. I also found many geographic words that were spelled differently. This required investigation, but I was greatly helped by period cartographers, so I have used the original spelling where possible. Some place names are no longer in use or have been replaced by more modern versions, which I have used. Several character names were also spelled incorrectly, but many later became famous during the Civil War. Thanks to military records, I was thus able to use the army spelling.

John was trained as what we would call a pharmacist and used many Latin phrases that are no longer employed, though many of his medical terms are still in use. He was also a bit of a hypochondriac so the work is peppered with occasional explanations of his health, which are sometimes amusing when compared with our current medical knowledge. I was surprised at the survival rate of the wounded soldiers, especially when considered alongside the death rate experienced during the Civil War. The only logical explanation that I can find is that the speed of the ball was considerably slower in the 1830s than it was thirty years later.

In writing this contemporary version, which I have titled *An Englishman in the Seminole War*, I have attempted to make John's story an easy read by those living in the twenty-first century. It is no longer presented as a series of letters, which often contained repeated or adjusted stories, but has been converted to chapters dealing with the various episodes of his adventures.

The original letters were intended to assist his more difficult son to navigate his adolescence, and for this purpose John frequently interrupted his tale to include personal insights and his own philosophy or spirituality. He was blessed with a keen insight and a naturally beautiful way of expressing his thoughts. Since they interrupted the flow of the story, but act as a window into his heart and mind, I have created a few chapters at the end of the book under the general heading "Bits and Pieces."

Slavery had a profound effect upon John when he was in America and this is easily observed throughout his tales. By the time John wrote his letters nearly thirty years after the actual events, not only had the great convulsion materialized, but many of the officers under whom he served had become senior officers or officials during the Civil War. This prompted John to express more on the subject of slavery and specific personages, which deserves its own chapter.

It is my hope that this tale provides both enjoyment as well as an opportunity for many in our society to briefly open a window upon events that may have a bearing on their own existence.

Acknowledgment

To Elizabeth, my wife, for her endless patience in allowing me the time to pursue this project

John Bemrose circa 1865

London, England, 1863

Preface

My son Weightman has been reading accounts of the deaths of various personalities, some of whose lives would be considered unfulfilled. These reflections upon the lives of others have such a profound effect upon him that he is evaluating the deficiencies in his own life. I am partly to blame for his condition due to my neglect in his upbringing, by giving too much time and preference to my work. As a parent, I believe it is my duty to respond to him using the advantage of wisdom that comes with age and have decided to share my own life experiences with him. It is my hope that my own youthful experiences contain some lessons that will be relevant to him.

My Dearest Weightman, when I look back and compare my current life of comfort with my early years of poverty, I notice that they were quite equal, with regards to happiness. However, reflection reveals many errors that I made as a willful, impulsive and inexperienced youth. Fortunately, I learned from my mistakes and used my gifts from God to improve my position. My hope is that upon reading this tale you will find contentment in your current situation and not further aggravate yourself.

I found the recipe for my life was based upon a firm belief in the presence of God, and as a child of God His presence should be evident in the way I conducted my life. Our purpose is His glorification and our conduct should mirror His love. We should be grateful for our work, which is to be performed in an honest, happy, diligent, and aggressive, though tolerant, manner. We should obey our superiors, even those who are unkind to us, and complete the tasks that they place before us. Our relations with others should be honorable and prudent. We must learn to forgive and forget. We are to grasp life in its entirety, develop our talents to the best of our ability, helping others to develop their own and, if we achieve success, thank God for our blessings. We should not long for, nor expect material wealth, since our appetites are never satisfied. If blessed with earthly goods, share them with our fellow man for that will bring us joy. I pass along these observations with a warning: Our hearts neglect our Maker, especially when we are free from suffering. Accept your pain graciously, stay the course and you will receive your reward. It would seem that God, full of love for His creation, knows our needs, and though we are not deserving, provides for us with ample measure. To be content, place your complete trust in Him and you will know His peace.

I must confess, I have not been His willing servant, but rather a wayward and careless assistant. I was more inclined to show favor to those who treated me well rather than deal kindly to those unable to return the favor. Since you may have inherited the same selfish disposition as I, do not be afraid to ask God to help you overcome your infirmities. Others are always in need of our help, rather than our opposition. For if we show through love that we can have pity for the afflicted, then over time, if we do not give up, we shall overcome the weakness and make a true friend. So let us ask God for patience, to subdue our rage and save us from the anger and hostility of others.

It is not easy to write this tale, but I surely must try as He, our heavenly Father, has promised: "What thanks have you for loving those that love you. But by loving those that despise you or use you, you will have treasure in heaven." My son, may you and I store up this treasure, for it will lead not only to happiness here but in the hereafter, and we should not accept the glory for ourselves and we would not, if we seek to do His will. For all the apparent good done without God's help is illusory and vain and cannot last. It is merely an impulse of the creature who panders to vanity.

My dear son you have seen how our family, using such blessings as health, strength, and worldly substance, have given ourselves over to drunkenness, gluttony, and all manner of selfishness as though we do not know the giver. Our guides have been blind and irresponsible. My hope is that we cease these awful traits and instead seek to attain the desire to search for better, more enduring worth in the Kingdom of our Lord, where there is truth, peace and love.

During this era of enlightenment, may all people of all generations see with a renewed light, the blessings and promises in store for all. Knowing these things, may each of us prepare our own hearts and lives so that we may not be condemned forever. For we are bound in love and gratitude to reveal these truths to our children, households, and friends, as well as to those who still sit in darkness.

Family History and Boyhood

When I was a boy I often thought about the origins of my family name and, during my travels throughout England, I found ours to be common only in the Fens of Lincolnshire. Primroses and Penroses are more common in the southern counties, so I could not imagine Baemroses springing up from out of the Fens. The spelling here is the way the elder folk used to pronounce our name, but now the "a" is left out and we pronounce it as we spell it.

I believe our family was originally Flemish, as we certainly are characteristic of that race and we do know that a colony of these people settled in parts of Kesteven and Holland. I cannot trace our family farther back than to my grandfather's uncle, who lived in the village of Stubton. This I learned from my Father's nurse, an old woman with whom I lodged when a schoolboy. In the evenings, we would sit round the fire and she would relate many particulars of our people. How they were hard-working, careful folk and that my grandfather lived with his brother Robert (the head of the Bottesford family). The brothers were orphans and lived with their uncle, who used to tell of this great-great-great-uncle as being a bedridden man and that he had lived so long in bed that his knees had become immobile, so that when they placed him in the coffin they had to place a large stone upon them for three days before they could get the lid of the coffin to close. All such minutiae would have remained unknown, had I not enjoyed the gossip of this old lady.

We chatted of bygone days, such as the manner of life in my grandfather's household. How the women would spin unitedly and how the evening hours (after the day's toil) were filled up with games such as racings, catching the owl, single stick, and wrestling, in which sport the master joined. After the burial of their uncle, the brothers Robert and Joseph lived together and united their savings until they married, at which time they separated. Our grandfather came to Westborough and worked a farm until it nearly ruined him, and would have done had not the American Revolution broken out. This raised the value of his flocks and his corn almost three times. Because he had always known adversity, he now profited by it through saving his profits. By the end of a long life, and having raised a family of five, he was worth possibly 10,000 pounds.

He was not the sole reason for his success, for he was blessed with a partner, one in a thousand, a woman who was indeed a treasure. Modest, quiet, full of love, and tireless in her household duties. She took pleasure in working with her needle for hours without becoming tired or irritable. She seldom left her home, was frugal in her housekeeping, yet generous to neighbors, friends, and family. Whenever I visited my grandparents there was always something delectable to eat and a little pocket money from my grandmother's generous hand. She read her Bible to a late age and was surrounded by friends of her own generation. She was the redeemer in the house of our grandfather, a true gift from God. She was a fine specimen of womanhood, beautiful to look upon, sweetly retiring, always with a beaming kind expression, conveying to the beholder a welcome and a love so apparent, that none could mistake.

When I think of my grandmother, I have pleasant memories of affection, love, and welcome. But when I think of my grandfather, I see a stern, miserly, and domineering man. He was energetic, with great strength and a determined spirit. Even to the last, I was afraid of him and his heavy walking stick. My grandmother was definitely his better half. Their children were John, Mary, Anne, Jane, and William, who were all fine people. Anne was the pride of her father and was what people would call a magnificent woman, full of her father's spirit and determination. As a result, she ruled and sometimes outraged him. Her passions were dress and extravagance and she was the only one who dared to untie his purse strings. She was her father's favorite, if for no better reason than she was his idea of female beauty and a chip off the old block.

My grandfather had a habit of pleading poverty when he knew he was growing wealthy. It was a ploy so that his landlord would not raise his rent, and to disguise his situation he would pay the rent on the last day, as though he was short of money. If his farm were owned by a distrustful or unfair landlord there would have been less disgrace, but his landlord was kind and considerate, generous to a fault, never prying into his tenant's affairs, and a fine old English gentleman. My grandfather's behavior was not only disgraceful but wicked, being a lie before God and man. Even though he was considered a very honest man, to my view, he was most unjust. The devious scraping together of his wealth was an insult toward his Maker, the ultimate benefactor. It is a sad blot against his name which ultimately will affect his descendants, for I have already seen the ill effects of it upon his son, my Father, who I think was the peak of honor and honesty.

Because my Father was the eldest son, he inherited his father's farm and became the tenant of the son of the dead and benevolent old landlord. The two men knew one another very well, since they were brought up together, but they were the exact opposites of their respective fathers. The truth of the previous generation's relationship had left such a stigma in the young landlord's mind that he was always ready to assume the worst of his tenant and this caused problems in the relationship. In addition, my Father received a commission as a lieutenant in the local militia and began to mix with other young officers from the surrounding countryside. Through them he developed a bad habit of drinking and a looseness peculiar to their class. He worked the farm for about twelve years and, though he was considered a good manager, his bad habits led him away from that monotonous life. His landlord, fearing for his own prosperity, would not rest until he had gotten his whole farm back. The result was my Father had his best fields taken away from him, which eventually caused him to give up the farm. It was a great misfortune for which he was not to blame.

Uncle William shared in his father's inheritance, but the boys went their respective ways. My Father sought to secure a respectable position in society through protecting his assets, while my uncle William almost lost his in reckless habits, for he was not financially disciplined and very thoughtless. I am grateful to God that he married well. He became a most loving father, which caused him to change his bad habits and even to read the scriptures. Filled with love and kindness, he became a model husband and father to the world.

My Father married Mary Wilson of Westborough, the daughter of Matthew Wilson. I knew little of my Mother's family except for her father, who was one of the kindest persons I ever met. He loved to create happiness and was never happier than when he was working on behalf of his grandchildren. Long after his demise he was lovingly remembered in the hearts of his grateful dependents.

After my Father lost the farm in Westborough, he moved to the village of Long Bennington where he worked another farm for thirty-nine years, but it came second to his political career and hardly produced more than weeds and refuse.

Several years later, during conversations with me, his previous landlord referred to the time of my Father's occupation. He told me that they should have never parted company, that he should have acted differently, and how bad advisors had influenced my Father. On one occasion he told me, "Mr. Bemrose, your family and mine had close transactions for forty years and your father ought not to have left, we could have worked well together." The parting harmed both families and showed how my grandfather's craftiness destroyed my Father's prospects. Even so, this gentleman was most kind and friendly to me and my children for over twenty years.

I was eight years old when we arrived at Long Bennington. For a time, we attended the village school, but behaved so badly that my Father moved my brother and me to another school, where the master was notorious for being a strict disciplinarian. While there we boarded with my Father's former nurse. It was not long before we were hastily called home for my Mother's funeral. She had died in childbirth and the baby died soon after.

My Mother was the only religious person in our house, and I believe that had she lived she would have brought us up in a more Christian environment, which would have better prepared us for society. She was a woman of purpose determined to do good, accepting as her main responsibility the proper rearing of her children. It was a great loss to lose her at an age when we needed her safe and guiding presence.

My Father was a politician and, after reading the works of Volney and Thomas Paine, a Free Thinker. He was a very kind and gentle person, full of charity and benevolent feelings toward all. He was often surrounded by his peers, which unfortunately exposed us to drunkenness and gluttony. With little Christian teaching or discipline we ran wild, making it necessary to place us under the supervision of a housekeeper, who was his second cousin. I wish that my Father would have been more a man of God than a man of the world, which was so highly prized. It is no wonder that, exposed to his bad influence, we wandered from the paths of honor and integrity.

After two or three years we were sent to Nottingham boarding school, where we were supposed to obtain some classical knowledge. Once more we came under the influence of people incompetent to train youth, having been poorly raised themselves. The master was very likable, learned, and well versed in the classics. The mistress was very unfriendly and, although a talented teacher and painter, was unfit as a manager and housekeeper. The assistants were badly trained. Soon they were short of cash and in financial straits, which caused great bitterness and daily arguments. His authority was compromised further when he sought our financial assistance through numerous small loans. We soon took advantage of his misfortune, becoming headstrong and rebellious. His wife's habits increased his despondency, and they became a miserable pair, thoroughly unsuited to manage unruly boys.

After I had been there about six months, he tried to exert his authority, but we rebelled and defied him in front of the whole school. A scuffle ensued, in which I kicked and struck out like a young demon, concluding the disgraceful scene by putting on my hat and leaving for home. I walked the twenty miles and reached home at six in the evening. To my Father's credit, I was welcomed only for the night, woken early the following morning, and taken to Bottesford where I was placed on the coach. I returned to my master in disgrace but unsubdued and unrepentant.

Our leisure hours at Nottingham were spent playing games of cricket and boxing, my brother and I becoming joint owners of a set of boxing gloves. On Saturdays and market days we were allowed the run of the streets when our master was only too keen to see our backs. He dreaded our return at tea time when we were frequently obnoxious, finding fault with the food, which was of poor quality. I look back on those school days with regret for the shameful treatment we perpetrated on that gentle teacher. My brother was quite beyond his control and I was hard to manage. Years later, when I had to correct my stubbornness and insubordination, I realized how boys require a strict environment for our own good.

We remained at Nottingham until I knew as much about algebra as my teacher, then we left to finish our education at a village school nearer home. Not long after our departure I learned that our master became mentally unstable. He suffered a depression and was admitted to an asylum, where I believe he died.

The master at my finishing school was most respectable, learned, and very knowledgeable, but quiet and shy, almost unable to communicate. I never knew anyone with so little instructive ability. He ran a profitable school and apparently managed all parish affairs, which I and others considered to be the source of his wealth. But his prosperity proved to be false for, after his death, his widow was left only £20 a year to maintain her and her two daughters. Once more I was subject to someone who was badly trained and only interested to use his profession as a means to make a living. His wife was his total opposite. She enjoyed her work, was companionable, and a good communicator with her friends and neighbors. She would have been most agreeable and useful with a more suitable partner. One of their daughters suffered from a mental disorder, while she also suffered from her many troubles which compounded as she aged. It was a sad ending to what I considered to be a well-organized household.

At finishing school, I was older and taller than the other boys and did not care to join in their pranks. This allowed me to spend more time beneficially in my studies and gain a degree of respectability. I made good progress and after a further six months I completed my training.

When I think about my youth and the various schools I attended, I reflect upon the number of teachers who are unfit to train the young. So many are employed for the wrong reasons. I also regret the lack of religious teaching at either of the two boarding schools that I attended.

Upon leaving school I was considered sufficiently educated to be apprenticed to Mrs. Ann E. Lowth, a country druggist of Oakham Ruts, and bound, after three months' probation, to serve six years with a salary of £75 per year. Mrs. Lowth was a person of considerable distinction, being the daughter and granddaughter of high-ranking clergymen of the Church of England. Her grandfather was the Archdeacon of Stowe and her father-in-law was the son of the Earl of Winchelsea's chaplain. Mr. Lowth had died about six months prior to my arrival and had left a prosperous business in a poor state. He was fond of horses, dogs, and all kinds of animals, and preferred to pursue his veterinary trade rather than his business. His bad habits eroded much of his retail trade, which he had built up over twenty years. During his latter days, and until his death, he was seldom at home, which resulted in difficult financial circumstances for his widow and children. This convinced me that, however good a business may be, it will soon be lost through neglect.

Mr. Wellington was our store manager and we nicknamed him Duke after the famous general since he had a similar nose. He was from Somerset, about twenty-five years old, and seemed quite capable of reviving the neglected shop. He was energetic, neat, and meticulous, but while attending to delinquent customers he reminded them about their outstanding debts. This upset our habitual debtors who exclaimed "It was not so in Mr. Lowth's time." Duke was most anxious to cultivate a good relationship with the respectable members of the community, which ultimately greatly increased our trade. The number of wagonloads of paints, oil cake, and similar supplies became so great and so heavy that our porter, Robert, and I scarcely had a minute's free time. Sales were generally slow in the small and poor village of Oakham, but our store became very profitable because our clients were mainly from the neighboring gentry, nobility, and clergy.

It was evident that Mrs. Lowth was brought up to be a well-educated, God-fearing, Christian woman. Whatever spiritual upbringing I lacked was soon altered through a daily routine of morning and night prayers and Christian counseling. She led a truly Christian life and treated me like one of her own, being always kind, considerate, and interested in my welfare. Any disagreements were generally overcome through her heartfelt concern for the welfare of her whole household. She ran a neat and orderly home and provided excellent meals of fresh and healthy seasonal food. She was a beacon of light in our district and, though some despised her for her superior sanctity, there were a few who joined her in helping the poor with her teaching and supervision of children and other charitable works. Her most loyal helpers were Lady Turner of Cold Overton, the Honorable Baptist Noel, Squire Finch of Burley, and the Reverend Jones. Her own children were brought up in her fashion, so it must have been especially difficult for her to train an unruly youth like myself who was so naturally inclined to disarrange everything.

Unfortunately her husband's habits had not been in harmony with those of his wife. His apprentice was allowed too much freedom. When Mr. Lowth routinely left the shop, so, too, did his apprentice, who became a drunkard, unable to work the counter. Consequently Mrs. Lowth was suspicious and critical toward her apprentices and imposed restrictions and standards that were hard for me to bear. At a time when I was looking for credit and trust from my supervisors and benefactors, I initially became despondent and filled with regret. Her training would have imparted stability, propriety, and wisdom to prepare me for society, but my childish mind and wayward heart became almost inaccessible to her wise corrections. Nevertheless, as my first year progressed, though the work was hard, I became more comfortable and hopeful.

Unexpectedly Robert, our old porter, a wise and discreet person, left us due to inadequate wages. He was an all-around worker who filled his share at the counter and was knowledgeable about oils and paints. His replacement was inadequate and added to my troubles by cleverly evading work, which I was left to complete after he had gone home for the night. My life soon became an intolerable routine of constant work from five in the morning until ten or eleven at night and, due to exhaustion, I occasionally made mistakes like forgetting to book goods sold in the ledger. Regardless of the hour I would be called out of bed even in the winter, and left to ruminate in the cold store until I remembered the omission. Sometimes I sat for an hour or longer before my memory would rescue me from my dilemma, allowing me to return to my bed in the small hours of the morning. As I sat, I began to think it was a cruel punishment, especially since it was fatigue that weakened my brain as well as my body. Becoming nervous and irritable, I committed more blunders, until I became listless and miserable.

The new porter was a fawning bootlicker who spent much of his time in the stable curling the pony's mane in order to make a big show when he drove his mistress out and about. He became my evil nemesis, a spy who reported all my indiscretions. Apparently friendly and professing to understand my troubles, he secretly tried to stab me in the back. Mrs. Lowth suffered much from indigestion and her doctor recommended morning airings in her little pony carriage. She was open to flattery and like all of us was pleased to hear good things about herself. The porter took advantage of his situation and was able to insinuate all kinds of wrongdoing on my part. This led her to sympathize with what the porter said and she became suspicious of my actions. This resulted in my losing the kindness and goodwill of my mistress and Mr. Wellington. Unfortunately, neither I nor Mrs. Lowth found out about this until it was too late.

At the end of two years of apprenticeship I returned home, only to find my brother William already there. He had lost his own position due to insubordination to his master, and I noticed that his behavior was likely to destroy the peace in my Father's household. I was able to confide my troubles to my Father, who advised how important it was for me to do my best and act bravely and honorably until the end of my apprenticeship. Then to avoid becoming an additional burden to my Father, I returned to Oakham before I was fully able to resolve my own predicament. Even so, his counsel had a profound effect upon me and, out of love and in order to please him, I departed with a fresh resolve to do my duty.

I tried my utmost to regain lost favor, but notwithstanding my resolve, my troubles increased daily. Once more I was overworked and overwatched, and as my workload increased, I suffered two or three more expensive accidents. The first was when I broke two bottles of methylated spirits. These events worried me excessively and I became depressed and unable to sleep either day or night. Unfortunately, I ridiculed the idea of religion and, having no relationship with my heavenly Father, I was unable to seek solace from Him when I was troubled. I fought hard to overcome my feelings and only found relief when I received a letter from home. It is a blessing when parents maintain communication with their children, for those sweet epistles calmed my troubled spirits. Whatever the distance, a letter will bridge even an ocean. In my case it was a rope of sand for as soon as I made a good resolution, I inevitably broke it when the first difficulty presented itself.

Soon I was confronted with my greatest problem when the porter confided a secret with me that I promised I would not divulge. He told me a lie, saying that Mrs. Lowth thought that I should be more careful with my money rather than waste it on purchasing seals and watch chains. The truth was that these ornaments were costume jewelry that cost me a few shillings. Later her son Henry came to me holding my trinkets and asked me what they cost. I boastfully exaggerated what I paid about ten times in order to aggravate his mother. Such stupidity showed what little regard I had for myself and, on this occasion, there were repercussions.

It was a fault of mine through life, when unjustly accused, to pretend to be guilty. On this occasion I continued to repeat the lie until I isolated myself from others, except for one companion. There was a young man who lived opposite the shop who I saw on Sunday afternoons when we usually strolled to the neighboring village. Mrs. Lowth carefully selected this gentleman to be my companion for she wanted to give me every opportunity to be properly and morally educated. She chose well, for he was well-groomed, an upright gentleman, and easy to converse with. At the time he was studying for college and eventually became the vicar of a parish in Northamptonshire. His father was an officer who served under Sir John Moore during the Peninsular War against Napoleon. Although I kept such good company on Sundays, the six other days working with the porter were most detrimental. His influence was so great that I succumbed to his constant insinuations and continued on my path to annoy my mistress and provoke my master.

During that time I developed an indomitable spirit and had little fear about making my own way in the world. I thought of writing to my Father to tell him that I would sooner give up all my prospects in life rather than bear the stigma of suspicion from anyone. But I could not follow through, not out of a desire to please my employers, but because my Father was already burdened by my intractable brother who was wasting his abilities at home. Inevitably that moment arrived when my integrity was in doubt, so I wrote to my Father requesting he come for me. He answered my letter suggesting that I was imagining and exaggerating my situation, which to some degree in hindsight may have been the case. Too late my passions were aroused and I became blind to the reckless consequences of my proposed actions. I determined that, as life had become so wretched, I would rather bear my indignities on my own, amongst strangers.

The porter continued to bring his cashbook to me every day for me to complete. It was a Saturday evening when once again he came with his insinuations regarding my mistakes. This made me so angry that I instantly threatened to explain everything to Mrs. Lowth and Mr. Wellington. I wish I had. I passed through the glass doorway and, as my hand rested upon the handle of their sitting room door, he caught up with me and protested. "For God's sake, Bemrose, don't go in. I'm sure it's all true, but don't expose me and get me fired; think of my poor wife and child." He managed to dissuade me from my wise decision, and I returned to the shop. Frustrated with all the lies and intrigue, I sacrificed my better judgment and told him that it would be my last night at Oakham. I would depart in the morning, as I could no longer remain to handle their money under such doubts and suspicions.

What sort of man would allow a youth to destroy himself and to leave the comfort of family and friends? He knew that his explanation would have straightened out the whole matter, although at his expense. Humanity can be selfish and cruel. The porter knew he had lied and also knew he was the cause of all Mrs. Lowth's doubts about me. He was a constant talker, a gossip full to the brim of other people's business. He had been a footboy in the employ of the idle aristocracy and was taught in the servants' hall to watch, cringe, listen, even imagine, and then report on all matters. He was a member of that class who are careful of their own skin as they scratch and claw their way forward over the backs of others. To this day that porter's character has taught me to shun all gentleman's servants, whom I generally find are too apt to know more secrets than is good for them.

Journey to America

I was sixteen and one-half years old in August of 1831 when I deserted my apprenticeship, my friends, and my family. In my determined foolishness I put in motion a crazed plan, which began when I asked Mrs. Lowth for permission to visit a gentleman clothier in Uppingham. It was a ruse that gave me the whole of Sunday as a headstart. I departed with a bundle made up of my most valuable clothing, which I intended to sell to add to my ready cash of four pounds. Rising early, I began my journey, but between Barley Thorpe and Langham I met up with my nemesis, the porter. To further confuse my benefactors, I told him that I was going on to Nottingham. I then walked to Melton Mowbray, a distance of about twelve miles, where I boarded a coach that was bound for Leicester. There, under a false name, I boarded another coach bound for Birmingham, where I remained four days, strolling about the streets and suburbs. It was in Birmingham where I began to consider my ultimate destination, but made no enquiries, fearing that I would arouse suspicion and be detained. I intended to head for the coast but was so ignorant of the general geography of my position that I was obliged to purchase a map, at the exorbitant cost of seven shillings and sixpence and which I still have to this day. I swore that no matter what happened, I was not returning to Oakham.

In Birmingham I stayed at an inn in the center of town, where the widow landlady, surrounded by grown-up daughters, was recently married to a young drunkard half her age. It was a house of confusion and misery far beyond what I had ever seen or imagined, and I was very glad to board the coach for Manchester, from where I continued by rail to Liverpool arriving early the following morning.

Full of confidence I explored the city and crossed the Mersey to visit the Battery. There I was shown around by an obliging artilleryman, whose behavior suddenly changed to contempt when I omitted to pay him the usual fee. Then I boarded the ferryboat for the return journey. Not understanding the procedure, I immediately went forward without paying the ferryman, who believed that I intended to avoid payment. He came and cursed me and, even after paying and apologizing, he still showed me so much animosity that I thought he would throw me overboard. I was glad to reach land in safety, but after meeting with such abuse I began to have serious doubts about leaving home. I reflected upon my position and the results of my rashness. Through my own fault and weakness, I was an outcast, a stranger to all and alone in the world. While I deliberated my situation, with no idea as to my next move I wandered about the banks of the river, the shipping wharves, and the docks. Eventually I came across a New York skipper, who asked me to purchase a passage with his ship. I began to imagine a journey to America. It would be the most suitable place for me, for the language was my own and her people were mostly our descendants.

To pursue the possibility I began to assess my resources, which were sadly depleted. I then found a one-eyed Irish sailor who was willing to assist me in making up my mind. During our conversation I learned that my new friend lived in a cellar at No. 19 Pudding Lane, not far from the docks. For a modest fee he suggested that I stay with him and I followed him to his humble abode, where he introduced me to his wife. The following day we went to a shipping office and made enquiries. Continuing my reckless plan, I pawned all my disposable clothing and watch. My friends found that I had disposed of my watch too cheaply and offered to pawn my gold chain. Having doubts about their trustworthiness I followed them to the pawn shop where they parted with the chain for thirty shillings. It had cost my Father about £7. Then, holding my cash and pawn tickets, they tried to elude me on their way home, thinking that I was unable to find their cellar, but I quickly followed and when I caught up with them demanded my money, which they handed over. Pooling my money, I was able to pay £2 for a passage to New York on the ship *Constellation*, which was to sail in a few days. In those days passengers only paid the passage from port to port and had to provide for their own meals, which cost me a further thirty shillings. I was left with nine shillings after all my expenses and only then did I begin to appreciate the finite value of money. I started to hoard my pennies when I realized that I would need every one of them.

At night I was separated from my hosts by a coarse cloth screen, which hung across the apartment. When my host thought I was asleep he tried to gain the support of his wife in a nefarious plan to rob me. Thank God his scheme was thwarted by his good woman, whose heart was set to seeing me safely on my journey. She even threatened her husband, saying, "Touch the boy's money or hurt a hair of his head and I will forsake you forever." She persisted until he promised to do his best to help me. Even in that wretched den moral principles prevailed thanks to a compassionate woman eager to help someone in distress. Following the warning he was true to his promise and I gained a friend, for he never tired of assisting me. Were it not for those two humble people, I could never have raised the money nor surmounted the difficulties I encountered in order to reach America.

My ship lay alongside the Georges Dock and, early one morning accompanied by my Irish friends, we boarded her before she moved into the stream. I remember our parting well; their warm wishes for my success in the new country and her tears, so like a mother's that, were it not for the difference in the quality of our clothes, the bystanders would presume she was my mother. When they left me, I felt I had parted with the last and truest friends of my native soil. I was especially grateful for their kindness and unhappy that I was unable to repay them for their hospitality. One consolation was that they held my pawn tickets and I hoped that they would be able to redeem them for their own use, especially my overcoat, which was almost new.

I became quiet and thoughtful after their departure, reflecting on how few of my middle class have lived amongst the poor. From my vantage at Pudding Lane, I witnessed scenes under an archway opposite the house, where street people spent the night and where they made their morning toilet. We ate very ordinary food, our main dish consisting of potatoes and salted mackerel. Our leftovers were shared with our more destitute neighbors who were glad to come for the crumbs my kind benefactor would give them.

We lay in the stream for two days waiting for a favorable wind and the remainder of our passengers. During this time, the Liverpool watermen acted like rogues upon their innocent and ignorant prey. As more passengers arrived, they were told that the ship was to sail imminently and therefore the watermen were able to exact exorbitant fares for the short trip out into the bay. The regular fare was one shilling, but some were forced to pay four and five shillings, and one even paid ten shillings. Such behavior was cruel since it was exacted upon those who could least afford to pay. Our fares to cross the Atlantic varied greatly and upon comparing notes, I found that some had paid as little as twenty shillings, while others as much as £4. I fared better than most, thanks to the wisdom of my Irish sailor, who advised me to board the ship while it was still alongside the dock.

Steerage was full to capacity, consisting of pigs of lead, crates of pottery, water casks, and emigrants, of which there were ninety-four of us in all. We were packed like cattle three and four in a bunk, or berth, three tiers high. It was a mixture of humanity with most of the people being Irish, the remainder English, Welsh, and a company of Italian musicians. The Irish and English were from the lowest strata of society, but the Italians were of a more respectable stock.

Our pilot came aboard as soon as the wind permitted and we were pulled out by a steamboat beyond the Black Rock, where he left us in the care of our Yankee captain. It was still daylight as we sailed along the English and Welsh Coasts, close enough so we could see the beauty of our native land. Here and there the undulating slopes and the base of the cliffs were studded with villas. On the other side of the ship the mountains of Ireland appeared in the distance. These scenes, though pleasing to my eyes, did not appeal to most of the passengers, who were leaving these shores with a sense of bitterness.

The ship was a thoroughbred New England Yankee. Upon clearing the Channel, the sails filled, our speed increased and, parting the waves, we surged out into the Atlantic. I was the first to succumb to the heaving and pitching and was struck down with seasickness. For three days I was miserable, helpless, and quite unaware that an English family had stowed me away in a bunk to look after me. Upon my recovery they brought me some tea and coffee and a little nourishment to get me back on my feet.

I was also the first to gain my sea legs. Others not so fortunate lay prostrate and miserable for three weeks or longer. Women tended to suffer more, and one Englishwoman would have died had it not been for the captain, who ordered her to be carried upon deck to breathe the invigorating sea air. Sailors generally did not like service aboard emigrant ships and openly expressed their disgust when sickness amongst the passengers brought additional work.

About a week into our voyage on a foggy afternoon we collided with a Russian vessel at about 4:00 p.m. I was standing on deck but did not see the ship until she was about fifty yards away, steering directly across our course. Our helmsman spun the wheel with all his might and foot by foot she silently crossed our bow. I was transfixed by the sight, anticipating our escape, but his efforts were in vain when our prow crunched into the stern quarter cutting away the cabin window and all its ornamental work. There was screeching, grinding, and loud cracks as the beams and planks tore apart causing splinters to fly in all directions. The women below deck screamed, and the Russians swore and gesticulated while a few fell on their knees and prayed.

Our captain was a cool, stern, and collected seaman as he delivered his orders. The mate and his men were soon active with their axes, cutting away all obstructions from the Russian ship, which projected over our deck and became entangled in our rigging. Conversely the behavior of the Russian captain was ludicrous as he displayed his rage and terror by cursing and gesticulating at our more fortunate and staid commander. I was afraid that events could escalate into something ugly, but our ships were soon separated and by morning our damages were remedied. Without seeming to miss a beat we continued our westward voyage.

Upon regaining my health, I developed a routine of reading, eating, and sleeping. I soon exhausted all the books the passengers carried and then borrowed all those that belonged to the sailors. Normally I could be found on deck reclining on a water barrel, reading a book. I was not a good cook, nor was I able to afford food that was tasty, so my meals were perfunctory and usually consisted of biscuit and water. All cooking was performed on deck and occasionally I made a little stir-about (a dish of oatmeal and water heated in a pan to make a pudding). Sometimes I was able to add a little ham or red herring as a luxury. This was a delicious change for me, as my usual condiment was salt since I had no butter or milk in my stores.

After about three weeks everyone became lousy. Lice were so numerous and industrious that they drove even the filthiest among us to greater cleanliness. They took possession of our warm berths and formed colonies in our shirts and underwear and even began to stroll on the outside of our clothing. A black coat particularly showed them to advantage by the contrasting color. I disliked them so much that I relinquished my berth and took possession of a box about three and a half feet long, upon which I slept the remaining portion of the journey. Though it was very cold I found it preferable to the heat and filth below deck. They eventually found the captain's cabin and those of the mate and the owner's son. Their presence was soon obvious throughout the whole ship's company as we all began to gyrate and scratch whenever the lice irritated our skin.

The sailors then received orders to heat a red-hot iron bar, which they placed in a tub of tar and brought it below decks before sunrise. The tub was carried throughout the steerage compartments producing such fumigation as to make everyone vacate their berths. The mate had a cruel nature and enjoyed this exercise so much that he planned it for a time that would catch us by surprise. I witnessed some ludicrous scenes when the tar tub made its appearance. Imagine ninety-four sleepy human beings, men, women, and children, quickly turning out of a dark steerage, many half dressed and some having on their neighbor's clothes. One morning a particularly audacious Irishman arrived on deck wearing a lady's corset. Naturally, it was all fun and appreciated accordingly.

After four or five weeks some of the passengers began to run short of supplies and theft became a nightly occurrence. I lost a piece of ham and my remaining stock of herring, while others lost more. To solve the problem, we held a council meeting and developed a watch, which consisted of four men each night; two from sundown to midnight, who were relieved by the other two who were on duty until dawn. This proved to be the perfect solution, as there were no more losses. My losses left me without any meat and only some biscuit and oatmeal, with which I prepared stir-about as my only nourishment. It must have agreed with me for I never felt healthier and was freed of my bad moods and headaches. I was so happy with the result that I began to speculate about what little sustenance the body requires. I remember planning that once I arrived back on dry land I would live on oatmeal and a plain diet, save my money, and return to England rich and prosperous.

I made a few friends on the ship; one was an invalid American sailor, better educated than the others. He was friendly and we had many pleasant conversations. I also became friendly with the owner's son, a young man who was a very quiet gentleman.

The captain was unsociable and the mate was an overbearing Yankee bully who was always bragging or fooling about, which often led to a cruel turn of events. He delighted when others suffered from one of his many pranks. His helpless victims normally ended up with a ducking or an ugly fall upon the deck. His games were so obnoxious and extreme that before long everyone disliked and was afraid of him. One of my English berth-mates dared him to combat and beat him soundly while berating him for his evil behavior. This had a beneficial effect upon the emigrants, but like all bullies, he had to have the last word. He often tormented a French sailor and if the man complained, he was forced to suffer additional duties. On one occasion the sailor was given the duty of tarring the rigging for so many days that he won the sympathy of the emigrants, who showed their disgust until the mate was disciplined by the captain. The mate responded with reluctant obedience, but in the end he cruelly used a rope upon his victim. The punishment was against the law and I hope he was fined upon arrival in New York.

Then one seaman died of a fever. A Welsh Moravian Mission clergyman officiated at the funeral. I never saw a congregation of so many faiths so devout or attentive to scripture, where all differences were forgotten in the solemnity of the occasion. Death was ever near and danger so apparent, with only a plank separating each of us from eternity. Following the ceremony, the remains of the sailor were thrown overboard.

Occasionally our musical company of Italians varied the monotony by playing tunes on the quarterdeck. They were evidently practicing to be ready to go to work upon arrival in America. When the weather permitted and the sea was calm, our captain approved of dancing, much to the delight of the Irish and the sailors. These amusements were beneficial to all, especially to the homesick and those who felt ill.

I slept with my clothes on, but because of the cold, the lack of nourishment in my diet, and the distorted position in which I slept, my limbs became very stiff. This caused me to be rather miserable at times, although I accepted these discomforts as the least of my problems.

Our vessel was on her maiden voyage and, though good-looking, was not a great sailor. She seemed to have little buoyancy and behaved like a tub, lumbering and pitching among the waves. We had expected to arrive in New York within five weeks and I had provisioned accordingly. Due to the extended time for the journey, I was forced to purchase twenty-eight pounds of oatmeal from a passenger, which reduced my remaining funds to four shillings and four pence. I was not happy, but due to my youthful confidence I imagined that all I had to do was land in America to recoup my finances. About the twentieth of September we passed to the south of the Newfoundland Banks. That day was very foggy and for the remainder of our journey the wind generally remained northwest.

We endured stormy weather for much of the voyage, with gales blowing from out of the northwest. The headwinds were so strong that even stripped to bare poles we frequently lost ground. Every morning passengers anxiously requested our distance from port and the answer was often that we were fifty miles nearer Liverpool. Such disheartening replies were received so frequently that many of us seriously began to doubt whether we would ever see land again. Bad news at sea invariably caused superstitious sailors to imagine all kinds of evil attributes towards the passengers. In our case they determined that there was a murderer amongst us.

During the gales the sea would develop into huge swells resembling mountains of water that obliterated the horizon. I loved the stormy weather and positioned myself at the bowsprit, where I could experience our submergence down into the trough and the subsequent ascent when the bow re-emerged upon the crest of a wave. Few shared my enthusiasm, for only the captain, the steersman, and I were on deck during foul weather. Our skipper would stand on deck for however long the storm lasted, but was seldom seen when the weather was mild. A ship under bare poles, in a heavy gale, is a glorious experience. There is something so invigorating and refreshing that it must be seen and felt to fully appreciate its unique reality.

After a storm we invariably attracted schools of porpoises numbering into the thousands. Upon nearing the ship they would split into two large bodies, passing on either side as though the keel cleaved them apart, until they rejoined their company at the stern. They were so numerous that evidently they enjoyed the calm weather or were stirred up from unfathomable depths. Occasionally grampuses and young whales would come within a few hundred feet of the ship, spouting up water through their blowholes to a height of forty or fifty feet, filling us with wonder as to the inhabitants of the ocean.

Though we were daily reminded of the immensity of our Creator's works, some lived as though He were not even there. A Moravian missionary and his companions were on board and were active in their faith, acting as our witnesses for God. They conducted evening services of prayer and praise, and a Sunday service on deck which was well attended. Such occasions attracted a large audience to worship, but also brought some who were more intent on mockery. Their private devotion at night, before retiring to bed, was conducted in Welsh, which created amusement and some abuse. One evening the leader, who was a huge man, grew fed up with the ridicule and lashed out at his tormentors. Threatening them, he said, "There was a time when I would have thrown three or four of you over my head like so many babies." Fortunately, they did not put him to the test, and neither did they repeat the insults.

Early one morning toward the end of September, a sailor cried out from atop the main yard the welcome news of "land ahead." Every heart, like mine, leaped with joy at the prospect of being released from our wooden prison and hoping to regain the comforts of life on terra firma. By that time, we were in a wretched state, filthy, with our clothes in deplorable condition, and many of us almost starving. Toward the afternoon we could see the lighthouse of Sandy Hook, which was located about twenty miles from New York. Just about that time several boats, each manned by four or five men representing the various newspapers of the city, came alongside. They were strongly built and lengthy and, after the clipper style, were good sailors. I heard that one of them had even crossed the Atlantic.

The boats brought alongside the first Americans I ever saw. I was expecting something different but knew not what. I stared at every fresh face that approached and could not help wondering where we had met, for they looked English, except they lacked the ruddy complexion. By the time they departed we were near the lighthouse, which was passed about nightfall. Then our captain ordered one seaman into the chain room to throw the lead and another to signal for a pilot by firing off a musket, which seemed to have no effect. The casting of the lead to determine the depth of water is common practice, especially after dark. For a landlubber it is a memorable experience due to the musical cadence in the operator's voice as he calls or sings out, "by the lead nine," meaning we were in nine fathoms of water. As it was a dark night our captain decided to lower our anchor and wait for daylight, but just as the crew were about to do so, a light was seen on our weather bow, which fortunately turned out to be the pilot. He was a fine-looking seaman and evidently well trained and educated. He quickly took charge of the ship and gave instructions to reset the sails, to which the ship agreeably responded. This made all the passengers happy to know we were back on track heading for our new home.

A short time later I heard a rushing sound growing louder. Another ship was approaching, and with a shout of "ship ahoy," our crew maneuvered our vessel just in time to keep from being run down. One of those enormous liners passed us, moving with terrific speed. Our vessels were so close that the wind generated by her passing raised my hair. I was on deck, so I still have vivid memories of the event, which was more of a sensation than a visual experience. The incident left me with an indefinable dread of what could have been a great calamity, but for the mercy of God. Even now I am able to see and feel that majestic ship swiftly looming out of the darkness and passing us as though running downhill at full speed. Beyond our encounter she gained her sea room and, like a bird on the wing, soon disappeared from sight as she leapt out across the trackless Atlantic.

We passed through the Narrows and came to rest in the Bay of New York. At two in the morning, we dropped anchor and waited for dawn and the doctor. We were so excited that few passengers slept and were awake to meet the sunrise. When it burst upon us, we were entranced by the spectacular scene. Some described the bay to be as beautiful as Naples, but to me it was simply beautiful. The Narrows was strongly fortified with batteries on each side of the East River. The one on Manhattan Island, a favorite promenade, was called Castle Gardens and was nearly opposite the Half Moon Battery of Governors Island. The two together would sink any enemy fleet that tried to pass. In front of us lay the fine city of New York, with its three hundred thousand souls, numerous spires, domes, and cupolas. To our right and near the city was Governors Island, with its high woody grounds. On our left was Gibbet Island (Ellis Island). Staten Island was off the stern in the distance and dotted here and there with villas. A medical officer was then summoned to inspect us all.

The doctor confirmed that there were no passengers with a fever to detain the ship any further, so the crew again set the sails and we moved toward the city. Most of the emigrants then began cleansing themselves. Those who were fortunate enough to have a change of clothes cast their dirty, infested clothing overboard. They then put on fresh, clean dresses, suits, and Wellington boots. As a result, there was a great transformation in those who had dressed so raggedly during the journey. They looked comfortable and clean, while I still felt lousy and worn. It was foolish of me to have used pawnbrokers to change much of my clothing for inferior contaminated garments that caused me weeks of discomfort. I had also made the mistake of wearing my best and only suit during the voyage. While I was perceived to be financially comfortable, I was in fact almost penniless.

As we sailed the last few miles up the harbor toward the city, I witnessed the most magnificent spectacle of shipping, including some fine steamers loaded with passengers. Finally we came to rest in Peck's Slip. These slips were used instead of docks and formed part of the shoreline that was excavated to allow ships to receive and offload their freight while at anchor. To receive the Custom House officers, the passengers were then ordered on deck and the hatches were closed. I experienced no problem from the Customs officials, as all my worldly possessions were bound up in a small bundle. My journey had lasted forty-nine days at sea, and I was happy to be released from a ship that, due to its poor sailing qualities, had kept us prisoners for so long.

Before I left the ship I noticed that some police had come on board and taken our mate into custody. It appears that no sooner had the vessel landed, than the French sailor made a charge against the mate and a warrant was issued. I do not know the results, though my sympathies were with the Frenchman, and I hoped that the mate suffered a suitable penalty for his cruel treatment toward him.

During the voyage there were numerous disagreements and scuffles which, owing to the discipline required at sea, could not be concluded. Sometimes the parties were able to exchange a few blows, but the matter was usually settled by the captain when he came upon the scene. He was a strong, thick-set man who would confront the belligerents with a slap on the cheek of each and then ask what they were fighting about. If this did not end the disagreement, they were soon cooled down by the mate and two or three other sailors who soaked them with numerous buckets of sea water, which invariably cured the problem. In some cases, fights were planned to continue when the ship reached land.

One incident could have had a tragic ending. An Italian musician had married a Manksman (from the Isle of Man) and while they were below deck, she had a heated argument with one of her husband's countrymen, who had been peeling potatoes. The old man of about sixty years struck her in the breast with a knife. There were cries of murder, but the ensuing Italian-style confusion quickly brought the captain and mate to the scene with their pistols. They subdued the old man with a rope, and he became repentant enough to be secured. Then they put him in irons and took him to spend the rest of the voyage in the lock-up room over the stern. I pitied the old man, so lonely and uncomfortable, especially when the weather was stormy. Upon our arrival in New York, he was brought to trial for cutting and maiming, after which I am sure he received further punishment. By the end of the voyage we had all experienced minor disagreements, but were so pleased to arrive at our destination that all was forgotten and forgiven, and we were able to part amicably in the knowledge that we would never meet again.

I had heard how immigrants were badly treated in New York, even how they were robbed of everything, but my own experience was quite the opposite. When New Yorkers visited the ship, they appeared respectable, while some passengers were more inclined to act as rogues. During my stay in the city I did not experience anything untoward or dishonorable, except a deed I witnessed, perpetrated by four of our passengers. Six of us spent our first night lodging at number 122-1/2 Cherry Street. In addition to a comfortable, clean bed, we were all served dinner and breakfast. In the morning we ventured out to see the city and became aware that four of our number did not intend to return to pay for their lodging. They also wished to tempt me and a young Irishman named Charles to join them in their nefarious robbery. Thank God we were not tempted, but parted company mutually disgusted with each other. When Charles and I returned to our lodgings, we advised our French landlady about the dishonesty of our associates and our regret that we should have joined company with such scoundrels. Though very sorry, she was not angered by her loss, realizing that it could have been worse if they had remained three or four days. The terms for board and lodging were three and a half dollars a week, but my remaining sum of four shillings and four and a half pence would not last more than two days.

This was a serious predicament for a well-bred young man used to the benefits of a good and comfortable home. I was forced to learn about the value and use of money the hard way, by having to go without. Though most distressing and inconvenient at the time, the experience has been rewarding and even financially advantageous. The hardships engendered a hope that my own children would not have to suffer the same as I but benefit from my advice and experience. I later learned that, following my departure, my Father's greatest worry was that I of all his sons was least able to overcome hardship, for he saw me as an impulsive and wayward child. My rash behavior at running away was a continuous source of worry and sorrow, and many thought that it would kill him. My thoughtless departure only compounded his fears that I was utterly helpless and gave him no consolation.

Our landlady's household consisted of herself, two grown daughters, and her husband, who was seldom at home. The first night for Charles and me was cold and very uncomfortable due to the sudden change from being shipboard, where we had become used to the sounds and movement of the vessel. Our anxieties faded when we were served breakfast in the morning, which I thoroughly enjoyed. The feast was so plentiful that I did not think it was healthy to consume all that was offered. I knew that people who were subject to sparse and ill-prepared food had to be cautious when exposed to unlimited fare, especially when served an abundant American meal, which invariably consisted of a variety of pastries, fish, flesh, and fowl.

Charles and I took a stroll into the suburbs. We walked so far out of the city we found thornapple trees (stramonium) growing in the streets. I wondered what it was and was told it was stink weed, the American name. It was also called Tames Town from an incident during the Revolutionary War, when soldiers mistakenly used it for greens when bivouacking on the banks of the Tames Town River.

As we strolled about, we noticed the different behavior of the people and I found they spoke better English than you would typically hear in England. We saw various fruits and nuts for sale that were strange to me and some, like oranges, were very expensive, costing $4.50 each, which was equivalent to six shillings. I noticed the city was full of small shops that sold cheap alcohol, which attracted neither of us. As we wandered around, Charles and I exchanged many confidences. I learned that he was neither a smoker nor a drinker. He was modest, well-brought up, well-read, and a splendid penman, who had received a good education and came from a good family. Apparently, his father had died suddenly without a will. Through the existing law of primogeniture (a feudal rule by which the whole estate of an intestate person passed to the eldest son) the estate was passed to his elder brother. Since he was no longer treated as a brother, but more as a dependent or servant, he was sent to plow, while his brother acted the part of a country gentleman. Ultimately, he became disgusted with his circumstances and decided to emigrate, whereupon his brother offered him £50 sterling and paid his expenses to Liverpool.

When I told him my story, he was alarmed at my lack of cash and generously offered me the use of his funds until I could find employment. He acted like a true friend, but the gesture took me by surprise, and I wondered why anyone would be so interested in my welfare. I wanted to be in control of my own destiny and had already decided to join the army, but Charles and my landlady would not hear of it. The kind French lady portrayed the soldier's life in dismal terms, saying, "Mon Dieu! If you see the pauvre rapscallions that come into de cety," meaning the soldiers that were stationed at Governors Island and Bedloe's Island. "You nevare can vish to put on de grey cloth, dey look like forecat (prisoners). Allons, mon enfant veritable, live with me, you would take care of de shop, you pass de waiter, then monsieur come home" (meaning her husband) "den ve arrange something. Mon Dieu! He is goode, vaite, vaite, me say temps vil." I began to reconsider my proposed actions, but to this day I still recall how my pride prevented me from using the Irishman's resources. However, her words of warning and encouragement gave me pause and, reflecting upon what my Father would advise me if he knew of my circumstances, I began to seek a position in a drugstore.

I learned a valuable lesson in charity from strangers and natives of foreign lands that I had been taught to despise. It made me pause and wish that Englishmen would know better than to malign their French or Irish neighbors. It saddened me to see English laborers selfishly deny their Irish brothers a morsel from their dinner. Much of the injustice in this world springs from ignorance, for even in poverty the Irish are generous and warmhearted. They open their humble homes to the needy traveler and would divide their potatoes and buttermilk with an enemy, even if afterwards he had to fight him.

I was surprised at the generosity and consideration given to me by those warm-hearted people. Charles seemed only too happy to treat me as a brother and fellow countryman. Often as a schoolboy, I had joined the mob to deride poor and ragged Irish laborers. In New York, where I was a stranger in a strange land, my unkindness was returned with generosity by the same once-despised race. Daily, while I was in his company, I was taught to admire him and to repent of my cruel and ignorant foolishness. I now love the Irish for this man's sake and I hope never to see a distressed Irishman without remembering the debt that I owe them.

Charles and I then spent our time searching the newspapers for suitable positions and going to the *Courier* and *Enquirer* news offices, where we placed our answers to advertisements. My friend was hoping for a clerkship, for which he was well suited, while I favored the drugstores. We searched untiringly for a few days but met with no success. This caused me to gain the impression that I was becoming a burden to my friend and I began to try looking for work at the dry goods and grocery stores, also without avail. An acquaintance then advised me to apprentice myself to the tailoring business for three years and, though the work seemed distasteful, my interest grew when I learned the trade was very profitable. Against my will I went to a master tailor to secure a position. When I arrived the master was away from home, so I awaited his return by watching a number of young fellows on the stitching board. Instinctively I felt the occupation would not suit me, and on the spur of the moment I advised that, though I could wait no longer, I would call again, without the slightest intention of fulfilling my word.

Shortly after going to the tailor's workshop I was introduced to a Dr. Post, a Quaker and a perfect gentleman, who was the senior physician at the New York Dispensary. He promised me a position either in his public drugstore in the city or at the dispensary, provided I could wait a fortnight (two weeks). The doctor's shop was beautifully outfitted and very clean, but I was filthy and still full of lice. Once again, my pride and sensitivity caused me to miss a great opportunity to restore my position, as I did not feel that I should become part of his respectable family and business. My kind landlady, who knew of my condition and objections, urged me to meet the doctor's time frame, but I dreaded the need for any further explanation. I was also too proud to become dependent upon my new benefactors and sought to escape. My chief desire became to leave New York and free myself from the dependency on the doctor, my landlady, and my dear Charles. He was ready and eager to support me, saying "His fate should be mine." But I could not bear the thought that he should suffer financially on my behalf.

I imagined that the best place for me was the army or navy. But I would not enter either while still in New York. Consequently, I rejected all of Charles's kind offers with gratitude, but thought it cruel to waste his precious resources any longer. When he found his entreaties were of no avail, he finally offered me a share of his purse, of which I gratefully accepted $2 to again start out alone in the world. To my shame I forgot his last name and failed to write it on my map of England, which was the only article that I kept throughout all my experiences. I believe that it was either Cowen or Cohen. I never forgot him and named my third son after him.

Some years later I met with an acquaintance of Dr. Post who told me that the doctor was one of the best men in the world. It was a pity that I was not forthcoming with him, as he was one of that small band of Christians who lived for others. I was yet to learn that God never ceases to provide us with opportunities that unfortunately we so often reject.

While visiting New York I received no assistance from any Englishman. On the contrary I found them cold, unapproachable, and suspicious. In my wanderings about the city, I met an American druggist who was always glad to see me at his store, and he befriended me by sending me to three English physicians with notes of introduction, but I was denied entry into their offices and surgeries. He was so philanthropic as to imagine that my countrymen would gladly help me. Many Englishmen of doubtful character migrated, so I propose their own circumstance developed in them a natural aversion to meet or assist any of their countrymen. The English culture of class respects influence or station and would naturally reject someone who was unkempt or ill-clothed, since poverty was considered to be self-inflicted due to a life of crime, impropriety, or indolence.

However, I also believe that had they known my circumstances, they may have acted differently. Once you get past that frozen crust which forbids familiarity, you will inevitably find how warmhearted we English are. When you are poor or cast down, an Irishman or -woman will sooner understand your situation, and I recommend you seek their assistance first. I have found that the French, German, and Spanish are even more accessible than the English, while the Scottish are a people of extremes, usually full of greed, but occasionally most generous and loving.

When I ponder this period of my life, I wonder what would have been the results had I acted more sensibly. Possibly my destiny required that I experience more hardship to make me self-reliant, for I followed a course that led to further suffering. During my stay in New York, I saw most of the city and was surprised by the architectural similarities with England. I had thought that, after a journey of so many thousands of miles, I would find great differences. The streets were more spacious, with the Bowery and Broadway being the most fashionable promenades. New York was the port of entry for all nations, and all nationalities were seen on her streets. The shipping was extensive and the steamboats were magnificent.

There and Back

I bade farewell to my kind hostess and her two daughters while Charles accompanied me to the stand of the Philadelphia line of coaches where we parted, never to meet again. I crossed the river to the village of Hoboken and then continued by coach to Newark, a town of six thousand people. With my friend's two dollars in my pocket, I was doubly richer than on my arrival in New York. After a pleasant ride, during which a gentleman farmer invited me to pass a week's shooting with him—which I thankfully declined— we reached Newark about noon. I disembarked and presented a sixpence to the coachman, as was my custom. He was taken aback and insulted by this gesture, at my trying to make him a beggar. "No!" he said. "We don't do so in this country." I was amused, as well as pleased, for sixpence meant more to me than it did to him. I wish that all people would cultivate this custom. He called himself independent, or what we would say in English was self-reliant, which should never be sold for a mere sixpence.

Newark was a pretty town situated about twelve miles from New York. It contained five spire churches, all grouped together as was customary in America. I visited all the drugstores I passed, looking for work, but was met without success. Once I was on the point of obtaining a job in a store that dealt in paints and oils, but the owner's wife did not agree with her husband. I then continued on foot toward Elizabeth Town, which was a further five miles. About one mile after leaving Newark, I turned off into a pretty, sequestered nook, opened my bundle, and spread out my midday meal. I was pleasantly surprised to find that it consisted of dainties given to me by my kind and thoughtful French landlady. The countryside was very beautiful, the weather fine, and my meal most enjoyable, all of which raised my spirits and added renewed zest to my solitary picnic.

I arrived at Elizabeth Town about sundown and found the tavern full, so was directed to an Irishman's home situated on the outskirts of town, where I was grateful to be offered a shakedown bed on the stone floor. We dined on buckwheat cakes, which I found were delicious. They were made on a griddle, each cake consisting of a ladle of batter which was soon cooked and eaten expeditiously. The Irish family appeared to be very comfortable and apparently prospering, most courteous and attentive and delighted to entertain me for a small remuneration. I awoke early, breakfasted, and then called at a chemical factory. There was no work available for me, so I proceeded on my journey. Elizabeth Town was small, like a village, and consisted of one long main street with a few shops on either side. The following day was a long march, and I did not arrive in New Brunswick until about 5:00 p.m. I chose not to seek lodgings in the town because of the expense and thought I could be accommodated at a cheaper rate at a roadside inn.

Soon after leaving town it became dark. I walked about another three tiring miles in pitch darkness when I suddenly made out something standing in front of me. Apprehensively I pressed on and came upon a large black and white Newfoundland dog, who immediately began to bark. He was not vicious, nor cowardly, for on my jumping aside, he quietly allowed me to proceed. Soon after encountering the dog I reached a tavern on the Philadelphia side of New Brunswick, where I was shown into a kind of bar. There I was questioned by a farmer, who seemed as ignorant of England and the English as the bulk of my countrymen are of the Americans and their country. I was tired and, not wanting to waste time in conversation, I made a plea of fatigue and went supperless to bed. I arose early, too early for breakfast, paid one shilling for the accommodations, and proceeded on my way.

My shortage of funds compelled me to avoid meals, but apples were abundant throughout New Jersey and were my principal food. Occasionally I bought a bottle of spruce beer and three cents worth of a cake peculiar to the country. New Brunswick, a town of ten to twelve thousand, was situated in a valley, but not very pretty. The buildings, which were built chiefly of brick, had a very old and worn appearance. There were more Negroes here than I had met previously, but they seemed dejected, though they were not slaves, as it was not allowed in the Jerseys.

I continued my journey on to Trenton and passed through Princeton, a small collegiate town, where I saw the students walking in pairs. There I gave in to eating six large oysters, for which I paid a quarter that I could not afford. It is said that the poor of London would spend their last pennies in this manner, which must have some truth, for I had been very careful with my funds. Then I met with a lone wanderer, and after a while walking together we sat upon a log for a talk. My companion was respectably dressed yet I found he was penniless. Since I was better off than he I offered him all the coppers I had, which amounted to three cents, for which he was very thankful. I found that vagrancy is scorned in America and is one of the fine traits of their character. I never met with a beggar during the time I lived and served in that country. At Trenton the tavern was full of young men, as if there was a feast or club. But as I had renewed my savings tactics I went to bed, arose early, and departed, paying only for the room. Trenton is situated on the Delaware River, and noted for the defeat of the British when Washington made a sudden night onslaught with about three thousand of his barefooted soldiers. They had marched through sleet and snow to do the daring deed. There was a fine wooden bridge over the river, with the roof and sides covered in shingles. It had three roadways: the center was for vehicles, while the other two were for the use of pedestrians. There was a small toll for passing, as there was at most of the bridges I crossed in this state.

The following day I walked through a countryside of apple orchards and came across some pigs feasting on the fruit. According to English custom I asked the farmer if I could take a few apples and he told me to help myself without the necessity of asking permission. The orchards were open to any wayfarer who would take the trouble to collect the fruit. Apples were plentiful and very tasty, yet of little value. Wooden zigzag fences used to divide properties and fields destroyed the landscape, along with the unpleasant sight of fields of large pumpkins.

I then passed through a part of New Jersey that was sandy and sterile. About one-fourth of the countryside was wooded and at intervals was settled by Dutch colonies. These people were stout, had clean habits, and lived as a close-knit society, but had difficulty speaking English. I called at various farmhouses for a drink of water and was unable to communicate my request other than by using sign language. At Bordentown I passed near the house and extensive gardens of Joseph Bonaparte, the ex-king of Spain. It was very rural and picturesque, and I could not help thinking that the brother of Napoleon had a better chance of happiness in Bordentown than when he was his brother's puppet on the throne of Spain. The landscaping was very European and beautiful, showing that New Jersey under proper culture could become very picturesque. As I neared Philadelphia, I found the hedges to be well trimmed and the countryside dotted with neat farmhouses and beautiful gardens. It was a great improvement over what I had passed through, where the farms and fences were in a sad state of repair. The last seven miles of my journey was truly picturesque and quite equal to English scenery. On the outskirts of the city, I passed several open barouches filled with dark gentlemen who were taking their Sunday recreation.

Because it was the Sabbath, I had trouble finding a place to stay. Eventually I managed to find lodging on North Front Street with an English family from Lancashire. I had walked thirty-seven miles under a hot sun; I was spent and quite lame. After resting my weary limbs and lacerated feet, I was truly glad for a little refreshment and retired for the night. I slept soundly and did not come down until late the following morning. I checked my cash and found that it had dwindled down to three York shillings, which was not bad considering that I had travelled nearly one hundred miles on foot. It showed me how little I required when compelled through necessity. I remained healthy under this sparse regimen, with the exception of my lameness, which was due to my previous day's exertions.

My first day in Philadelphia was spent in leisurely wandering around the city. The plan of the city was perfect, being laid out in streets running north to south and east to west and intersecting each other at right angles. Everywhere I walked I found to be very neat and orderly. The wealthy lived in the suburbs in spacious homes, with gardens that were very beautiful. I strolled over the greater portion of the city until quite fatigued, when I retired to my room to contemplate my next course of action, considering my destitute condition. I had been spending recklessly and realized that my resources were gone. I was also quite aware that my shabby appearance did not help me to secure a position in the drug trade. To compound my problems, I was still troubled with lice from the ship and knew that nothing short of steam of sulfate in a hot oven would kill them. Since I only had one suit of clothes, I was in a helpless condition and thought that my only chance to become clean and comfortable once more was to enter the army and get rid of all my filthy clothes, which had become truly hateful to me. I was aware of my predicament and, though my heart was not in agreement, in thoughtless desperation I determined to become a soldier or a sailor. My only comfort was the probability that many others followed my course of action for similar reasons.

The following morning I applied at the Navy Yard, thinking I would prefer the life at sea as a mariner rather than service on land. Upon hearing my accent, I was told that it was necessary for me to be an American, but if I really wanted to join it could be done simply by saying that I was native-born, which apparently was a common occurrence. I was tempted to deny my country but stopped when I realized the fallacy of swearing to serve a nation honorably and truthfully, yet to begin such service with the use of a lie. I further questioned that, if it was good for the Navy not to have aliens admitted, why not enforce the law, but if it was not of any consequence, then why not expunge such a law. I determined to take the true and honest course, for which I am thankful, as it has brought me many blessings over the years. I also learned that the Marines were paid $6 a month without a bounty, whereas the Army pay was $5 monthly, with a bounty of $12, one half received upon enlisting and the remainder due after the first muster into the service. I then made my way over to the Army enlistment office, which was situated at South Fourth Street.

The man inside was dressed as a gentleman and, when I saw him, I shyly moved back toward the door while muttering that I was looking for the office of enlistment and begged pardon for my interruption. He followed me from his desk, where he was writing, and said, "And so it is, young man. Do you wish to serve the United States?" On answering his smiling questions in the affirmative, he told me that he was the sergeant, and that the lieutenant could not be seen that day, as he was otherwise engaged. He suggested that I call back on the following day. This upset my plans, as once more I had been childishly thoughtless and had spent my remaining coin at an Irishwoman's shop in the suburbs just a few hours before. I was too proud to explain my destitute condition to the sergeant but promised to call again the next day and arranged a fixed time for my interview with the lieutenant.

October 31 was a fine day with mild weather. With no money to pay for lodging, I thought I would take a chance and spend the night under a hedge or in a barn on the outskirts of the city. Immediately I headed for the suburbs hoping to find a comfortable resting place, but it was a long walk before I reached open country. Dusk was upon me and I was unable to find somewhere suitable in the dark, which made me anxious. I decided to return to the city to ask the Irishwoman where I had spent my last penny for a loan. Retracing my steps, I thought I was lost when her house came into view. I walked in, sat myself down, and told her my needs, promising to repay her out of my bounty. I asked for a shilling and said that I would repay her within a few days, as I had made a commitment to enlist the following day.

She was compassionate and, as she counted out the coppers, she remarked in her native accent, "If ye be honest ye'll repay, if you're not, it shall be bad luck to ye, but I little the poorer." Thanking her for the loan I returned to my lodgings, only to find there was no need to have worried myself about money. An old Englishwoman, the mother of the owner of the house, asked me to write a letter to her family in Manchester, England, for which she gave me a shilling and a drink of brandy out of her private cupboard. Once more I considered myself quite rich and was able to purchase a meal before I retired to bed. I well remember her words describing to her friends how cheap it was to procure ducks, turkeys, fowls, and many other luxuries that were not easily available in England by members of her class. As I wrote, my thoughts reflected upon how all that meat was still unavailable to anyone such as I, who had no money.

The following morning I packed up my belongings and reported to the recruitment office. I was accepted by Lieutenant Day, who gave orders for the corporal to take me to see Dr. Smith, the surgeon. The doctor believed that he had an intuitive knowledge of people and could assess them by their manner, speech, and appearance. He eyed me over during the examination and asked, "What countryman are you?" I replied, "English." Whereupon he answered, "No, you're not, you're a Frenchman." I smiled and told him that he was mistaken, but it was to no avail, for he became excited, saying, "Don't think you can deceive me, you're French, your speech and manners are French." "Oh, sir!" I laughingly rejoined. "I'm no Frenchman and do not know the language. I wish I did." "Ah, well," he said. "You're of French extraction, everything proves it, your manner, your name, and your appearance all favor my first idea of you." So we left it at that, for "A man convinced against his will is of the same opinion still." The doctor was so confident it baffled the corporal, who witnessed the exchange and saw how much I was amused. There was something excessively ludicrous in being sworn out of my own identity. In any case, whether French or English, I was considered healthy, which was what I required for me to become a soldier.

I was passed to a magistrate to whom I swore to serve as a soldier in the United States Army for five years. Since I enlisted on the first of November 1831, I was only sixteen years and three months old. Eighteen years was the lowest age, according to law, for the government to recruit, but as I was an alien they either waived the rule, or entered on my paperwork as being of the correct age. Also, because I was so far from home, there was little chance of my being sought after for release. After receiving half the bounty of $6, I was outfitted with the army standard winter clothing, which consisted of a jacket and trousers of gray cloth, blue cloth cap, and boots. The facings were yellow worsted lace for the artillery and white for the infantry. My civilian clothes were gladly discarded for $3, so that I felt very flush with cash. I also had a roof over my head, excellent food, and the finest white bread I ever ate. Even now, I still long for the bread of Philadelphia. The sergeant and his family were nice people and seemed comparatively prosperous. He was an old soldier and served against the British in the last war, but there was not the slightest boasting or bragging from him. He had evidently seen a good deal of life and was quite cosmopolitan in his ideas. He was extremely kind to me and I was very grateful for the sudden change in my circumstances. Immediately I began to hope for better days.

While in New York I wrote a letter to my Father that contained all the details of my actions since my flight and gave notice of my intended journey to Philadelphia. I did not write in Philadelphia, as I thought I would be moving almost daily. This was an error, as I remained longer than expected and I later learned that my Father never received my New York Letter. This only goes to show that it is always best to correspond at every opportunity.

I remained in Philadelphia about two weeks, during which my time was spent foolishly and unprofitably. In the evenings, for six and one-quarter cents I could visit a public dancing saloon. There I met a mixed bunch of men, consisting of English, Irish, Dutch, and Americans, and coloreds, but all of the lowest grade. The dance hall, which was long and roomy, belonged to a tavern and was very suitable for music and dancing. At one end there was a raised platform for the orchestra, which comprised gentleman musicians of color. There were usually two violins, one tambourine, and one triangle. My young mind was soon overwhelmed by the new sights and sounds, languages, and pointless arguments, such as the superiority of peat whiskey over Monongahela, cherry brandy, and applejack, a common spirit distilled from crab apples.

The party often deteriorated into a general melee of Irish howling, women screaming, French crossing themselves, and Dutch swearing. The fracas would inevitably climax in an indescribable uproar of many tongues, with broken jugs, bottles, and fragments of violins flying in all directions. The city watch would bring the festivities to a close and they nabbed a few to spend the night in the city lockup. Though I sometimes joined in the fun, I preferred not to drink or dance, as I found it more amusing to be a bystander rather than a player.

On more than one occasion, I and some vagabond recruits joined a company of Negro musicians that met nightly to practice in one of the back streets. Our intention was to supply them with drink in order to get them drunk, which was accomplished by dusk. We then followed them through the streets as they swayed and stumbled while playing "Yankee Doodle" or "Hail Columbia." The antics exhibited by these comic musicians in their drunken state were laughable beyond belief and brought citizens streaming from their homes to join the cavalcade, shouting with laughter. I sometimes wonder whether the musicians were playacting or reacting to the liquor.

The irresponsible behavior exhibited by some off-duty servicemen gave soldiers a bad name. Even Negroes in those northern states, though badly treated, were met with more consideration. We were generally considered lazy drunkards and often received insulting taunts in the streets. Soldiers join up for many reasons, some, as I, through necessity or foolishness, some through sudden pique, and others through choice. I was of the opinion that, if the government wanted to improve the general character of the troops, they could offer better pay to attract a better-educated class. This could have gradually cleansed the army of most of the undesirables and thus gained the respect of the community. On the contrary, naval officers and enlisted men were generally held in higher regard. They received better pay and were considered more eligible for a position in society than equivalent army officers.

The *Pennsylvania*, the largest man-of-war in American service, capable of mounting 140 guns, an impressive sight to behold, lay in the Navy Yard at Pennsylvania. She sat in a dock supported upon layers of wood to keep her dry and in good condition.

I believe that the evil of some is permitted for the good of others. Among our recruits was one whom we referred to as an old soldier, for he had already served three years as a Marine. This man taught me a valuable lesson, which I hope will act as a warning to others. He was an insatiable drinker, a scoundrel, and a swindler who, like quicksand, dragged good men down to their destruction. Knowing all the dens of iniquity, he used this information to systematically relieve us of our money. When he could not induce us to purchase his drink, he would request a loan, which invariably went unpaid. On one occasion he took us to a rum shanty, which he described as a place for fun. At the liquor counter we were given a mixture more potent than any medicine I had mixed. It did not kill but prepared us for the destruction of our souls. I saw there were also women at the counter, imbibing the same poison. They were such a debased group that I shuddered to think that I was there with them. I managed to persuade all to leave, including the old soldier, who assumed an innocent attitude. I thank God that I had enough courage to speak out against ever entering such a place again. A few days later, the same wretch led us to the same den by a more circuitous route. I departed at once, but others remained, including James Hamilton, a young Scotsman and my bunkmate. James was well-natured, very generous and amiable, but a little too lighthearted. He fell into danger and though I tried to help him he was apprehended by the law and brought to justice.

Many Americans were drinkers, believing they could pass through life in an irresponsible, inebriated state. The truth was that they were ruled by their desire for alcohol, where they lost their conscience and often developed criminal habits to satisfy their own gain. Some became the robbers and murderers that were daily depicted in the newspapers. To this day I thank God for sparing me from such evil. I was still a child who, just a few months previously, was enjoying the comfort and safety of Mrs. Lowth's household. It was remarkable that I was kept safe and fortunate so that by the time I reached Philadelphia, I had acquired enough experience to recognize and keep me out of serious trouble.

Philadelphia was the first place where I was able to exercise my independence. It is where I learned to smoke cigars and to drink, though moderately. Expressing my new habits and pursuits caused me to forget my duty to repay my debt to my considerate Irish landlady. One morning I awoke feeling ashamed that I had failed in my promise, which should have been repaid immediately after receiving my bounty. I felt like a fool having allowed my mates to sway my good intentions. Had I waited much longer I would have spent all my money, and I would have hated myself. I went at once, paid the money, apologized for my neglect, and spent an additional half a dollar with her, to enable her to help another destitute. I wish I had acted more wisely and given her my five-dollar bounty. She would have kept it for me and prevented me from wasting it. I am unable to remember one good thing we did with our bounties, and never in my life have I spent money so aimlessly or foolishly.

I also became acquainted with a good and kind man named George Washington Call, who was a native of the city. He entered the service either through an act of pique, or a problem with his family. He was a comb-maker by profession and was able to earn more money in a week than he would earn in a month while in the army. George never walked the streets, fearing that he would see an acquaintance or client, as he considered, like all Americans, that he had degraded himself by enlisting. He was well-built, about six feet tall and as straight as a forest pine. We served together for five years and became like brothers. He was true and upright, one of the bravest of the brave, every inch a soldier, but full of affection. He was my image of an ideal American but had a slight tinge of sadness in his disposition, which made me try and lift his spirits at times, especially when he was thinking of home and his beloved sister. Every time I think of George it brings back pleasant memories, for he was very kind to me and called me his son of the rendezvous from the first time we met.

The term of service of the recruiting corporal had nearly expired and I was offered his position, to remain in Philadelphia as a member of the recruiting team. Unlike England, where recruits were either cajoled with lies and drink or beaten up, while all accompanied by fife and drum, Americans applied at their own leisure at a recruiting office. The responsibilities were more for a clerk and included writing, taking the recruits before the surgeon, and ultimately accompanying them in squads to the general depot in the Bay of New York. While I felt competent to assume the duties, I wanted to see more of the country. I excused myself from receiving the honor of such a distinguished promotion, and about two weeks later I was ordered to pack up for the Bay of New York. The balmy and beautiful Indian summer ended on the morning of our departure, when the streets of the city were covered with a thick layer of snow that had fallen during the night. After we boarded the steamboat for Wilmington, we found most of the passengers sitting below deck, around a stove, chatting and gambling, a custom very prevalent amongst Americans. From Wilmington, we took a line of coaches for New York and I noticed that we passed along many of the same roads that I had travelled upon during my outbound journey through the Jerseys.

After traveling all day we arrived in New York about nightfall. Then we waited at the Castle Garden promenade for a boat to take us to Bedloe's island, which was nine miles distant from the city. Upon arrival on the island, we were paraded in the dark before the commandant, Captain Belknap, and our names were called. Afterwards we were ordered to our quarters to retire for the night. There were about three hundred recruits on the island, which was also used as a supply base for all the surrounding forts and posts. I remained there for five weeks, which seemed like a very long time, especially since we were subjected to conditions imposed by a corrupt and dishonest garrison staff.

I nicknamed our commandant Captain Deadknap, as he and his sergeants were rogues who robbed the recruits of more than half their rations. When an old soldier arrived with a fresh batch of recruits, he was always taken to a berth where he would not see what was taking place. I later learned that these crooks carried out their thievery for nearly three years, before they were found out and disciplined. The orderly sergeant managed to run away with his ill-gotten gains, but Belknap, along with his other subordinates, was sent to Green Bay, the Siberian station for officers and men who had misbehaved. I was cold and hungry for the entire time I was stationed on Bedloe's Island, and regretted having spent my bounty money, which would have been very useful during those days.

We were given two meals a day. Breakfast was at eight and consisted of a pint of chocolate or coffee, which tasted like dishwater, boiled pork, and a small portion of bread. Dinner was served at two and included a pint of tasteless, watery bean soup, some more boiled pork, and another small portion of bread. We then fasted for eighteen long hours until breakfast the following morning. Our camp commandant and his aides arranged the meals so that, through hunger, they could systematically empty the pockets of all the new recruits. Belknap was the proprietor of the sutler's store, and arranged through his orderly sergeant to open it in the evenings around the time the soldiers would be most hungry. Having a monopoly, it was very well patronized during the long cold winter evenings. Unfortunately I, like other members of our detachment, no longer had any money, due to our extravagance in Philadelphia. In addition, the camp was lax and disorderly, and the men were careless, while those who were unscrupulous seemed to receive more consideration than those carrying out their duties. To have stayed long in such surroundings would have eventually demoralized any body of men.

That year the weather was bleak, and the cold was intense. At night I went to bed hungry, looking forward to the meagre meal in the morning. Yet I was never stronger or healthier, making me think that too much food may cause many of our ailments. I also had to do my own laundry, since I had no money to pay others. There was no drill and little discipline on the island, which the following examples show: I mounted guard with a rusted musket and crooked bayonet, a weapon which I could not use in self-defense. Once, when I was on guard, my orders were to prevent anyone from removing wood from a heap which was stacked near the wharf, unless ordered to do so by the sergeant of the guard. During my shift, the captain of a New York boat called a pirogue, which was employed to bring stores to the island, requested a few sticks. I stuck my rusty firelock into the ground by the bayonet and, shouldering a load of wood, carried it myself to the boat. On another occasion, when I was assigned guard duty, I was visited by the sergeant of the guard, who made no mention of the fact that I was without my weapon while strolling along the sands in search of oysters.

The cold was so intense at night that, when it was my turn to mount guard, I kept myself warm by chopping wood or strolling the beach in search of oysters. One night I remained too long while picking them off the rocks in the shallows. Not realizing how the cold had taken hold of my body, I suddenly became numb. I began my return to the barracks, but the wind and driving snow cut through my clothing and I became exhausted, leaving me with barely enough strength to save myself. I hardly recall how I reached my quarters but know that had I stopped for even a short time I would have sunk down in the snow and quietly drifted off.

The views from Bedloe's Island of the city and surrounding islands were most picturesque. As I feasted my eyes on the beauty of nature my heart was often heavy from the want of comforts and proper sustenance. I often thought about visiting Charles, my Irish benefactor, and our French landlady, and wanted to apply for a pass, but I knew they would be disappointed to see me in uniform. New York was nine miles distant by road, yet no more than three miles looking across the water. When I was on duty early in the morning, I would hear the great city awake from slumber. Initially the sounds were faint, but grew louder and louder, until you knew that the streets had filled with life. Sometimes I could distinctly hear the rumble of vehicles and the beating of hammers.

One day while walking atop the fortifications I met a young recruit reading his Bible. William H. Scofield, a native of Connecticut and a schoolmaster by profession, was to become one of my best friends. He had joined the army in preference to suffering the daily grind of a district school. Though he was morally and religiously raised, he, like the rest of us, neglected his prayers and was led astray by the ways of the world. The Bible is necessary reading to cultivate wisdom, but few soldiers sought strength or comfort from scripture. I doubt I saw ten copies in my five years in the army. The only religious people I knew were General Clinch and a few Negroes who worshipped God in spirit and truth. The Negroes were the most faithful people, and my hope was that God would not forsake them to find their freedom.

We were very glad when the day came to select four bodies of men for the southern stations or forts on the Atlantic Coast. I was fortunate to have a Doctor Moore inspect me as, during my examination, he turned around to another surgeon and, tapping me on the chest, remarked, "This is a healthy boy. What's your name? What's your profession?" I answered, "A chemist." "Oh, indeed, what is calomel?" To which I answered, "Hydrargyri submurias." "That will do, let's see how tall you are." I got into the standard and measured only 5 feet 7 1/4 inches. He then kindly said "Stretch a little." Then he called out to the post officer, "About five feet seven and three-quarter inches. Captain Belknap, this man is wanted in the south, I have a good berth for him, he is wanted as hospital steward." "He won't do," said Belknap, "he is not tall enough for the artillery." "Oh, what's that signify?" asked Doctor Moore, "he is not required for the ranks." "Can't put him down," answered Belknap roughly. "He must go to the infantry."

For many years I harbored malicious thoughts of Captain Belknap, resulting from his unkind treatment toward me upon finding out that I was an Englishman. Resentment toward the English was not common amongst Americans, but in his case there was good cause, since he had been wounded by the English in the Battle of Fort Eric in 1812. Most Englishmen I knew in America lacked honesty and were not held in high esteem. Considering I did not leave under creditable circumstances, it would be reasonable to suppose that many others did the same. However, I was almost always met with geniality and kindness from nearly all civilians, officers, and soldiers. So much so that I have always maintained a high regard for Americans.

The rough response from Captain Belknap had the desired effect for it caused Doctor Moore to take up my cause. "Come with me and we will appeal to Major Twiggs." "Major," said the doctor, "I wish this young man to go south. He is very healthy with a sound body. He will do well there and is required in the hospital." The major was a tall and gentlemanly officer, who had full command of the distribution of troops. He questioned me kindly and only found that I was a half-inch too short, whereupon he graciously waived the requirement and ordered Captain Belknap to put me down for St. Augustine, Florida.

After inspecting the troops, the different squads were paraded separately. Then Major Twiggs, in a friendly manner, passed through the ranks asking each man his name and trade. I later learned that this was a ruse to find out if any man had entered under a false name. In one case a stammering man was unable to remember his alias. The major immediately told him, "You are a scoundrel, sir!," intimating that a black mark would go with him to the captain of his company. I was glad that I had not entered the navy under false pretenses, and counted this as another warning to always be truthful, no matter what the situation or possible consequences.

Major Twiggs and I crossed paths with one another in Florida about four years later when he was the colonel of the 4th

Regiment of Infantry. Later he held the rank of brigadier general, commanding two thousand men in Texas, but being a Southerner, at the commencement of the Civil War he disbanded his troops and entered the service of the Confederate States as a major general. I was sorry to receive such news of someone who befriended me. Though he was useful to me, I considered him to be a traitor to his country. I am sure that there were many Southerners who would not have agreed with me. I learned that he died in 1861, bereft of everything except his command as a general in the Southern Army. His son-in-law's property was confiscated during the turmoil that followed the Civil War.

St. Augustine, Florida

Eventually the day arrived for our departure and we embarked upon the *Amelia* packet ship that was bound for Charleston, South Carolina. A military band played, and our comrades cheered as we marched down to the wharf. We pitied those who were left behind in that den of starvation, a station where the treatment of the soldiers could be classified as no better than cruelty to animals.

The passage was tolerable until I became seasick and sat on deck upon a chest and vomited until there was nothing left. Suddenly the ship lurched and threw me with the chest against a companion ladder that was fixed to a trapdoor over the hold. We struck with such force that it dislodged the ladder and opened the trapdoor. I fell through down into the hold below. Falling about eight feet I landed, luckily, jockey-fashion astride a barrel of vinegar. My comrades rushed to the opening fearing that I was hurt, but seeing me mounted upon the cask, they burst into peals of laughter. This signaled the beginning of a terrifying hurricane off Cape Hatteras. Rope after rope snapped, allowing the canvas to fly uncontrollably. Sensing danger, the captain commandeered the troops so forty-seven Grey Jackets helped the twenty Blue ones bring the ship under control. Though I was terribly sick at the beginning of the gale, I was completely cured by the crash, which shows that the excitement was beneficial. Even as the storm raged and the waves grew mountainous, my stomach was soothed and became calm.

We arrived in Charleston after a week's passage and my party was sent to Fort Moultrie on Sullivan's Island, about seven miles from the city. The other detachments embarked on a steamboat for the Augusta Arsenal in Georgia. Fort Moultrie was noted as the stronghold that was defended bravely and successfully against the British Admiral Parker. While there I suffered from a severe cold and acute pain in my right side, but soon recovered owing to the comforts at the fort.

We waited on the island for ten days for the packet schooner *Agnes* that plied between Charleston and St. Augustine. Soon after boarding I lost my cap overboard and was on the verge of jumping in after it, when I was held back by a lieutenant. I then had to cover my head French-style with a cotton handkerchief. This did not protect me from contracting a head cold, accompanied by excessive blood in my head that was only relieved by periodical bleedings from my nose.

After two days at sea we arrived opposite the St. Augustine bar and the pilot boarded us from a small boat like a whaler. He spoke in broken English, as he was from the island of Minorca. As we crossed the bar, the channel was so shallow that we occasionally touched the gravel bottom. The bar at St. Augustine was continually shifting, so it was the duty of the pilots to sound the channel after each storm, as it could be very dangerous. The coastline was bleak, causing one member of our party to remark, "It was the remains after the world was finished." We passed Anastasia Island to our left. The shore was rocky, but the interior looked wild with marshes, creeks, and almost impenetrable thickets. A lighthouse stood out on the higher ground. The rocks were formed from small seashells and sand and crumbled quite readily. It was not fit for building, but it did stand up well as a material for sea walls or breakwaters. On our right was the mainland, with a level and sandy, but very barren, beach. It was separated from the city by the North River, so named because it originated in the country about thirty-five miles north and within five miles of the St. Johns River. Our schooner then spent about two hours beating up the inlet, which led to the city.

The first view of St. Augustine was very picturesque, owing to the varied style of architecture. An old Spanish fort, called Fort

Marion by the Americans and Fort St. Marks by the builders, was situated on the extreme right. It was built in the time of King Carlos II of Spain and had a large inscription on the walls of the sally port, "Spain, once the most powerful Nation." The streets were very narrow, and the architecture was a mixture of Spanish, half-Spanish, and American. This ancient city of St. Augustine, East Florida, was founded on Friday, the 7th of September 1565, by Menendez and was, by more than forty years, the most ancient city of the United States. At the time of my arrival, it was the most beautiful and most favored watering place in the land, and full of splendid hotels. St. Augustine was situated upon an inlet, erroneously called a "river" by the inhabitants, which ran south from the city for about twenty miles before it joined once more with the ocean at a place called the Matanzas. That outlet had a bar similar to the one opposite the city, which we had to cross on our arrival. The water of the inlet separated Anastasia and Fish Islands from the mainland. The island of Anastasia lay about one mile east of the city and unfortunately absorbed most of the sea breeze.

Upon our arrival at the wharf, an officer was ready to receive and conduct us to our new home at the St. Francis barracks, located at the extreme southern point of the city. Upon our arrival we were reviewed by Doctor Weightman, the post surgeon. I was in a miserable condition with bloodshot eyes, my head wrapped in a cloth, and a lame foot due to frostbite. Consequently, I was immediately placed upon the sick list. We were then ordered to join our company.

We were introduced to our future comrades in a large barrack room that was also the sleeping quarters for the company. On either side of the room were rows of three-tier bunks for the men to sleep singly. The men of the company invited us to take a position of honor, seated upon a long bench before a large wood fire. They gathered about us in friendly groups and immediately began to ply us with questions, such as where we were from. They soon learned that an Englishman was among the new arrivals, which prompted a long-nosed individual to call out from one of the bunks, "An Englishman, where is he?"

He was pleased to see a fellow countryman, as he was the only one in the company. He shook my hand warmly and would have embraced me if it were possible for an Englishman to do so. Gilding had been a respectable man in Liverpool, who fell in stature and eventually became the coachman for Colonel Henry Thomas Dummett, the commandant of English troops in Barbados. When the colonel absconded with the pay chest containing the pay for his troops, Gilding accompanied him and his family in their clandestine flight to Florida. While he and I were conversing, there was another shout. "Which one is the hospital steward?" asked Tones, the previous steward.

Having been given three chances by Doctor Weightman, he was let go due to his addiction to stimulants. Tones was the son of a wealthy Virginian planter, a surgeon by profession and consequently most suitable for the position, if he controlled his habit. Unfortunately, money was easily available to him from a bank account in the city and his friends did nothing to discourage him. He admitted that on the last occasion, he allowed all the wine to run out of the cask. "As you see," he said, "I have no-one to blame but myself. The doctor is kindness itself and would do his best for me, but I am such a fool for I won't let him." He wound up a fine speech regarding Doctor Weightman's excellent qualities by saying, "If anyone goes to heaven, it must be the doctor."

It was the habit of Major Gates, who commanded Company D of the second regiment, to meet and examine the newly arrived enlisted men on the first morning after their arrival. We were ordered to stand before him in one row, where he went from one to the next interrogating each individual. He ordered each man to extend out his right arm horizontally and to hold that position as he was questioned. This was to determine whether anyone could do so without showing a tremor. At the time I was still weak and nervous and, not realizing the importance of the questions, I foolishly answered them with an almost childlike innocence.

"Can you drink out of a spoon?" A question which referred to someone who drank Stone Fence, an equal mixture of rum and lager, that was favored by confirmed drinkers who used it to calm their stomachs first thing in the morning. The mixture, of course, was taken with a spoon and hence his query, which I did not understand and answered with a smile. "Oh yes, sir."

I soon recovered from my ailments and was then allowed the freedom to visit the city. This seemed like an unusual kindness to me, as my comrades were not allowed a similar privilege. Later I learned that the liberty was used to assess my behavior, as I had not instilled any confidence in either the surgeon or the major, owing to my pitiful performance and swollen appearance upon arrival. Major Gates, who was a good and kind officer, held a deep-seated aversion toward drunkards and believed that he had the ability to discern one upon first acquaintance. In the end they realized that they were mistaken. Doctor Weightman told me the reasons for their suspicions and confided to me the troubles they had with the previous steward, who was a drunkard. Dr. Weightman then explained all the duties and responsibilities of a hospital steward and promised that if I were suitable and performed my duties satisfactorily, he would assist me in my studies and look after my interests like a father. If, on the other hand, I was negligent, dishonest, or lazy, I would be removed from my position and be returned to the barracks to do my duty in the ranks.

After all my experiences, and not quite seventeen years old, I found myself installed in an office, placed in command of men, and in charge of a large building containing dry bedding, wine, spirits, molasses, tea, chocolate, and all kinds of stores needed for the sick. When I recall the sudden and prosperous change in my circumstances, I am amazed at the benefits I received in this far-off land. I knew that I was not worthy, but I did not recognize then, as I do now, how indebted I was to the fatherly and loving hand of my God. Thankfully, I recognized my responsibilities: that if I wished to succeed, my work had to come first.

My duties in St. Augustine were light, as there was only one company of artillery under the command of Major Gates stationed at the fort. He was assisted by Captain Gardener, one first lieutenant, two second lieutenants, and one assistant surgeon. There were fifty to sixty men in barracks.

Every morning doctor's call was beat at 7 a.m., and I had to be inside the barracks to find out from the orderly sergeant, the first sergeant of the company, and the sergeant of the guard if they had any men who had reported sick. If there were, they were escorted by me to the doctor. Severe cases were ordered to the hospital, while the others were either placed as sick in quarters or returned to duty. At 8 a.m. the surgeon visited the hospital, and I had to accompany him in order to receive instructions regarding the various patients. In all cases it was my responsibility to dispense medicines and to see that the matron got the proper food stores for the day. Every morning I had to make a full report of the sick, which included particulars regarding the number received that morning, those who returned to duty, and those who remained on the sick list. The report was signed by the surgeon who then presented it to the commandant. It was also my duty as the steward to supervise all matrons, ward masters, and attendants, or nurses, to see that each fulfilled his or her specific duty and to report all neglect or inattention. All complaints from the sick were made to the surgeon or commandant through the steward only. All necessities, drugs, and stores were obtained by the steward using quadruplicate requisitions, which had to be written neatly and plainly. These were signed first by the surgeon, then by the commandant, and then they were transmitted to Washington for further approval and signature by the surgeon general or commissary or quartermaster general as the case might be. They were then returned to the commissary or quartermaster of the post as vouchers to be used for the delivery of hospital goods.

The wardmaster had to take charge of the sick men's accessories, furniture, and bedding in the different wards. Attendants or nurses were assigned according to the number of patients in the hospital, as were matrons, whose duties were to cook and wash.

All requisitions, returns, and inventories were made out quarterly and forwarded to the head of the department. It was also my duty to keep a meteorological diary of the weather; keep an account of funds and medicines; prepare the minor pharmaceutical preparations; attend to the purchase of fish, flesh, and fowl and all the odds and ends required for the convalescent. My duties, though not arduous, were numerous and required my constant attention.

We were inspected by the commandant and his officers weekly and monthly. My pay was an average calculation of about £35. per annum. I had to purchase my clothing and one ration. I received my pay at irregular intervals, and did not receive my first pay at St. Augustine for six months. I used my first pay to write a letter to my Father, in which I stated all the particulars leading up to my departure from England, my various journeys, and my current situation at St. Augustine. After a period of four months, I happily received the following letter from my Father:

Long Bennington
August 30, 1832

Dear John,

I have to acknowledge that I have received your letter and it has brought me great relief, for I have been in a sad state of mind concerning you and I cannot help but think that you were too rash in taking such a step. But as it is so, we must look forward and hope for the best. As far as advising you what to do for the future, I must also leave that entirely to yourself. England is getting into a dreadful state, both in the country and in London. You must know I went to London after I received your letter to know how to act in your case. Your Uncle Horspool, on my behalf, has undertaken to send you £30, as soon as he can find a proper channel to send it by. Sending it by letter we found would not be safe. So you see, you may have received it before this letter, which if not, you may expect it any day.

From your letter I see you have signed up for 5 years, but I cannot determine what is best. Whether you should return or stay your 5 years, or whether you should accept the situation offered to you by the gentleman who wished to take you. Provided you think through the matter, I will leave the decision up to you. I am sure there are regulations that you must follow, which you know and I do not know. We thought the £30 might gain your liberty to return home, or you could use it to better your situation in America, if you see a good prospect. I urge you to keep writing every half-year or so, for I shall feel very anxious to know how you are doing, or whether you are in need of anything. But please do not stay in the country any longer than necessary, especially if you are uncomfortable.

I must mention that I called at Mr. Mills of Stamford when I went to London and he seemed very sorry about your circumstances. I also found that you had sent a letter to Mrs. Lowth, who has since returned all your belongings. Your sister claimed your umbrella to hold until we all meet again, if we shall live. Life is very uncertain at present so if you think you will not be returning, please keep writing, or I shall suspect that you are dead. Therefore, if you receive this letter before the £30, wait awhile in expectation of it and then write to inform us of it. Tell us what you think of America, how you are getting along and what you think of doing in the future. I believe we would all be better off in America, but that can't happen at present.

Dear John, I have nothing further to relate and nothing worth noting has occurred among us since you were at Bennington. I must repeat that I find it more difficult to make a profit now than a year or two ago and I am afraid I shall lose some principal. People are getting poorer and William is idling at home. Joseph is at Fisher and Fillinghams in Newark and doing well I hope. They all with Cousin Jane send their best love to you. I hope all is for the best and I sincerely wish you all happiness. Don't be unhappy any longer than necessary.

I remain your most affectionate Father
John Bemrose

You will notice from my Father's letter that his first wish was of my well-being. Here was forgiveness, love, anxiety for my welfare, and money transmitted at the first opportunity to help me if required. I was reminded of that beautiful parable in the New Testament, the Prodigal Son, who, after he wasted the legacy he received, was welcomed back with open arms by a loving father. This analogy between earthly and heavenly love is all we need to know. Love is a gift from our heavenly Father, proving truly that "God is Love."

As I became familiar with my duties, I grew comfortable with my situation and decided to complete my time in the army. As mentioned in my Father's letter, I had written a resentful letter to Mrs. Lowth, my old mistress. In it, I compared her treatment toward me as being similar to that of a Negro slave in Florida, which was wrong and a great exaggeration. Mrs. Lowth's was a place of training, where the work and discipline were meant to prepare me for a more responsible position. If only I had been patient and accepted my course, I would have succeeded. In the end my indiscipline and pride got the better of me and became the cause of my own demise.

Most men who give up their apprenticeship training usually meet with misfortune. Some die while others become drunkards or just waste their time away. I was fortunate for my God to put me into the caring hands of Doctor Weightman. I could just as easily have been under the command of a tyrannical officer. The more I learned about the doctor, the more I admired him. He was extremely kind to me and became a true friend for the whole time I served under him. Everyone loved him, and all were ready to serve him, for he took pleasure to ensure that all in his care were comfortable and happy. It was his wish that I should study medicine and he gave me free access to the library in his quarters and was happy to help me with my reading. Naturally, I followed his advice which prepared me to attend lectures in medicine at some time in the future. He promised that at the end of my service he would introduce me to some of his medical friends in Philadelphia who would determine the best way for me to secure an entrance to a suitable medical college as a student.

Dr. Weightman was part owner of a plantation situated on the St. Johns River, which is about eighteen miles west of the city. He spent his annual three months' leave on the plantation, during which time he usually engaged Dr. Porcher, the post doctor, to act for him. I came to know and developed a good friendship with Doctor Porcher. On one occasion he confided in me his regret that I had entered the service and he also informed me that he could obtain my release if I produced a birth certificate, as I was a minor at the time of my enlistment. This was a gesture of kindness but I was so happy and comfortable working with Doctor Weightman that I failed to follow the matter through. I remained at the hospital for a further two or three years, during which time I concentrated on my studies. It was my daily custom to arise early to read and write my medical journals, as I found that I retained the substance of the work when I wrote it down. I read Wilson on diseases of hot climates, Bell's *Anatomy*, and also Cheselden's. Occasionally I drew anatomical figures with my pencil. On another occasion Dr. Porcher gave me three days of instruction and practice with the scalpel, when I dissected many exterior layers of muscle. Dr. Porcher loved his work with anatomy and through his instruction our friendship increased. As a result he became more insistent that I should obtain a proof of my minority from home so that he could obtain my discharge. I wrote to my Father and the following was his reply from home:

Long Bennington
March 16th, 1834,

Dear John,

You will find the first part of the letter taken up by your sister, who I'm afraid you will find is a good deal like me, a poor scribe.

We began to think your letter took too long as it was nearly three weeks longer coming than any of your former letters. Your Uncle Horspool made two or three inquiries by letter to me, thinking it very long before it arrived and has advised me to write to see what is the matter. He has been very anxious after your welfare, but thank God it arrived at last and has given me the most satisfaction of anyone. I sent it up to London the day after I received it, which I know will also give your uncle great satisfaction. What with receiving the money and the way you spend your time, makes me look forward with great anxiety to seeing you in England. Then if we live, we will conclude what to do for the best, whether to stay in England or not. The farmers' situation is desperate, with nothing but ruin before them, except for those that were able to secure their independence during the Good Times.

It was your wish that I should send the date of your birth, which is January 16th, 1815. Consequently you were nineteen last January the 16th, so therefore you would be a few months past twenty-one when your time is up. Your share of the interest from your Uncle George will doubtless be allowed from the time you are twenty-one up to the time you arrive in England.

Your brother William, I am sorry to say, does not know what to do with himself, for all his delight is shooting and fishing, and he never shows any interest in his books. Therefore, he must have forgotten what little he did know, which causes me great uneasiness to see him so thoughtless.

Dear John, I can't think of anything more worth relating, for everything in the neighborhood is much the same as when I last wrote. Therefore I have to announce we are all very well and likewise your Uncles Rowbotham's and Horspool's family and hopes these few lines will arrive safe and find you in good health.

I remain,
Your Affectionate Father
John Bemrose

I had followed Dr. Porcher's advice in vain. The coming and going of letters over a distance of nearly five thousand miles took several months and when I eventually received the above letter, I found it to be useless. Army regulations required that a document must be signed by either a magistrate or the pastor of the town or village where I was born. It also required the signatures of at least two respectable householders. Since I was unable to comply with the regulations, I was obliged to stay my term.

Fortunately, I was happy with my situation and my work. I was in the best of hands assisting Dr. Porcher and, though I suffered from periodical attacks of fever and bouts of homesickness, I could not have been happier. Even when I look back over the years, I realize how he valued me and became like a father to me. The gratitude I felt created in me a desire to be useful and become indispensable to him as a help and a comfort. We loved each other with that kind of love, shown in silent attentions to one another. If the doctor suffered, I was ready to aid and if I were foolish, he came with succor and advice, for he knew my weakness and my peculiarities and he saved me from myself. He was kindness personified and to work and weary for him was a joy. To do the wishes of those who love us is very gratifying, though Christianity asks us for more.

The major was especially considerate and would frequently spend an hour in the surgery when he entrusted me to look after his children's minor ailments. He always had me receive my pay in his own quarters, where he would kindly offer me a seat at the table. This would have been viewed as uncommon treatment by the paymaster, as it was quite an exception for any noncommissioned officer or private soldier to sit in the presence of a commissioned officer. He was courteous to me on all occasions, even before other officers. The major obviously had his own reasons, but my belief is that he respected my sobriety, especially since he was the one who had suspected otherwise upon our first meeting. Unfortunately, after his departure I unintentionally made an enemy of Captain Drane, his successor, which occurred as follows:

Captain Drane had a vacancy for his own orderly sergeant and offered me the position. I did not want to leave the hospital and refused the promotion, even though Dr. Weightman had given me his approval to make the change. The pay was a little more, but time rather than money was my real issue, as I wanted to retain the opportunity to study. Captain Drane had been raised from the ranks during the war against the British and was nearly illiterate. He probably hoped to secure a sergeant who could write well and keep his accounts. But I loved working in the hospital under Dr. Weightman, who treated me very well. Captain Drane was unhappy that I did not accept his offer and for the remainder of my term I was a victim of his occasional anger. Most of the time he was unfriendly and would often take delight in annoying me even in petty matters. Over time I learned to cope with him and avoided confrontation by giving him a wide berth. I also knew that I had my doctor to protect me.

During my stay St. Augustine was divided into two towns, called American and Minorcan, where a large open square was the line of separation. The fish and meat market abutted the inlet on the east. The Episcopal Church was on the south side, with the Catholic Church and the courthouse directly opposite on the north. The Athenaeum rooms and post office were situated on the west. In the center of the square stood a column with an inscription upon it: *Plaza de la Constitution*. The city was populated with about three thousand Minorcans, two thousand Americans, and about one thousand comprised of Spanish, French, Dutch, Irish, English, and many people of color.

The Minorcans were referred to as Turnbull's Negroes. Doctor Andrew Turnbull, an Englishman, had brought their forefathers to his plantation in Florida from the Balearic Islands, off the coast of Spain. This was during the period from 1763 to 1784, when Florida belonged to the British. He had promised that they would work off their passage and keep, after which they would be employed at a fair wage. Instead, he kept them in bondage until some of the men rebelled and made their escape through fifty miles of woods to the city, where the affair was handled by the authorities. The result was that their companions were released from their unjust and cruel servitude.

The division north of the square had three streets running north for about half a mile, which were intersected by five or six streets running east and west. That was the most populous part of the city. At the extreme north stood the ancient stronghold of Fort Marion, or Fort Marks, that was built by the Spanish. It was an immense construction and stood in a commanding position of the channel. The walkway atop the walls was very spacious with plenty of room for artillery and troops. When I was there, it was mounted with 32-pounders. The interior was a quadrangle and bombproof. A deep moat surrounded the walls and was designed to allow water to enter at high tide. There was a glacis around the fortifications defended by large cannon. This fort, though apparently strong, was silenced by battery from the opposite island, when the British last invaded under General Oglethorpe. There were still signs of the damage that was caused.

Two public thoroughfares of about six hundred yards long ran south of the square through the American quarter. They were intersected by three streets running east to west. During the Spanish years, St. Francis barracks was a monastery located at the extreme southern end of the city. It was a reasonable structure, surmounted by an octagonal cupola from which you had a good view of the sea, looking directly over Anastasia Island. About a hundred yards farther south was the hospital and married soldiers' quarters. Half a mile south of these were the ruins of the Spanish arsenal and magazine, situated within a quadrangular turreted wall of considerable strength. The arsenal fell into the hands of the British when they constructed a defensible structure during the night, just 200 yards from it. This surprised the Spanish garrison and made the magazine untenable.

St. Augustine is the most ancient city in North America and was the seat of government under Spanish rule. The ruins of the original Government House were still partly standing, along with the ruins of a convent. The city was almost surrounded by water as the St. Sebastian River takes a circuitous course from the north and enters the inlet about a mile from the southern suburbs. To depart the city for Picolata and Tomoka to the south, there was a large wooden bridge over the waterway that was about a quarter of a mile long. The city was mainly supported by the orange trade, but also by periodic trade from planters who lived beside the St. Johns and along the coast at Mosquito, Tomoka, and New Smyrna. There was an excellent fishery, as the Minorcans were expert fishermen.

The countryside adjacent to the city abounded in a variety of fruit orchards, including oranges, peaches, figs, pomegranates, quinces, melons, citrons, limes, and grapes, and the woods produced wild oranges, huckleberries, and prickly pears. The principal vegetables were sweet potatoes, pumpkins, tomatoes, cucumbers, squash, and vegetable marrows, which were abundant. Onions, cabbages, potatoes, carrots, and turnips were raised but were not of the best quality. Indian corn, or maize, was very good and grew to over ten feet high. The climate was most favorable for the growth of sugarcane and cotton. Some French families grew mulberries to form silkworm colonies, which were well established in several groves by the time of my arrival.

The climate of St. Augustine was healthy. The air was mild and pleasant, notwithstanding the high temperature. It was a favorite winter resort for invalids from the North and was recommended to those with consumptive habits. More than 200 invalids stayed in one of the many boarding houses, while the hotels were usually filled with the planters and gentry.

The chief occupations of the city dwellers were fishing and hunting the wild deer, but there were also trades such as cigar makers, carpenters, and blacksmiths. Shoemakers and tailors were notable exceptions, as clothing, shoes, and implements all came from the North. A monthly schooner named *Agnes* plied between St Augustine and Charleston, South Carolina, and a weekly packet sailed between Charleston and New York.

The Minorcans were unsophisticated but very amiable, civil, and good-mannered. They always greeted passersby courteously with a "buenos dias" in the day and a "buenos noches" in the evening. As Dr. Porcher had permission to practice medicine amongst the citizens, I saw much of them. I was warned to be wary of them and their knives, but my personal experience proved otherwise. They spoke a broken English that was pleasant to the ear. The young women were handsome and practiced clean habits, but after marriage they became slovenly and unkempt. Their eyes were black, as was their hair, which was long and strong. They usually displayed a smile of contentment and a thorough absence of anxiety. The looks of the dames, or older ladies, varied dramatically from night to day. In the evening they were tastefully appareled, their hair in ringlets and covered by a Spanish veil. By the following morning the same pretty and well-arranged belle of the evening looked disheveled, with unkempt hair, unwashed face that showed vestiges of pigment, stockingless legs, and slippered feet. The males were generally slovenly and wore light jackets and trousers, with large, slouched straw hats. This was the dress code they all adopted, for the summer heat varied from ninety to one hundred and ten degrees in the shade, making comfort, not appearance, the main consideration. Their wants were few, their fortunes small, and there was no craving after excess. A little rice, some fish, and fruit were sufficient. So little fresh meat was used that one steer supplied the entire city each day. Mutton was not used, as a sheep could not live in Florida due to the sweltering heat.

The houses were built of shellstone quarried from Anastasia Island, opposite the city. The roofs were shingle and painted red, while the walls were whitewashed. Almost all the houses had balconies projecting from the second story, while many had latticed windows, which were shut at night. The Minorcan homes looked dreary with their latticed windows painted Venetian red, while most preferred the American homes that had a light and jaunty look. Their woodwork was painted light green, the roofs were of slate, and the stonework walls were painted white. They were cooled by allowing the air to pass through green Venetian blinds in the windows.

Sunday evenings were particularly carefree since the sacredness of the day was considered over by 6:00 p.m. The townspeople then amused themselves with dancing and serenading in the streets, or billiards indoors. The fandango was the popular dance. I often followed in the rear of the crowds that followed serenaders, who were usually accompanied by half a dozen musicians. These public affairs were very popular with the Spanish beaus. When the music ceased upon arrival under a chosen balcony, the lover would step to the front of the crowd and gracefully doff his straw hat, while wishing his "cara puella" good night, which she acknowledged with a plaintive, "buenos noches."

St. John's Eve was the great annual festival of the younger citizens, who would parade around the city in costume and then complete the festivities at evening balls in masquerade. During the day, the ladies represented ancient chivalry, mounted upon handsomely caparisoned steeds, while the gentleman wore the costumes of ancient dames. These groups toured the city and entered the more distinguished homes for refreshments. Two or three shrines were specially constructed and placed strategically throughout the city. Their large wooden frames formed a recess that was beautifully and tastefully decorated with flowers and draperies. In the center of the recess was placed a representation of Christ, apparently of silver, which was lit up by the glare of a hundred tapers. The custom was to present the gentleman that first viewed the altar with a bunch of flowers taken from the decorated pile, which he gracefully received from the hand of the lady proprietor. The receiver in turn was expected to host a grand ball the same evening where he was crowned the king of the feast and leader of the dance. I was enthralled by the scene, which was brilliant and grand with a total absence of gluttony and drunkenness. Everyone seemed lighthearted and happy. I personally did not like the way they mixed the sacred with the frivolous, but on reflection that was preferable to the way we English spend Christmas, with music and psalms in the early morning sung by befuddled, gluttonous performers.

When a death occurred in a Minorcan family, it was considered a mark of respect to view the corpse. The body was placed for public view on the street where the deceased was laid out and decorated in finery and surrounded by eight large silver candlesticks, which burned both day and night.

Funerals were full of pageantry, and once I was part of a procession at a Catholic soldier's funeral. We marched to the music "The Dead March in Saul." I was paired with an old Scottish ordinance sergeant called Crosmond, who was 6 feet 2 inches in height, while I was a little over 5 feet 7 inches. We were a ridiculous pair, as he had a long slouching gait which years of drill had not cured, while I had not been drilled at all. My marching was most unprofessional and not helped by the slowness of the music. We were stationed in front of the corpse and were supposed to walk abreast of one another. Crosmond could keep the beat, but he gradually pulled ahead of me and the procession due to his lengthy stride. He would exclaim good-naturedly, "Bless me, John, keep the step." Then I would retort, "I can't, stilts are necessary to keep up with your long legs." In this awkward manner we arrived at the church, the corpse was carried to the center aisle, and the priests went through the Catholic ceremony, after which we marched again for the burial ground. One priest led the march, positioned about ten paces in front and carrying a silver crucifix. Another priest closely followed the first, carrying the prayers that were used in the service, and he was followed by my Scottish friend and me. Following the interment, I hoped that my difficulties would have vanished for the return journey, but the music struck up "The Merry Man Home to His Grave." Worse and worse, the step quickened and Crosmond responded to the liveliness of the music with invigorated legs. I sped along, out of breath and out of step, until we were the laughing-stock of both soldiers and citizens. Even the officers chuckled when, finally, the commanding officer gave the word to halt and sent for me and Sergeant Crosmond. We were then placed in the rear, which prevented the sergeant from leaving me, and we managed more appropriately. After that exhibition, I never attended a funeral as a member of the procession. To prepare myself for future marching duties I presented myself to the drillmaster and received instruction, which enabled me to pass muster more creditably and comfortably. The Catholic priest charged $80 as remuneration for his and his brother priest's share in the funeral.

The reason I was an undrilled soldier deserves an explanation. When I arrived at St. Augustine hospital, a color sergeant named Yeoman was living in hope of being the next steward. He had made a strong case to both the surgeon and commandant, but as he was known to be dishonest, he was denied the position. My arrival completely squashed his chances because he understood that, if they were unable to get someone who understood medicine, the position would be granted to him, as he had administrative qualities which included being an excellent penman and scholar. Consequently, Yeoman was unfriendly toward me and came to the hospital ordering me for drill, which in my innocence I attended. While he was putting me through the goosestep, Dr. Weightman called at the hospital in search of me. Finding that I was absent he asked the matron, who told him I had left with the sergeant. He immediately came to the Piazza overlooking the parade ground and called out to me to leave the ranks. He asked how I came to be drilling and I told him the sergeant had given me an order. At once he became angry and informed me that I was to obey orders only from him and the major. "In future," he said, "remember you are not to allow the sergeants to take you from the hospital, for you are under my direction. In the event a sergeant comes with any orders to the hospital without the commandant's or my signature, kick him out." The truth was that I was unfit to march, when in hindsight I should have been trained in all the skills of my trade. You never know when you may be called upon to perform a service that is expected of your position.

During the time I was stationed in St. Augustine I had the opportunity to witness the conditions of slavery. For the most part, I found the slaves were treated humanely, and the hard-working Negroes had the ability to redeem themselves from their unnatural state of bondage. It was common practice for slave owners in St. Augustine and the adjacent parts of East Florida to grant slaves their freedom, if they could pay for it, for this was Spanish law. Typically, they were not worked severely. Their tasks were generally completed by noon and they had the remainder of the day for themselves. Every Negro was allowed their own garden, pigsty, or pen to keep a pig or cow and almost all had chickens. With proper care of their own animals, which they were allowed to sell, many were able to emancipate themselves.

Unfortunately there was an exception in the law that excluded Americans and plantations from the Spanish custom. Plantation slaves were eager to avoid the increased hours of working the fields, which denied them the benefit of leisure time, and they generally sought alternative work. Since there were more applicants than positions, employers were able to choose their servants. I lived in Florida nearly five years and do not recall a single case where a plantation hand was able to obtain his liberty.

There were also masters who were unfit to own slaves, such as Bulow, a Prussian, who was an atrocious monster and despised by his fellow planters. He was the largest slaveowner in the St. Augustine area and resided at a handsome plantation house called Bulowville, located about forty miles south of the city. Charles Bulow owned over three hundred working hands and was very wealthy. When I first met him, he was quite young and handsome, yet bereft of any good traits in his character. He was intemperate and quarrelsome with his peers, tyrannical to his dependents, and a murderer of three of his slaves, one of whom he shot during my time. The slave was working as a marker at one of his master's shooting matches, when he made a mistake that angered Bulow, who immediately shot him dead. The territorial slave law exacted a fine of $500 for a life, which this monster paid three times. If an owner was unable to pay the fine, he was then imprisoned for one year.

Only in a slaveocracy could laws be made that sanctioned brutality and inhumanity. Slave owners were quick to flatter themselves and soothe their souls when their slaves received good treatment. The system cultivated a horrible distortion of human nature. "My slave, I protect. That free nigger is to be pitied." Such delusional charity enabled owners to be self-deceived rather than to do what was right. But such arguments were valueless to me since the laws were made by and for the oppressor. It was a fortunate slave who lived under a caring master, but others who were not treated kindly had no avenue of redress. Young masters became sensual, drunken, unchaste, and evil as they learned about the demoniacal power they possessed. There was no surprise that in their lust they quickly exerted their newfound might against a weak and defenseless people, who from the cradle were instilled to be inferior creatures, chattels. I came to view slavery as the greatest abomination on the face of the earth.

A public slave auction occurred once during my stay at St. Augustine. It was a disgusting display that was beyond my imagination. Buyers quibbled like cattle jobbers over the physical attributes of those being marketed, while fathers were separated from sons and daughters parted from their mothers. Marriage ties were annulled, sons brutalized, mistresses and their daughters dehumanized.

It is not difficult to blunt your feelings and be induced to excuse any abomination that becomes accepted as normal in society.

Christian ministers in the South were already part of the system, so who was the guardian of morality? I had to thank God that I remained aloof and prayed that in His mercy, He would keep me clear of the unclean traffic. It was my observation that when a man becomes enslaved by vice, however benign or prosperous it may be, it develops a blot of iniquity within and, like a cancer, will eat our very soul and let loose upon the land a deadly pestilence.

I was there when Bulow died, and his young son brought his father's corpse to the city for interment. They came by water and, as was the custom, the Negro boatmen sang to the stroke of the oars. Bulow made them sing his own composition, a line of which I record:

"Old Bulow is dead and gone to hell and here lib young Massa doing well."

Fort King

In the winter of 1834 our garrison at Fort Marion received orders to march for Fort King, the Seminole agency. The purpose was to strengthen that command then under Brigadier D. L. Clinch, pending negotiations between the Seminole tribe of Indians and the United States agent, General Thompson. The following is an account of the difficulties that existed between these Indians and the United States government at that time.

In the treaty between the United States and Spain of 1795, it stipulated that the Spanish government of Florida should restrain their Indians from committing hostilities against the United States. Then by treaty on the 22nd of February 1819, the Floridas were ceded in full dominion and absolute property to the United States, at a cost of fifteen million dollars. In this treaty there was no reference to, or provision for, the Indians, in any manner whatever.

At that time the white population was centered in and around the cities of St. Augustine and Pensacola, while the interior was sparsely inhabited by the Indian Nation, which consisted of less than six thousand men, women, and children. It was said that the Indians, known as Seminoles, were banished from the main body of Creeks in Georgia to make a home for themselves in the wilds of Florida, where they increased in number.

These natives were lawless and known for their frequent raids upon the cities to capture Spanish and Minorcan women for ransom. Even when I lived in St. Augustine, it was not uncommon for someone to point out a woman who had been ransomed.

These and other uncivilized habits presented serious questions as to whether the natives could ever become good citizens, or productive landholders. There was never any question that a large territory with twelve hundred miles of coastline, acquired at such great cost, would be left in possession of the Indians. To solve these problems, it was agreed to move all the Indians to a reservation and to provide them with a generous annuity. At the Treaty of Camp Moultrie in 1823 the tribes were granted five million acres in central Florida, while Congress agreed to pay the chiefs specific annuities and other benefits.

The Indian Nation had distinct boundaries about two hundred miles north to south and about eighty miles at its greatest breadth. Tribesmen were not allowed to leave the Nation without a pass from the agent or they were liable to punishment. They governed themselves. If an Indian was found guilty of a misdemeanor he was tried by a number of his chiefs, who were at the same time the judges and executioners. But if an Indian trespassed upon the lands of a settler he was reported to the agent, who appointed a council of his elders or chiefs to punish him. If a settler mistreated or retaliated against an Indian, then the agent would take action against the settler. If an Indian required redress from a settler, the expenses were covered by the government.

It was common for the natives to come to St. Augustine in groups of six or eight, to barter their skins, venison, raccoons, and squirrels for rum, shot, powder, and groceries. In all such cases they had to have a pass from the agent. They presented a very picturesque appearance when they were in the city. The chief of the party marched first, straight and as impassive as the pine of his native forest. On these occasions he was decked in all his finery, with his long dark hair fantastically dressed with feathers of wild fowl, eyebrows dyed black, and underneath his eyes a semicircular rim of red paint, with large silver rings in his nostrils. If he was a great brave, his ears were slit and elongated, so that they rested upon his shoulders. His body was covered with a tunic that fitted tight to the breast and was covered with circular pieces of silver of various dimensions that were beaten out of dollars, half dollars, and quarters, sometimes amounting to thirty or forty pieces according to his wealth.

When an Indian travelled he wore all his wealth, which reminded me of well-to-do Englishmen who dressed up to show off all their finery in public. His sash or belt was of worsted, of various colors, and prettily decorated with beads. His moccasins were made of buckskin, with the inner flaps turned down and lined with silk worked with beads. His leggings were made of worsted, similar to stockings except they were of many colors. They were bound round immediately above the calf with worsted sashes similar to a belt, only of less width. The chief's family usually followed, mimicking the same direct, cautious gait, but were dressed more plainly, as few possessed leggings or moccasins and, if they did, they were without decoration. Women usually accompanied these parties as they were the packhorses, laden with skins for barter in the city. They were neglected by their men and treated no better than slaves. They cultivated the soil and looked after their children and cattle. They carried their papooses upon their backs in a kind of wallet. Only once, at Fort King, did I see an Indian man carry his offspring. That man was affectionate and playful with his child, which was very uncommon to members of their race.

Within a year the Indians were unhappy with the arrangement. Acting through their agent, the Indians made known that there was insufficient game to supply their needs on the lands they were offered. In 1827 a Mr. White was appointed commissioner to offer sufficient land, west of the Mississippi, in exchange for the Florida lands. Eventually the Indians agreed to send a delegation under Major Fagan, the former agent, and the current agent, to examine the lands. After they viewed the country, the location and boundaries were marked out satisfactory to all parties. The lands agreed upon were situated in the wilds of Arkansas, west of the Mississippi River. Upon their return they made a favorable report which led to a meeting at Payne's Landing on May 9, 1832. Sixteen state commissioners and fifteen chiefs of the Nation ratified the Treaty of Payne's Landing. The treaty was then signed by Colonel James Gadsden, who represented the United States.

The first article of the treaty called upon the tribes to relinquish their lands and agree to emigrate. The second stated that the United States would provide compensation for all the improvements in Florida and pay certain annuities. The third provided for goods to be delivered after their arrival on their new lands, the fourth provided blacksmiths, and the fifth a valuation of their cattle holdings in Florida. The sixth article agreed that the United States would pay $7,000 for slaves and other property alleged to have been stolen by the Indians. The seventh article provided for their removal within three years after the treaty, and for their subsistence for one year after their arrival in their new home. The winter of 1834 was agreed to be the last before the Indians set off to their new home. The governor then fixed the spring of 1835 as the time of their departure.

Following the treaty the Indians returned to their long homes at their respective villages, which were generally built upon the margins of large round ponds, common to Florida. At the time every village or pond had a chief and subchief who were favorable to the treaty. The head chief, or great Pond Governor, known as Hicts, was also favorable. This Indian had mixed with the whites during a long life and was by far the most enlightened of his Nation. Consequently, he held great sway in the councils of his countrymen.

We departed St. Augustine in December 1834 for Fort King. Our first day's march was short, due to the men being intoxicated, and we stopped for the night at Twelve Mile Swamp on the Jacksonville road. This was my first night camping in the open air. After the troops had stacked their arms, they busied themselves cutting lightwood, which is the remnants of standing pine that had been burnt by fires or scathed by lightning. The resin is driven inward and consequently it is very flammable. It was collected in piles to cook their rations the following day. Then they each cut themselves a space around the fires for their couch. The scrub was so thick and the ground so uneven that I slept little my first night camping out.

On the second day we arose at four in the morning to make preparations for our journey. We made twenty-one miles, passing through woodland with immense pine trees. Every four or five miles we crossed small running streams, whose banks were covered with a thick growth of brush, live oaks, cedar, and hickory. The soil by the streams was superior and was called hammock lands by the settlers, whereas the pine barren was comprised of loose sandy soil that supported sparse outcrops of grass and occasionally palmetto and huckleberry bushes. That night we halted near a farmhouse, which was located about three miles from Jacksonville.

It was very different from the farmhouses I knew in England. This was a log building that had spaces here and there, which admitted mosquitoes along with the breeze. The roof was shingle, flat pieces of pine about two and a half feet long by eight inches wide. The building had a stoop in front, where the occupants passed the cool of the evening. The adjoining buildings or outhouses were wretched-looking places. The garden was bare except for about forty to sixty storks that were left standing. The grounds were separated by zigzag fences. Some fields were cleared, while others were covered by dead trees that had been cut down. It was the custom to fell a portion of the forest each year, so that as the soil wore out, farmers had fresh land ready for breaking up.

Arising early on the third morning, we reached the St. Johns River by sunrise. Our crossing to Jacksonville on the north bank was delayed until noon, due to our large train of wagons. At that point, the river was about two and one half miles wide, very shallow for about a hundred yards on each bank and colored a reddish brown from the impregnation of vegetable matter. Jacksonville was a small town, about thirty-eight miles northwest of St. Augustine and fifteen miles from the mouth of the river. It comprised about one hundred and fifty wooden dwellings. Ships as large as brigs and schooners came up to the town. There was a local newspaper and two or three large general trade stores.

During the few hours we spent in town the officers had a great deal of trouble trying to keep the men out of the spirit stores. One man became convulsed by the heat and drinking raw rum. Eventually drunkenness got the better of our troop, so by the time we were six miles clear of Jacksonville we were obliged to call a halt for the night. On the following morning Dr. Weightman suffered a fit while eating his breakfast. I was taken by surprise and felt rather inadequate when I could not find a suitable remedy. It must have been caused by his lack of rest and undue excitement from the previous day. I felt very sorry for him, especially since he had shown me so much kindness on the march by inviting me to join him at his meals of grilled fowl that was prepared by his Negro manservant.

On the second day out of Jacksonville, drunkenness again was a problem since the men had clandestinely filled and hidden bladders of rum in their knapsacks. We were only able to progress fourteen miles, which was another example of how liquor destroyed the soldiers' abilities, making them unfit and incapable of progress.

In the mornings, my stomach muscles were much inflamed and swollen. Many of the men had sore feet and some had considerable skin chafing, especially those who wore their full uniform. Once the march was resumed, my aches and pains went away and I did not suffer much.

Our fifth day on the march brought us to Black Creek at noon, a navigable stream that flowed into the St. Johns. On the west bank there was a small village bearing the same name. It was situated about thirty miles from its entrance into the St. Johns and twenty-eight miles south of Jacksonville. Once more we were delayed crossing the stream and progressed no more than ten miles on the opposite bank. By that time, we began to look the worse for wear, with our faces, hands, and clothes filthy from the black resinous smoke of the fires. We had already used up our bread, so we were forced to make unleavened bread, using stagnant water to form a paste with our flour. The dough was wrapped around a piece of wood which was stuck in the ground and placed near the fire. The stake was turned at intervals so that the dough was equally baked. Frequently I dined on raw pork and this kind of unleavened bread, possibly with greater relish than I experienced with professionally prepared food. Sometimes the inner part of the dough was half-baked, but it did not matter as I was in good health and could stomach anything. As a result of such expeditions, I learned that hunger was a good sauce that made any food tastier. Another discomfort was to wake up in the morning to find my blanket saturated with a heavy dew, which had formed in the night. I was surprised that it had no ill effect upon me.

Over the following two days we marched on a southwest course which took us fifty miles through Alachua County, before we encamped near Micanopy, a village of about one hundred and fifty persons. The country between Black Creek and Micanopy was picturesque, being hilly and studded with lakes and ponds. I noticed that the people seemed to have ghostly pale faces and flaxen hair, which showed evidence of cachexia, probably from a habit of eating dirt. They were a community of Crackers, who subsisted mainly on Indian corn, bread, and hominy. I found them to be very cunning and extortionate, since they tried to sell their produce for treble the value, only because they were able to command their own price. Fresh milk was a great treat, as it was very scarce in the city. They also distilled a very noxious and harmful rum, which they sold to the men. The spirit, called new rum, had a very sour smell and an acrid flavor. When a soldier was found intoxicated in the wilds and was asked where he got the rum, he would invariably reply, "I tapped a tree." After leaving Micanopy we passed by the edge of a large prairie, the only one I had seen. It was full of high grass as far as one could see in any direction. To me it was a wonderful sight, a luxurious sea of green stretching to the horizon. We halted at the edge for a while simply to enjoy the exquisite beauty of the landscape that was new to us.

We passed McIntosh's plantation, situated about three miles from Micanopy and about half a mile from Lake Orange, which was about four miles wide and twenty miles long, looking very pretty in the distance. The route to Fort King from Micanopy was almost one continuous thicket. The trees were not as huge as they were by the St. Johns, since the forest here was much younger. On the eighth day we passed Witumpky about one hour before sunset. It was nothing more than a store opened for the purpose of trading with the Indians and was situated about six miles from the fort. We spent one more night in the wilds and arrived at the fort the following day at 3:00 p.m., completing our journey of one hundred and fifty miles in nine days, meeting with no accidents on the way.

Florida is a land of flowers, so named by the first explorers. During the spring season the forests and swamps and margins of ponds or streams teem with magnificent flora, the water lily predominating. Much of the state is covered with immense pine forests; in the hammocks there are cedar, live oak, and hickory, and on the prairie spire-like palms. Beneath all these magnificent lords of the forest will be found various cacti plants, prickly pears, palmetto clumps, prickly ash, love apples, wild grapes, and oranges and here and there the luscious fruit of the huckleberry bushes. Where man has settled there are plantations of cotton, sugar cane, or pineapple. Maize grows ten to twelve feet high and corn, watermelon, squash, tomato, artichokes, peanuts, and sweet potato are grown throughout. There are verdant peach and orange groves, with occasional fig and pomegranate, the fruit of which arrived by cartload at the St. Augustine market. The lakes and rivers teemed with mullet, drum, sheepshead, angel- and devilfish, with innumerable oysters and crabs. The banks of the streams were populated with gopher and land turtles that were particularly delicious. I thought of what it would look like in the future for its natural beauty and daily bounty far exceeded its daily requirements. It is probable that Florida would become prosperous, great, and happy in the future.

But we named Florida the land of snakes, for many kinds abounded throughout the state. This led me to believe that beauty in nature must coexist with terrible death-dealing animals and reptiles. The rattlesnake was the most dreaded reptile. It was common for the musicians to destroy them on the march, cutting them in two with their swords while they lay basking in the early morning sun, across an Indian trail.

Fort King was a large wooden barracks, beautifully situated upon rising ground about thirty miles west of Lake George and about forty miles from the Gulf, or western shore of Florida. At the time of our arrival, it was manned by a company of about 250 artillery and 60 infantry under the command of Captain William Graham. General Clinch joined us two weeks after we arrived, as the commanding general during the negotiations.

General Thompson resided there as the Indian agent at a salary of $15,000 per annum. He obtained his rank under General Jackson during the war between the Creek Indians and the United States. He was a very amiable and compassionate man, always kind and never weary, but his good nature made him too trustworthy of the natives. If ever a man fulfilled the sacred trust of his government, General Thompson was that man. The duties of an agent were to protect the Indians from the connivance and encroachment of the whites and to distribute amongst them the gifts and annuities provided by the government. The Indians referred to him as their white father and entrusted him with all their difficulties, while he called them his children. The Nation was also provided with an armorer to keep their rifles in order. His salary was $800 per annum and he was subject to the agent's authority. The settlers were also under his jurisdiction.

Upon our arrival I was confirmed in my usual duties as hospital steward. The steward of the post, who carried the nickname of Boss, made room for me, at a personal loss of four dollars and fifty cents a month. I did not consider this fair, but when I shared my thoughts with him, he told me that he was rather pleased, as he did not feel confident to fulfill the extra duties that would have been forced upon him. Boss, a New Yorker, was a good-natured, friendly, and genial man, always ready to do his best. I was very grateful when he was retained as wardmaster during my stay at Fort King.

The Indians came into camp in great numbers and appeared cleaner than those I saw in St. Augustine. Most of the males were over six feet tall, but rather narrow-chested. Hunting was their chief occupation, so their arms were not well developed like their lower limbs. Their features were regular, except for a slight prominence of the cheekbones, some flatness of the nose, and rather thick lips.

They were very dirty, especially the women. The common mode of washing was to fill their mouth with water, I suppose to warm it, then spit it into the palms of their hands and apply it to their faces. The men were modest, whereas the women cared little about how they exposed their bodies.

The women were stoutly built, owing to their laborious life. Some were quite handsome, but the majority were ugly and frequently grotesque and misshapen. They were fond of necklaces and finery, such as silver drops and rings in their ears, which hung upon their shoulders. The wealthy wore a sort of vest with a petticoat tied above the waist very tightly, which created an appearance of obesity that was esteemed by them to be a height of beauty. The poorer classes wore no vest, with the top half of their body naked to the waist. The hair was worn in plain braids, one half being combed from the top or middle of the head over the forehead forming a semicircle reaching both ears. The remainder was combed back tightly and collected in a roll on the back of the neck. I suppose these women desired to look appealing, but their fashion reminded me of our prisoners in jail, who had their hair cropped to hang over their brows.

They were very fond of bleeding themselves. On the march, when tired, they would rest at the first brook and cut themselves either with needles or the teeth of the gar fish. They sliced themselves in parallel lines, straight down the muscles of the thigh and leg, which they then washed with the water of the brook, thereby taking off the soreness of the muscles. This refreshed and enabled them to continue their journey with renewed vigor. During my stay at Fort King, I bled many of them, which they seemed to enjoy, continually exclaiming at the site of the purple stream of blood "inclemaischa," which means "good" in Indian. I had often heard that Indians did not suffer from toothache, but my own experience was different. They frequently applied at the hospital to have their teeth extracted, an operation they bore most stoically.

The Seminoles were not shy and were adept at begging. One day my assistants and I were returning from a visit to the barrack commissary to draw rations for the sick in hospital. As we were crossing the green with our stores we were waylaid by a party of Indians, and had some difficulty in making our escape without losing the stores. They hounded us with exclamations of "Gimme some oochena," which means pork, and "tuggilaggi," which means bread. Bread was a great treat for them, especially compared to their aaufka, which was boiled Indian corn that was kept until it turned acid.

Toward the end of March 1835 General Thompson, the agent, held a talk or counsel with the chiefs to prepare them for removal. At first, he was quite optimistic, but that changed to disappointment when the majority voted to prolong the departure time. The council was held on top of a raised platform, or promenade, that was built between the barracks and used to drill the garrison out of the hot sun. It was raised on piles about ten feet from the ground, the same level as the quarters. I believe the architect must have been afraid of snakes and other reptiles that abounded in the neighborhood, secreting themselves between the logs of buildings and even coiling themselves snugly between bedsheets.

The principal chiefs of the Nation sat upon benches along one side of the platform, while General Clinch and his officers, in full uniform, sat facing the Indians on the opposite side. General Thompson sat with his clerks, who took notes. In the space between the officers and Indian chiefs stood a Negro interpreter, nicknamed King Cudjo for the stateliness of his gait and manner that originated from paralysis of one side of his body. Cudjo was supplied with quarters and rations in the garrison and a salary of

$15 monthly. He was a runaway slave and consequently spoke in the common Negro slang of the plantations.

There were about two hundred and fifty Negroes living with the Indians; some were slaves, but the majority were runaways from the plantations of Georgia. These Negroes were supposed to have great influence with the savages and were thought to have joined with Micanopy to incite the majority of the Nation in council and declare themselves averse to removal. The ex-slaves probably thought that they would be reclaimed by their owners, but the agent, foreseeing this potential problem, gave notice to the tribes that the government intended to indemnify the affected slave owners.

It was the policy of slave owners not to educate their Negroes, which made it appear that they were incapable of culture or civility, and therefore not fit to be free. From my own observations and communications with the Negroes who lived among the Indians, I never met with finer people than the runaways. Freedom had given them a manly carriage quite opposite to their dejected brothers on the plantations. Though they lacked formal education, they were very smart and well-spoken, equal, if not superior, to the poor whites, or Crackers of the wild. It became my firm belief that if America freed the slaves and allowed the races to amalgamate, they would provide a fresh impetus to her population. The mixture of the races would not deteriorate, but rather improve the stamina of the people, for I noticed that the children of mixed color were physically superior to their progenitors. Where could they find more magnificent frames than the male and female mulattos and quadroons?

General Thompson was the first to speak and he was followed by Hoate Micco, who gave a brief talk stating the reasons why the meeting had been called and asked that the departure time be postponed. Jumper, a well-known warrior who had fought against Jackson in the first war, was next to rise. He was a tall, thin, and aged savage who spoke at length with impassioned gestures. At the end the general asked Cudjo to translate. Cudjo began, "He say he like this country berry well, he born here, he not like to leave in his old age. He say, Micanopy sent him to say so. He also say, that after the last war, when the hatchet was buried, you promised no more to trouble his children. He say, he sign at Payne's Landing, but now dey had anudder governor and he must obey him. If he say dig up de hatchet, he is ready, he fear not death, it is his duty to die for his people."

General Thompson, pointing to General Clinch and the soldiers collected at the back, then said to Cudjo, "Tell him that if he breaks his troth with us, that I shall be obliged to call upon the white warriors to force him." Upon receiving the translation, the noble warrior jumped up and, spreading his arms wide, he stood in the graceful position so easy to the savage. With eyes flashing and his countenance transformed into a scornful look, he occasionally punctuated his speech with bursts of derisive laughter. Excitedly the agent asked, "What did he say?" "He say talk not to him of war. Is he a child dat he fear it? No. He say, when he bury de hatchet, he place it deep in the eart wid a heavy stone over it. But he say he can soon uneart it for de protection of his people. When he look on de white man's warriors, he sorry to injure dem but he cannot fear dem. He fought dem before, he will again, if his people say fight, he must and will obey."

Coahadgo then made a few remarks, stating that he thought it rash for the agent to threaten his people, since whatever the elders agreed to in council, it was their law to obey.

Charlie Omathla, one who had visited the new lands, was the next to speak. He was a fine-looking and friendly Indian who was supposed to be very rich and enlightened. His dress and manner gave the impression of a substantial grazier, which I suppose he was, as he owned a large herd of cattle. He was frequently seen in camp and was the chief of a village nine miles from the fort, called Omathla's Town. He seemed a free and easy, very sociable man, who was received by General Clinch in his quarters as an old acquaintance. Charlie spoke for some length and his speech was more genial than any of the other speakers. Except for the language he spoke, I could have imagined that he was one of the settlers, so free and easy and so like a farming man.

"What did Charlie say?" enquired the general.

Cudjo continued. "He liked the agreement of Payne's Landing. It was made by the fathers of the Nation and he hoped that he would always abide by his word. He said his word is his oath. Can he break what was agreed upon and sought after by his people? No, the talk of Payne's Landing was a good talk, if he denied it, his father will know that he is a liar. He said that you, the agent, had been very kind to his people and he hoped that you would go with him to his far country. If so, he is ready. Where you are, he said he would like to be."

General Thompson then replied, "Tell him and Coahadgo that I shall accompany the Nation beyond the Mississippi and that I shall protect them there, as I have strived to do here, to the utmost of my power, and authority."

John Hicts, the son of the former Pond Governor, spoke a few words, stating that he had no wish to leave Florida and that if some elders had formerly made an agreement, he thought it was not binding upon the Nation at this time.

During the proceedings I took notice of Sam Jones, an old but ferocious-looking Indian chief of the Miccasukys who was not at the treaty signing. He was reclining carelessly against the barrack partition. At times he seemed dissatisfied with the proceedings and stamped his feet in great rage. Occasionally he shook his white head, evidently wishing to show his utter contempt of the agent and surrounding officers. This Indian had always been against the exchange of lands, so I was not surprised at his impatient manner during the talks.

The parties had been in council for several hours when suddenly the platform upon which they all sat gave way under the weight. Everyone fell to the ground, which resulted in a most ludicrous scene. I was standing at the edge of the chasm and could not help laughing to see the fat and lusty General Clinch, with the agent, all the officers, and Indian chiefs, sprawling on all fours forming a medley of human bodies. The officers and some of the Indians were in high spirits, laughing at their sudden downfall. But there were other Indians who did not understand the accident and they rushed out from the supposed trap, screeching most awfully. When General Thompson regained his feet, he was quickly able to dispel their fears and, through his fatherly manner, succeeded in calming their suspicions and doubts.

The accident adjourned the council for another time with an understanding that Micanopy himself would attend. Powell made a few remarks during the above talks and spoke of his friendship for the whites. It was his wish to comply with the agent provided it was the will of the elders of the Nation. This Indian was called by the whites, after his father, a Scotsman, but he liked to be known by his Indian name, Osceola, or the rising sun. He was a Tustenuggee, or subchief, in the councils of his countrymen. He was reported to be the most agile in the hunting grounds and a very famous sportsman amongst his people, particularly with the Indian ball game. He was a fine, active-looking Indian, not quite so tall as most, being about 5 feet 10 inches in height, thin, with compressed lips and very regular features, owing possibly to his being a half-breed. When he spoke, it was with a smile, appearing very good-natured. He was known to the agent prior to our arrival at the fort and was presented with many handsome gifts, supposing that he would assist in bringing over the rebellious portion of the Nation to his wishes, for he had always been agreeable to the intended embarkation. Lieutenant John Graham and Osceola were almost inseparable. When we lived at Fort King during the time of peace, they were daily seen with one another in the community. Both shared a strong love of field sports, and it was a very common sight to see both of them returning to camp after a hunting expedition in the woods. Lieutenant Graham was a fine specimen of a man, measuring six feet five inches tall, young, and doubtless very interesting to his Indian friend. I was also friendly with the lieutenant, who had great pleasure in loaning me books. He was also a frequent visitor at the hospital with our young surgeon, Dr. Clark.

The above description of the talks is not perfect, owing to the Negro interpreter's limited vocabulary of Indian and English. He may have understood the Indian language sufficiently to converse with them, but to change a language with such a paucity of ideas into our own probably required more knowledge and skill than King Cudjo possessed. As a consequence, when he was asked to more fully elucidate the meaning of the speakers, he tended only to react with a grunt. "He say he no go, dat all he say like."

During my posting at Fort King I was fortunate to see an Indian war dance performed as an amusement for our officers. The site chosen was a most picturesque area about four miles from the fort. It was a beautiful spacious opening, surrounded by drooping ash and weeping willows that had been cleared of undergrowth by the natives. Fires were lit up at regular intervals on the outside of the circle at the extreme edge of the clearing.

I arrived at the rendezvous at eleven o'clock at night shortly before about three hundred warriors arrived. They were accompanied by a number of Indian women and children dressed up in all their finery. The dance commenced about midnight when a lone warrior sprang from his squatting posture into the center of the opening with a loud whoop or shrill cry, where he whirled round and round. He was followed separately and successively by about 200 others. This great body of warriors was picturesquely dressed, and they presented a fine sight as they whirled round in a compact mass. The individual routine was to spin around quickly three times, while making a low moaning or humming noise, and finish with an electric, shrill, and piercing whoop that rang through the forest as it curdled one's blood. The process was repeated over and over again.

The scene was exciting, as light from the fires created moving images on the edge of the forest that conjured the appearance of a fairyland, but the screeching of the Indians dispelled the illusion.

There was something cruel in the sound of the war whoops that foretold of murder and bloody deeds, and brought to mind images created from our readings of Irish cries and Gaelic frays. Toward the end of the dance our officers entered the maze, joined hands with the Indians, and danced until the perspiration flowed down their faces. Imagine the heat generated from two hundred and fifty screeching dancers whirling around for two hours. Yet these Indians did not appear tired when it was over, whereas our officers were exhausted after fifteen minutes of jumping and were obliged to sit down to recover.

Afterwards our officers and the chiefs separated, shaking each other's hands, laughing, and wishing each other well. About that time, I and two of my companions were seen by Captain Drane, my restless tormentor at St. Augustine and on the march. He came up to me and smilingly asked, "Did you know you were here against orders?" I answered in the affirmative, stating that the novelty of the proceedings had overcome my duty to discipline. Fortunately, I was not under his supervision at the time, accountable only to the medical officers and commanding general. My station, along with the hospital, was outside the guards, so in effect, I did not break the order. Since I did not pass a guard, I did not think Captain Drane was entitled to interfere, but he alone amongst all the officers could not let the occasion pass without finding fault with me. If it was for the sake of discipline, he was correct, but I believed that it was a continuation of our old feud. In any case, I saw the general at eight the next morning holding my report, which he did not refer to. On the contrary he was most kind to me and only made courteous enquiries regarding the sick in hospital.

The dance was organized for the amusement of the officers and possibly to cement friendships, but when I look back upon the occasion I imagine how it might have ended in tragedy. The order was that the natives and the officers were to attend unarmed, while the rank-and-file were to remain in barracks, an arrangement that set the stage for a possible massacre. If General Clinch could have foreseen future events, he would not have approved that his officers would meet the savages four miles away in the woods in the dead of night. The general had seen service in the first Seminole War and had known them in peaceful times, since his plantation bordered their lands. His experience taught him to trust their word, and as he was of a chivalric disposition, he saw no need for caution. I ascribed our deliverance to God's beneficent care, for who else had implanted in these children of the wilds a spirit of truth and honor.

To judge the natives properly required a thorough knowledge of their way of life, their laws, and customs. The Seminoles were easily governed during peaceful times, but when the war hatchet was unearthed a huge change came over them. Their laws relating to war were cruel and included arson, murder, and scalping, but that was expected from savages. Even our own wars between civilized nations often tended toward barbarism. The Seminoles justified themselves by their laws, as do all nations. Their general rule was to use every strategy, whether fair or foul, to protect themselves, and any method to injure their enemy. Their code recognized their enemy as the white man, whether man, woman, or child. Every scalp in their belt, and every death of their foe, meant one less enemy. War by its bloody code changes all. Vengeance, deceit, and lies become virtues while truth and honor are pushed to one side.

While I was at Fort King I had an opportunity to witness the tracking ability of the Indians. Three were employed to assist a few soldiers to track deserters. The slightest indent in the sand, pressure upon or disturbance of leaves or a blade of grass, provided them with enough information to follow their quarry. The trailers pointed out every detail about when the runaways had stopped to take a meal, or to rest themselves. They could hear a footstep from a great distance, especially when they pressed their ear to the ground. They noticed every bird or squirrel on the topmost branches of lofty trees. Nothing escaped their acute senses.

They were very dexterous at playing a game of ball that consisted of two sides of the young and most active braves. Each man held a hickory stick of about two and one half feet long that had a small circular wicker basket fastened tightly to one end. The basket could hold a ball of about three inches in diameter. Each side had a goal set apart and opposite each other at a distance of about half a mile. The game commenced from the center, where the ball was thrown up in the air. Each party had players positioned so that each was able to catch the ball in their basket, while preventing the opposing players from doing the same. The art seemed to be to station themselves to recatch the ball by their own players, then carry the ball from hand to hand down the field, to the opposing goal, in spite of the efforts of the opposition. Great dexterity was exhibited in those games as players caught the ball when it flew through the air or hovered over the competing players. It was an exciting game and a sight to behold and admire.

Indian marriage ceremonies were simple. Friends and relatives of the parties would meet at an appointed place in the woods, being careful to have the bride ready for her lord's arrival. She was accompanied by other young females. The bridegroom arrived mounted upon an Indian pony ready to smoke the pipe of friendship. Indian ponies were short and very strong, with great stamina and valued equally to the cost of a horse in Florida, worth from forty to fifty dollars.

The ceremony commenced when the groom removed a number of colored sticks of unequal length from his belt. He presented the sticks to the assembled damsels. His bride was aware of the color to select the shortest stick, for that won the prize. When those preliminaries ended, the groom placed his bride upon his pony for what was probably her first and last ride. Once seated he put spurs to his nag and carried her home to his village. There she spent the rest of her life as a squaw, a most degrading and wretched existence much like that of a slave.

One day a deputation of Indians arrived at the agency to receive their government annuities. They represented about 1,500 men, women, and children who were bivouacked half a mile outside the fort. Gifts were given to each family according to rank; some chiefs received $50 with blankets, others, $5 dollars and a blanket.

I took a walk with a companion through their camp and found that we were a curiosity to the native children who followed in our footsteps, chattering incessantly. The men eyed us carelessly and stoically so that they would not betray their feelings. They had to seem impregnable before the white man at all times.

Much has been said about the agility and wrestling capabilities of the Indian, but I found them to be inferior when competing with our men. Even Osceola succumbed in a trial of strength with one of the infantry sergeants. In many contests with our soldiers, the Indians were generally weaker and the soldiers the stronger, if not quite so agile. When defeated, the Indians did not sulk. They seemed to enjoy the fun and laughed loudly at their failure. On occasion I stood among them as they viewed the soldiers at target practice, and noticed how they felt superior. And when they saw our men practice Indian fighting in the woods, their faces would express a sense of the ridiculous, intuitively conveying to me their knowledge of our inferiority as their opponents in their native habitat. I am confident it was during those five peaceful months, that our enemy saw our weaknesses and developed fighting tactics superior to our own. How often we assume an air of superiority over a native enemy, only to deprive ourselves of the opportunity to learn their ways to develop better tactics of our own.

The Indians were very partial to rum but in time of war, unlike the white soldiers, they resisted the temptation. During feast times they would get outrageously drunk, in which state their passions would become inflamed and, but for the watchful care of their squaws, they would cut one another to pieces. At such times the women took the precaution to hide their knives, foreseeing the possible consequences.

Many Indians had grown so close to the trappings of civilization that some were willing to accept menial tasks. Their love of tuggilaggi (bread), would lead them to work as servants to obtain it. Some washed clothes, others helped the cooks. I, too, had a young man of about nineteen or twenty who made his home with us at the hospital and became a willing water carrier. But when the time came to choose, he left us in the hour of danger.

Interaction with Indian women was rare. If any man addressed a young female, they would receive an extended wide-open stare, the pupils seeming to enlarge at the indignity shown by addressing them. I suppose it is the same in our society, where it is rude for a man to approach a woman before an introduction. Even in the wilds of Florida, I found that there was some degree of etiquette.

The spring close to the fort was in a most picturesque setting, shaded from the sun by embowering trees. The water was very pure and very cold and most refreshing. About four miles from Fort King there was another beautiful natural curiosity called the Crystalline Spring, which was the head of the Ocklawaha River. The river ran within two miles of the fort and entered the St. Johns River five miles north of the northern extremity of Lake George. This river was used to bring provisions for the troops from Picolata in a purpose-built, flat-bottomed boat. The one-way trip took eight days. Picolata was situated on the St. Johns, about seventy miles from its mouth and eighteen miles northwest of St. Augustine.

I visited the Crystalline Spring with Tyndale, a brother Englishman. We began the excursion without much planning and had to cut down a sapling to use as a paddle. The small boat belonged to the infantry and we found it secured upon a ledge of rocks three or four feet above the water. While trying to launch the craft I slipped into the water, which had a quicksand bottom. Realizing my situation, I held on to the boat for my very life, for I knew well that if I let go my hold there was no chance of escape, though only three feet from the shore. I was not concerned about the ducking, for at that time of year it was most refreshing, and the water evaporated quickly. If the accident had occurred after sundown, to ward off a cold I would probably have returned to the fort for a warm bath and bed.

Having received a little training from a Minorcan in St. Augustine, I was a proficient paddler and managed to get to the head of the stream in a short time. There we found a large expanse of water surrounded by precipitous rocky banks, about twenty feet above the waterline. The bottom of the spring was also rock, the depth of which was thirty-seven and one-half feet, according to our measurement. The water was so clear that a sixpence dropped from the boat was clearly seen resting upon the bottom. On looking over the side of the boat, the water magnified the distance so much that it made it look like the bottom was as far away as the sky was high. This springhead was supposed to be the same explored by the first Spanish navigators, Ponce de León and de Soto, who gave it exaggerated virtues and called it the "Fountain of Youth."

I injured my back during my stay at Fort King. A young, tall, and strong Yankee was always trying to wrestle me to the ground, but my vanity prevented me from suffering defeat. My short stature was an advantage when I clung to his waist, ensuring that he would also fall if I fell. One day he jokingly threatened that if I did not let go, he would break my back, as he feared being tripped. He then gave me an Indian hug until my back gave a crack and I fell, motionless, to the ground. For three weeks I suffered greatly and could only go down steps backwards, as placing my heels on the ground would cause me excruciating pain. For over thirty years I have suffered daily for my stupidity. My friend Boss cheerfully became a great help to me. The general good spirits of everyone at the station and the daily change of scene filled up my days. If it were not for this accident, I would look upon my time spent at Fort King with pleasant memories.

On April 23, 1835, the Indians once more met in council on a cleared space about half a mile outside the camp. Large stakes were driven into the ground upon which were spread the branches of trees, which acted like a shade to protect the assembly from the excessive heat of the day. Micanopy was present but had little to say except that he would not agree to removal.

Jumper, the best orator, then spoke, but as I was unable to understand the translation, I left. Apparently he spoke metaphorically, comparing the Nation to a tree of the forest, the branches of which are the children, the leaves the hair of the head, the sap is the blood, and the bark is the clothing.

"If, then," he said, "you spoil the tree of its bark will it not die? There is nothing to carry the nourishing sap to support the branches and if you lop off the branches will they not die? Such then is the case with my people. Take them from their forests and thickets, where from childhood they have wandered, will they not pine and die also? They will be unused to the forest of the new country, they will sigh for the home of their childhood. Also, if you throw the seeds of dissatisfaction amongst them will they not devour each other? If by force you separate them, obliging them to go to the distant country, will they not wish to be again with their friends and their fathers? Yes, my white friends, ask your own hearts, should you like to be sent from your home, separated from your people, and sent into distant lands against your will? Allow then the same feelings in the hearts of the Istichatty, so that I may call the Isteradka my friend and brother."

He concluded by asking for deferment of the period of removal, until all the people agreed to the conditions. He spoke for two hours and I managed to return in time to hear Cudjo's short translation. In any event, his delivery was quite equal to many public speakers.

Charlie Omathla spoke, agreeing upon removal and the validity of the Payne's Landing Treaty, but hoped the agent would give his people another year to prepare themselves and sell their cattle.

Osceola made a few remarks which upset General Thompson. He said his people were unanimous in their wish to remain in the lands of their birth, and that it was not for young men such as himself to dispute what their elders had agreed upon in council. He was bound to obey for Indian law ruled, "If any Indian subverts the councils of his country and sides with others, his life is forfeit and he is liable to receive death at the hands of the first Indian he meets." He also said that the Istalustys were against removal. They had lived together as friends for a long time and it would not be honorable to desert them.

The sound of the Indian jargon during the above talks was reminiscent of a colony of jackdaws. Every sentence ended with "cha," which prompted an immediate response from the crowd of Indians with "inclemais cha," and "char," which reminded me of our English response under similar circumstances of "hear, hear."

There were many other speakers, such as Alligator Chief, Black Dirt, Yachee Billy, Hicts, Coahadgo or She Wolf, and Hillchi-ti-Micco. The tenor of all the orations was against removal and for delaying the date of removal. The general and agent then agreed to give the Indians until the following year, with an understanding that they were to be ready the following spring.

The Indians then returned to the Nation, with the exception of three who were especially friendly, and Black Dirt's tribe who wished for removal. Missicippi, known as Old Diddy, was a resident at Fort King for so many years that he was considered a fixture. He also fled upon the declaration of war, which was no surprise as he was teased and bullied by the soldiers. They told him "Missicippi Olewargus and Missicippi iepus Diddy." He would respond, "Missicippi Alewargus Iepus and Missicippi inclemais cha."

Return to St. Augustine

We remained at the fort about two more weeks after the council disbanded and were then ordered by the general to return to St. Augustine. We retraced our steps through Micanopy to Picolata, a distance of fifty-six miles along an Indian trail that was completely overgrown with thickets. Each morning our pioneers set out two hours before the troops to cut a road, so it was fortunate that we were encumbered by only one vehicle. The men suffered much from the excessive heat and a shortage of potable water. It was my custom to drink through my handkerchief and to masticate blades of grass to keep off thirst. Some were foolish and swallowed whole cupfuls of filthy water, yet the more they drank the more they required. At night the mosquitoes and sand flies were greatly annoying, and our clothing got covered by a kind of flea which lived in the sand. After five months at Fort King and six days of grueling marching through dreary and houseless country, we were thankful to be back in St Augustine.

Our return to St. Augustine was more grueling than the march to Fort King and I determined that troops could not move through Florida during the summer without suffering serious ill effects. There were heavy dews at night, followed by hot, humid days. Our men suffered agues, edemas, and general debilities on a daily basis. Between Micanopy and Picolata we did not pass a single house and met only one individual who, when asked how far we were from the river, said "You are upon the banks," which caused us to continue until 11:00 p.m. that night, when darkness obliged us to halt. The following morning, we found the river to be three miles further, or at least twelve miles from where we met the Cracker. The typical distance between the Cracker holdings was ten to twelve miles and was considered as nothing. As we neared the city of St. Augustine, the view of the cupola and spires in the distance were most welcome and we were all pleased to return to our old quarters.

Early in June an express arrived with details of outrageous, insulting behavior by Osceola toward General Thompson, the agent. On June 3, 1835, the general reproached Osceola for inciting the Indians that refused to leave Florida, which irritated the savage so much that he broke into a rage and drew his knife to threaten the general. He was immediately disarmed by the guards and placed in irons, but on the following day the kind-hearted agent, against the advice of Colonel Alexander Campbell Fannin, the commanding officer, released him. The colonel was an old Indian fighter and knew the character of the Indians. He was always cautious and never trusted the savages. He cautioned the general against such mild treatment and told him that he expected Osceola to become his most determined enemy. The pride of the Indian is so strong that he cannot forget the least insult and will go to any length to achieve vengeance.

Expresses began arriving that complained about numerous bands of Indians raiding and robbing planters along the east coast. A detachment of troops was ordered south, with instructions to drive the Indians back over their lines. Dr. Weightman was appointed to accompany them, but as he was unwell, I was assigned in his place and a few days later received my orders from General Clinch. Our destination was the mouth of the Indian River, a distance of about eighty miles. I had no desire to leave St. Augustine. We were back in the city for little over two months and I was still in a weak state, having been bled a few days previously and still suffering from my spinal injury and an enlargement of the spleen. However, it was my duty to forget my aches and pains, so I prepared my medicines and packed them in saddlebags, as I was assigned a horse.

We departed on June 13, 1835. Our troop consisted of fifty men, and just before departure an order was read out on parade that the command should obey the wise admonitions of the newly commissioned doctor. This was my first attempt at quackery, and I did not display any air of confidence as I sat astride my nag using my saddlebags as my saddle. I was never much of a horseman, which was soon noticed by Sergeant Potter, who was amused and prompted to make jabs such as "You look more like a snip than a surgeon for men going out to battle." Another asked, "Doctor, where is your needle?" followed by, "Pardon, most noble officer, I meant your lancet." So onward we jogged, with my comrades joking at my expense.

About thirty miles into our march the countryside seemed to flourish, and the soil looked excellent for raising crops of sugar or cotton. There were many plantations along this coast, probably owing to the convenience for shipping the produce, most of which was rum.

After several days of severe marching, we were all exhausted and it became my turn to laugh. But the lads were so lamed and sunburned that I did not have the heart to retaliate. Sympathetic to their plight, I occasionally gave one of them a ride or a drop of cordial out of my saddlebags. On our route we passed the Fannin plantation and Colonel Dummett's large one at Tomoka. The proprietor was the colonel, whose coachman I had met when I first arrived in St Augustine. The Negroes came out in a body and squatted down on the roadside to see the soldiers, which I suppose was a novel sight for the poor isolated creatures. They appeared to be a sad, battered group, poorly clothed in comparison with the blacks of the city. These slaves seldom saw white men except for their master and overseer. Their almost total isolation, lack of variety, and change of scene and association made them nearly imbecile. Where was the justice? The colonel was able to live in luxury, have a town house, a plantation residence, and a beautiful home upon the heights at New Smyrna. The Almighty had blessed him with a fine Englishwoman for a wife, three beautiful daughters, and a handsome son. I met his wife and daughters at their town residence, where I was struck by their English ways and bearing that reminded me of home.

I wondered why they would choose to become southern slaveowners, which bound them to trafficking in blood. There was something warped in a man's mind who, for money, cast away his birthright to become a slaveowner, especially if that person has known and enjoyed civil and religious liberty, but then this colonel already had a corrupt character.

We halted for a day at Mrs. Anderson's plantation on the river in order to clean and refresh our wearied bodies. She was a good-looking, well-educated widow who lived in the city and was noted for being a very humane owner. The facts were somewhat different, when I saw the conditions of her forced laborers having to live in wretched pens instead of houses. The plantation was a dismal scene, with buildings falling into a state of decay and women living in huts not much better than dog kennels. Mrs. Anderson, a Catholic lady blind to her most apparent sin, probably eased her conscience through confessions and penances.

The river in these parts was full of very large, though timid, alligators. Early in the morning they would lie upon the water and blow, making a noise that reminded me of cattle lowing in the distance. When a party of us wished to swim in the stream, before entering the river we would send out a loud shout and the monsters would simply disappear. When they were gone, we took their place fearlessly and carelessly. Though much was said about the vaunted alligator, with its terrible looks and armored skin, the natives were not afraid of them and I never heard of any instance of their attacking a human being.

We left Ambrose Mackay, from Oundle in England, at Tomoka, as it was impossible for him to go any farther. Two days later we reached within fourteen miles of Mosquito, which the men called, "sand fly," owing to the great number of those annoying insects. I could protect myself at night from mosquitos with a mosquito net, but could not keep away the sand flies, which were no larger than a grain of sand. Upon our arrival at Mosquito, Captain Drane took the most able men with him, crossed the inlet, and went to the head of the Indian River, a favorite resort of the Indians in their fishing expeditions.

The mid-portion of the east coast of Florida was level and the soil on the hammock lands was considered fertile. The flora along the route was magnificent and it was easy to understand why the country was named Florida by the early Spanish explorers. The hammocks were wooded with hickory, cedar, gum, and bay trees, but were not so large as those bordering the St. Johns. The pine barrens were thicker than in the interior, with more undergrowth that included palmetto and huckleberry bushes. The thickets were almost impenetrable with wild vines, sour orange trees, and mulberry scattered throughout. There were more running streams near the coast than in the interior, but fewer lakes or ponds. The people were healthy and possessed more of the comforts of life than their counterparts at St. Johns and Alachua.

I remained at Mosquito with four patients who were suffering with ague, plus the men who did not continue to the Indian River. Mosquito was a small village on the west bank of the Mosquito Lagoon near the inlet to the sea. Many ships of light tonnage were at anchor in the lagoon, and I expected that over time New Smyrna would become an important shipping town, as its location was so convenient for the numerous plantations in the area. Inlets and creeks dissected the country in all directions and seemed navigable for small craft. I predicted that if the South could rid itself of slavery, this portion of East Florida, which had a most agreeable climate, would become well populated. The white population of the area were energetic and optimistic and seemed prosperous compared to the listless slaveowners who lived in tumbledown homes.

About four miles south of New Smyrna was a splendid, almost palatial, residence that belonged to an Englishman, Judge David Dunham. It was the most beautiful and spacious residence that I had seen in Florida. It was so immensely large I wondered why anyone would erect such a mansion in the wilds, since it was solely a bachelor and his slaves living there.

One morning during my stay at New Smyrna I hired a boat to cross the inlet and view the coast from the ocean. We were well rewarded by the most beautiful sight of coastal scenery, stretching from north to south in an exact straight line as far as the eye could see. The most beautiful beach I had ever seen was pure white sand, dazzlingly grand under the bright sun. I collected many curious shells, the best of which I took back to St. Augustine. Many wrecks were visible along the coast, which seemed to heighten the grandeur of the scene. We rowed to the lighthouse where we found the drunk keeper and his wife. Go wherever you will, and you will find someone afflicted with this debasing habit.

On our return trip we were battered by a ferocious storm, the like of which none of us had previously experienced, with hailstones that were large and painful. After crossing the inlet, we were passing within view of Colonel Dummett's residence when I saw the colonel on the lookout. When he saw the blue uniform, he hailed us and after pulling the boat ashore, Sergeant Potter and I made the ascent to the house. The colonel was eager to show us his hospitality, a trait that was common to all slave masters. At the time his young granddaughter was staying with him. She was a fair-haired girl who reminded me of my Saxon countrywomen. We drank to his health and parted mutually gratified, but I could not help thinking how much better for his peace of mind if he had honorably retained his rank in the British army. The sight of soldiers filled him with regret, as there was no escape from his guilt. I thought of what a man will do for the sake of money, even to sacrifice his honor.

Young Dummett joined us as we left his father's place. His lifestyle was limited to shooting, fishing, and drinking, but he was delighted to converse with me, a fellow Englishman, to share his homesickness for his ancestral home in Devon. I felt sorry that such an educated young man was forced to hide in such an arid wilderness, but his life was to change abruptly when hostilities broke out and he was made a captain of the Florida Rangers. I subsequently heard that he was an energetic officer, ready and capable of meeting the enemy on his own turf.

The members of our party who had continued on to the Indian River returned after two days, having not met with any natives. They brought with them a packhorse loaded with drum and sheepshead fish that they caught in the river shallows, which ran out about half a mile. These were larger than those I usually caught in St. Augustine. On our march we met an Indian woman, who fled into a thicket when she saw the soldiers. After a short chase she was caught and brought before the captain. Our interpreter questioned her and found that she was employed by one of the planters to bring him venison. She was made to understand that this was not allowed without a pass and that she would be punished if she were caught in the future.

Our journey to the south and back spanned three weeks, travelling about three hundred and twenty miles. It was an arduous trek with few results, made difficult by the excessive heat in June. Many men fell ill and weak with agues, which meant that I had enough work attending to the sick. I was especially pleased that we did not meet with the enemy. As we wound our way through the woods, we may have thought we were safe, but upon reflection even an encounter with only twenty of the foe would probably have led to our slaughter. Our bayonets and muskets would have been of little help against the Indians, who were armed with rifles. Just another one of the many mercies from God that kept us safe from harm. If our journey had been taken in winter it may have been enjoyable, as it was not monotonous since we frequently came across plantations. Following our return to St. Augustine, I resumed my old duties, which were far preferable to the gypsy life we led on the march in the Everglades.

Gilding was the Englishman I met on my first day after arriving in St. Augustine. He was the coachman for Colonel Dummett and had assisted him to abscond from the West Indies with a military pay chest. Gilding became an opium addict and spent his days so dependent upon the drug that he was always in debt. Constantly in need of money, he was adept at securing loans that he was unable to repay. I was his only exception, for the love of his country and his countrymen was so great that he could not find it in his heart to do me wrong. Once I berated him over his behavior, which affected him to such a degree that he was overcome with remorse and cried like a child. So great was his grief that I was careful never to allude to it again.

His parents were hotelkeepers in Liverpool where he had been a veterinary surgeon by profession. By the time I knew him his life was a wreck, his having been forced to leave England for reasons I never knew. By the time he worked for the colonel he was sufficiently compromised to join him in his crime.

Gilding was brought to me at the hospital and was under my care when he was subpoenaed by the court to make an affidavit on the colonel's behalf. I did not pry into his secrets, but it was reported by those who knew the facts that he had made a false oath. He was so dangerously ill that he was taken to the court in a vehicle, wrapped up in blankets. He returned with a terrible appearance and lived only for a day or two more, dying an awful death, cursing with his last breath. How thankful we have to be for honorable parents and good examples. Gilding was a most loving man who was fond of his country and cherished the companionship of Englishmen. With better company his fate may have been quite different.

Effective March 25, 1835, new orders were implemented regarding the enrollment of men into the service. The minimum enlistment was for a period of three years, with an increase in pay of $1 per month, making the pay for a private soldier $6 per month, but there was no longer a bounty upon enlistment.

On one occasion Sergeant Potter invited me to accompany him and others to a camping trip in the woods. We set off from the inlet south of the city and after three or four miles of rowing we entered a creek, which led to our destination. Our craft was a large, flat-bottom scow that allowed us to make our way through shallows that were only twelve to fifteen inches deep, but in which grew long grass that impeded our progress. When we reached our destination, we plunged into a delightful deep pool of a creek that was hemmed in by the wilderness. After a short swim I found a log on the bottom to rest my feet while I held on to an overhanging willow. I began to pull myself up and down when suddenly the log moved from under me. Not thinking I was in any danger I sprang upon the bank to see where the log had moved. All of us searched without any result until the woodsmen carelessly remarked that it must have been an alligator under the bank. It probably had no other chance to escape observation when we all suddenly dove into the pool from various directions. The occasion seemed very funny at the time, yet it had such an effect upon us that none of us dared to enter the water again.

While the men foraged for wood, the sergeant and I erected a shed to shelter us for the night. We lit a large wood fire in front of the entrance and cooked up a quantity of fish we had obtained for next to nothing. Our dinner was served up on the bottom of a bucket and was most delicious, and I suppose was made even tastier due to our exertions and the primitive conditions. We passed the evening singing songs and telling tales while our pinewood fire lit up the surrounding wild expanse of woods.

I rose early the following morning as I was to be present at doctors' call. The woodcutters gave me good directions to return to the city. First I was to stay on an Indian trail, and then on reaching a certain point, I was to turn northeast. Having had no experience traveling in the woods by myself, I was soon lost and wandered about until the sun was high. Eventually, losing all presence of mind, I became overcome with anxiety and in despair fell to the ground where I beseeched the aid of God. My urgent plea bought me calm and hope, so that I made another effort and found that I had been walking south. I turned and began to run, which I kept up for at least an hour, when I came upon a post indicating that I had found the right path for the city.

Reenergized, I pressed on and before long I was rewarded to see a distant clearing, with the sunlight breaking through the woods. By the height of the sun, I knew that I was too late to make my morning's report, so I completed my journey at a leisurely pace.

When I eventually reached home, I was informed by Lieutenant Dancy that I had been missed and he gave me a friendly reproof for being absent without leave. The lieutenant was one of our best and most efficient officers and he reminded me that, with so many sick in hospital, I had acted foolishly while Dr. Weightman was on furlough. I was wrong to consider myself my own master and the lieutenant, who usually treated me with great consideration, did not neglect his duty by screening me from a well-merited reprimand. If Captain Drane had been at the post, I would not have been so fortunate and would probably have been subject to a trial by court-martial.

On another occasion, acting with more discretion, I received permission from the doctor to go hunting. I locked up the hospital and, leaving the key at his quarters, I departed with Sergeant Potter. We secured a canoe for the day and landed on an island about two miles north of the city. My friend Potter was a prankster who delighted in practical jokes. He pulled his first stunt just when I was disembarking from the canoe with a gun in each hand. He made the canoe lurch and I fell into the water, which utterly delighted him. We then pulled the canoe ashore and commenced beating the marshes for marsh hens and wild fowl, with little success.

We were away from the boat about three or four hours and upon our return found that the canoe was gone. The tide had risen and carried our boat away, leaving us prisoners on a barren island. Hoping the craft had not drifted far, we walked along the side of the creek without success. Potter was not easily discouraged and was an expert swimmer. He disrobed, made a bundle of his clothes that he tied to the end of his gun, and placed it upon his shoulders. He estimated that the creek was about two hundred yards wide, but found when he had covered about one-third of the distance that it was probably 400 yards to the opposite side. He turned and started to swim back, but I could see that his gun had fallen from his shoulders and that he was spent by his exertions. To save him from drowning I rushed in and was just in time to bring him ashore.

Since Potter was exhausted we decided to pass the time shooting until the tide fell. Then a shot-corn became fixed between the ramrod and barrel of my gun. To extricate it I was obliged to fire it off, but it fell on the opposite side of the stream, which I had to cross to regain it. I undressed, keeping on a pair of cloth trousers and my boots, plunged in, and swam eagerly to the opposite side, fearing that if I swam slowly the tide would get the better of me and carry me out into the inlet. That was a mistake, as I failed to save my strength for the emergency that occurred when I realized the running tide had increased my swimming distance. I could not make the distance, nor could I return, as I had crossed more than halfway. I became flustered and lost buoyancy, which caused further exhaustion. On the point of drowning, and with death facing me, I rallied myself with renewed vigor. Many times I have swum four times the distance with ease and the water was not cold. I fought the waves until my body became numb from fatigue, and unable to continue realized that I was doomed. At that moment I felt the same overpowering sense of God's presence that I had when I was lost in the woods. My feet fell useless below me and I was on the point of sinking when I touched bottom, though still fifty yards from shore, standing in water not quite up to my armpits.

This was yet another mercy bestowed upon me when I was no longer able to help myself. Eventually I found my ramrod, but my fear was so great that I did not want to make the crossing. After resting, Potter urged me to recross, but he was unaware of my first difficulties. After a while my fears abated, and I decided to give it another try. The distance was not great, and I thought I might do better without my trousers and boots, as they certainly were great impediments. With the ramrod in my mouth and naked, I again ventured into the stream and arrived on the opposite side with ease. With nothing but my cap, shirt, and jacket for protection from the elements, I spent two more hours running and jumping to keep warm while waiting for the creek to lower, which allowed us to cross back to the mainland. It had turned out to be a day of hunger and disaster.

One day two companions and I visited the marshes on the south side of the city on a hunting expedition to shoot wild fowl. In the process of scattering the birds, I had to run through bogs and marshes and, while trying to jump clear, I missed my footing and landed on the edge of a mud pit. I gradually sank into the stiff cold clay mud up to my armpits. The surrounding grass was so tall that I was completely out of sight and began to cry out for help at the top of my voice. It soon became obvious that nobody could hear me. I would have soon sunk into the mire had I not had the presence of mind to rest myself on my gun, placing it horizontally across the pit. Eventually I was able to use it as a lever to extricate myself from the deadly trap.

On another gunning excursion I shot a bird which fell on the other side of a stream. I pulled a board from a dilapidated old building to use as a paddle, and unloosing a canoe made for the game. When I reached the center of the creek, I was met by a swift current at a point where three streams joined. The flow soon overpowered me and my frail paddle and was carrying me swiftly out the inlet. I quickly realized that my only chance of reaching land safely was to swim. Taking the boat chain in my hand I jumped overboard, dragging the canoe behind me, and after considerable time and fatigue I reached terra firma.

My friends and I arranged to spend a day on Anastasia Island, which was opposite the city. When we grew weary of scouring through the bushes and viewing the stone quarries and lighthouse, we took to the sea to practice surfing. The surf was very high, at least twenty feet, and dangerous, but as there was a sandy beach I thought it was manageable for a careful average swimmer. I would recommend all seamen learn how to surf, as this trick could save many shipwrecked sailors who are unable to safely make their way to shore through a heavy surf. Our party was well primed with rum and I, having had my equal share, decided to swim. Losing command over myself I swam out almost a mile, when my companions began to shout that I should return. Though I felt supremely confident to continue, they were adamant that I return. Fortunately, I responded to their calls, for if I had ventured much further, I may not have been able to make it back to shore. Many lives are lost when inebriated swimmers foolhardily venture out too far. Eventually the alcoholic high wears off, reality returns, and if all their energy is spent there is nothing left in reserve to fuel the exhausted body.

When I returned to the city and it became known how far I swam beyond the lighthouse, I was told I was lucky to get back alive, as the waters along that part of the coast were full of huge sharks. It was said that if a man or dog ever fell overboard, they would be consumed at once. I should have known better, for many times I had seen the dorsal fin of a shark cutting through the water in the creeks as well as opposite the hospital. St. Augustine and Pensacola are notorious for these large fish as they are regularly seen by the fisherman and natives, who are quite knowledgeable about the various kinds. Some fishermen caught sharks and delighted in drawing the huge bodies high upon the beach as a warning to strangers. Young sharks were good eating but we only used the tail, which was required to be skinned. It was delicious but so are all fish that are skinned, such as catfish and eels.

I retell these escapades because of the problems associated with them, but they also record most of my recreation during the five years I was in America. Considering my many difficulties it was just as well that I did not spend much time at play, for, judging from my own experience, the less mankind occupies itself in foolish frolics the better. I have learned that more accidents and lives are lost by play than by work.

From the time I left Mrs. Lowth's to the time I returned to St. Augustine, I avoided any duty to God. There were opportunities to attend some Bible preaching, but feeling no compulsion, I stayed away and never became part of any religious community, except for one occasion when I attended one service at the Episcopal Church. From my point of view the inhabitants of St. Augustine were nearly all heathen, apart from a few Negro Baptists whose place of worship was very near the hospital. Yet when I found myself alone, lost in the woods with no help, or with starvation and death before me, I called upon God. His presence seemed to surround me as though His was the only eye that could see my plight and ear that could hear my plea. I knew in my heart that His was the only power that could save me, yet my mind was always ready to deceive and lead me astray.

I have happy memories of St Augustine, due mainly to the amiable nature of Dr. Weightman, whom we referred to as "Fine Old Dick." He was a polite, refined, and genial gentleman, full of fun and fond of the young. Often you could find him surrounded by a group of boys, usually the major's children, but equally often in the company of ragged Minorcan urchins. Although in his early fifties, he kept himself young, relishing in the joy of his youthful associations. Only once do I remember him angry, and it was with one of the men for lying, trying to obtain hospital stores under false pretenses. The doctor never forgot his rank or position and had too much sense to risk causing any lapse of discipline by fooling around with those connected to his department. We looked upon him as our protector, father, and friend and served him with love.

He willingly served all those in his care. Working under him I learned to value the blessings of peace and unity. He held an almost magical power over the hearts of men, women, and children. When payday arrived, it was his delight to see Matron and I receive our correct pay, and on those mornings you were sure to see him approaching the hospital with a pleasing smile on his face when he told us his errand. Whenever he had an extra lump of ice, a barrel of mutton, or a pineapple that had arrived by schooner, he would never forget to say, "Steward, will you have a lump, a shoulder, or a quarter?"

Almost every day he dined at the hotel in the city. On each occasion Manuel Vilonga, his black Spanish servant, would take a bottle of claret from the hospital stores and place it next to his plate. Then, in a gesture of courtesy and friendship, he would offer the wine to those seated near his table. That wine was a symbol of his wish to maintain some degree of his generous Virginian hospitality, for which natives of that state were renowned. Some may imagine he did this to gain popularity, which it did. But those who knew him also knew that he delighted in giving to any stranger.

Manuel was a hired Negro slave who belonged to a Spaniard living in St. Mary's, Georgia, about one hundred miles north of St. Augustine. His was a life of happiness working for Dr. Weightman, but I could not help but wonder what would have been his situation if something happened to Dr. Weightman. Under such circumstances Manuel would have had to return to his owner. It was difficult for me to imagine the misery such a change would make in his life, and I believed that the grief would lead to the death of the poor man. Manuel loved Dr. Weightman with his whole heart and had even become relatively wealthy in his service, having saved up about $700. His wife and family lived in the city and occasionally I visited them at their cabin. They belonged to separate owners who lived more than a hundred miles apart, but slavery meant that they could not think of a future. The heartbreaking reality was the inevitable separation where all the children went with the maternal side of ownership.

Major Gates, the commandant, was a fine, gentlemanly soldier, not a strict disciplinarian, but fond of order and sobriety. I was always graciously received by him and, possibly to please me, he gave me full responsibility over the medical needs of his children. He was a kind old man who would often spend an hour in the surgery, talking over his youthful days spent in the North.

Captain Gardiner, though a strict disciplinarian, was most kind and considerate to his men. He was small in stature but very energetic and every inch a man. He was a very honorable person who took great pleasure in trusting his men, and they in return held him in such esteem that he seldom had to regret any misplaced confidence.

Lieutenant Dancy, our first lieutenant, was very clever, spirited, and energetic, yet so genial and kind he was never overbearing.

Lieutenant Smith, our young second lieutenant, was a great favorite with the men, who found him most charming and well-mannered.

With such officers our company was highly regarded, which helped to create a culture of cooperation among the men. I had already made firm friendships with Sergeants Scofield, Potter, and Caull from the time we were all together as a squad at Bedloe's Island, and I came to regard Company D, second artillery, as a truly fine body of men. We ranged in height from 5 feet 9 inches to 6 feet 3 inches, but I was the smallest and apparently the most fragile, since I was treated with great care by almost all and referred to as the small English boy. Sergeant Crosmond, a six-foot three-inch old Scotsman, became another true friend of mine over a period of four years. He always gave me excellent advice during my first two or three years in the hospital. Eventually he became an ordnance sergeant in charge of Fort Marion and never left the city. I was happy for him as the march against the Indians would never have agreed with him. During the entire time I was in charge of the hospital I was always respected for my work, and for the five years that I served I only had to send two men to the guardhouse. In both cases liquor was the cause. Though I was a mere boy, I was able to command stalwart and older men with love and patience. Such fortunate circumstances allowed me to be very happy in my position. My patients also placed great trust in me as I had in them. The bond was so strong that I became a kind of banker, or keeper of deposits, for those requiring safety for their funds.

One Sunday morning I obtained a copy of Burns's poems and, in order to read them quietly, I strolled into the woods. I walked and read, oblivious to my surroundings, until I had finished the book. Upon evaluating my situation, I found that I had strayed more than ten miles from the city and that no matter how quickly I returned to the fort, it would be after nightfall. At the time I had six or eight patients in the hospital and was holding about $800 for them in my leather trunk. I did not announce how long I was going to be away, but when I began my stroll my intention was to return by noon. When I did not arrive by teatime, my absence created considerable consternation as it was very unusual for me to be away longer than two or three hours. One patient had over $200 in my care, and he became suspicious to the point of having my trunk broken into. The trust the others shared in me overruled him, but they waited anxiously for my return. Daniel Daly, a man from Northern Ireland who did not have any money on deposit, explained to me afterwards, "I would not consent to have your trunk molested, but since the situation appeared to be in their favor, we agreed to wait until the following morning. If by then you did not appear, they would take the responsibility." Can you imagine such men having such a strong bond of trust as to leave me holding $800 in a trunk in a public room?

There was something very noble about the men of Company D, for I daily witnessed many deeds of kindness shown to those who were sick. When any soldier became dangerously ill, their comrades would obtain passes to come and visit them, bringing little gifts. It was the custom for the guards coming off duty to have the following day free to visit the city. It was a moving sight to see them first pay a visit to the bedside of a sick comrade. Even if the patient was one who shirked his duty, or had lost friendship with them, still he was never forgotten in the time of sickness. It was due to this camaraderie that even the worst characters were rehabilitated through the efforts of their fellow soldiers.

Doctor Weightman had an uncanny ability to know when a man was telling the truth and even liked a man who admitted to his wrongdoing. On many occasions I witnessed his desire to teach the truth. "Ward, I see you have been drinking?" "Yes, Doctor, I had a little too much," would be the soldier's reply. Then the doctor's countenance would beam with kindness and he would send the man to hospital and give him every attention.

One day an Englishman named Evendon from Kent enlisted and I escorted him to be examined by Doctor Weightman. Upon stripping, it was noticed that he had a malformation of the spinal column, which was natural from birth. Since this indicated a weakness, the doctor was not inclined to pass him. But Evendon was alarmed, for his heart was set on joining the army. Suddenly he began to relate all his handicrafts and varied accomplishments. His explanations were so amusing that he won over the doctor and commandant and was enlisted.

Shortly after, Evendon began to show up on the doctor's list to avoid his duties. This irritated the doctor, who began to wish that he had not accepted him. During one of his visits the following exchange occurred, which shows the growing annoyance of the doctor. "Well, Evendon," said Doctor Weightman. "You here again, what's the matter with you now?" "Oh, hurting very badly and weak in my back, Doctor, not able to stand my duty," replied Evendon. "Why?" said the doctor, becoming slightly annoyed. "Did you not tell me when you enlisted how clever and able you were?" I only recall three occasions when I witnessed my American parent showing his vexation in public, and on all three, fraud or lying seemed to bring out his worst behavior.

Evendon returned on another occasion and again lied to Doctor Weightman about the cause of his illness. Since the doctor now considered him to be both a liar and a coward, Evendon was sent back to his quarters to receive minimal care from myself, along with a dose of suitable medicine. Soon after, Evendon became so ill that I was obliged to transfer him to the hospital to receive better attention. When Dr. Weightman saw him in the hospital, he exclaimed in anger, "Damn a liar's legs off." Evendon then realized his mistake and was sorry that he had offended the kind doctor. For days he lay and moaned until eventually I requested the doctor to see him again. Evendon admitted his faults with tears of contrition, which were met with the greatest kindness and forgiveness by Doctor Weightman. These two men, the lowborn Englishman and the noble American gentleman officer, became fast friends. I can still hear Dr. Weightman saying, "My poor man, you should not have told me a lie, what pain you would have saved yourself. If you were only truthful all would have been forgotten."

The expert treatment from Dr. Weightman, along with kind attention from his comrades, made Evendon a better man. He was naturally clever and only required the will to succeed, eventually becoming one of the most useful men in the company. Before his enlistment he lived in the backwoods and understood all woodcraft. He could kill a steer and dress it equal to any butcher and then cook it as well as any chef. He had lived with the Indians and knew their culture, way of life, and language.

The following is another example of the great camaraderie that existed in Company D. We received news of Indian irregularities near Volusia, which was located about eighty miles southwest of St. Augustine, just south of Lake George. A platoon was dispatched under the command of Sergeant Potter, while the medical charge was given to Private Jones, our previous steward. He was a surgeon and considered a good practitioner; the right man for the occasion as long as rum was not available. After a few days, the entire platoon fell sick with a malignant typhus. By the time Jones fell sick, they had already buried three of their number and Sergeant Potter gave the order to return to the city. Their comrades responded immediately, each doing his best to help their friends. Carriages from the city were dispatched to fetch the sick, who received great compassion that was witnessed by all. It is not fair for me to highlight a particular case, but I cannot help being witness to the brotherly behavior shown by Sergeant Scofield to his friend, Potter. Denying himself rest, he was seen at the hospital providing never-ending attention and every comfort for his friend with a maternal care. No brothers could have felt more for each other.

Americans are unlike us English. They seldom save their money and delight in owning comforts and boasting about them to one another. No decent person is allowed to remain in need, for in depending upon one another, the misfortune of one man is considered a loss to the whole community. They do not consider themselves to be superior to one another and are not ashamed to receive help. They are great communicators, which keeps them out of isolation and prevents selfish habits.

I do not recognize the same qualities amongst the English. In my own extended family, I have witnessed a father rejecting his daughter from his heart, subjecting her to poverty and the mercy of strangers, even though he had plenty. To make matters worse the girl's brother adopted the same attitude. Such selfishness damages our own hearts and is harmful to society. I have seen deceit in friendships where hospitality is used to obtain a favor in return. Unfortunately, English charity is seldom extended to those less fortunate. We are in the habit of sending an apple to where there is an orchard and forgetting about God's poor.

I served three years in St. Augustine before Captain Drane arrived. He had been a poor man who, for his bravery, was commissioned from the ranks during the war with the British. When his comrades had retreated, he manfully stood firm, firing a piece of artillery that checked the onward rush of the British. Knowing too much about life in the barracks left him with a suspicious disposition, probably based upon his own previous behavior. He was overly proud of his rank and position, which meant that the slightest infraction by men of lower rank was perceived as a serious breach of respect. He mistrusted those under his command and created huge problems out of petty situations. It was not long before he filled the guardhouse with prisoners and the sick bay with patients. On one occasion he requested that I accompany him to examine eighteen men whom he had paraded in double rank across the guardroom. All the men had reported sick to escape his tyranny.

A story circulated that, at the time of his commissioning, he was suspected of stealing a goose and was seen marching around with the head of the dead bird hanging from his knapsack. His men eventually learned his disposition and, like good soldiers, accepted their new yoke. In the end he grew in wisdom and gained a respectable name in Company D as a practical but disciplined officer.

Captain Drane did not have any supervisory status over those employed in the commissary, quartermaster, or medical departments. With the exception of inspections, he knew that we answered directly to the heads of our respective departments. This irritated him and he developed a form of jealousy toward us. Once he told me that we were of little use as soldiers, but I replied saying that we had our work to do, often when he and his men were at rest. This was especially true on the march, when the commissary sergeant and I were always busy up to a late hour, I with my sick and the sergeant with his stores.

I did not escape his notice and frequently suffered at his hands, for Captain Drane delighted in finding fault in my work. Eventually he brought out the perverse Bemrose nature and I foolishly became impertinent and disrespectful. Considering that he did not take advantage of my impudence, I should have held him in higher regard.

These are some examples of his behavior: One morning I was passing through the barrack gates where he was standing. On saluting him he addressed me, and I answered by saying "Yes, sir." This mode of speaking did not suit him, for he would have preferred, "Yes, Captain."

On another occasion in the barrack square, I passed and saluted him. A few minutes later I met him again while passing through the piazza, and I neglected to salute him. He came up to me and, stopping me, he asked: "Do you know who I am, sir?" I answered: "Yes, sir." "Who am I then, sir?" he smilingly asked. Now it was a peculiarity of his to smile when displeased, but I was not aware of it at the time, so I smilingly answered, "Captain Drane, sir." Then he asked me: "What are you smiling at?" "You smiled at me, sir, and it was quite natural to smile back at you." Then, black with rage, he shouted: "You did not salute me just now." "No, sir," I answered, "I did so just below in the barrack square." But this was too much for him, and impolite. "You don't salute me now, sir," he shouted, determined to have it, when I instantly brought up my hand in salute with the rejoinder, "I salute you now, sir."

I had an unfortunate way of omitting this type of salutation to all officers and it passed muster with all, except with Captain Drane and one other officer.

Lieutenant Smythe, an Irish disciplinarian who lacked common sense, was once offended when I passed him without making the proper salute. Regulations stated that a salute was obligatory, to be done at least once to the same officer between sunrise and sundown. As I passed through the officers' quarters, I continually found it necessary to salute according to the law, but found it foolish to repeatedly salute the same officer several times in one hour.

I also lacked tact, which could have caused me much harm. Once I asked Captain Drane to authorize a requisition for mold candles for the hospital. He smilingly turned to me, saying: "I think you are extravagant. What do you do with them?" I proudly and foolishly answered, "I don't sell them." So it was that we had a constant war, which I probably could have halted had I been more subservient. Dr. Weightman, who always considered the welfare of his staff, complained to me because I did not take more care of myself. "If you fall ill, Steward, what am I to do?" The captain took the opposite course, saying that I was not treated like the rest, which was true for I was favored, but that helped to ensure that I provided the proper care to our sick, wounded, and worn-out soldiers when required.

Once when Dr. Weightman was on furlough, Captain Drane took advantage of the situation and found fault with my appearance. He complained that I did not look like a soldier, that I suffered from a lack of discipline, and that I should come to receive a proper uniform. When I applied for the clothes, he ungraciously threw them at me. As they did not fit and were useless to me, I became angry, which so upset him that he threatened me with a punishment that he dared not execute without the sanction of a court-martial. I told him to go ahead, but to remember that if he did, I would demand a full investigation. I then requested an exchange of the clothing. Meanwhile our altercation had attracted the notice of a passing sergeant who, not knowing the particulars, tried to help me out of good will. Out of pride I waved him off, saying, "I was allowed proper clothing by the government and only that will satisfy me." Suddenly Captain Drane calmed down and told me to follow him. His behavior had changed and he magnanimously met my wishes, treating me with an unusual degree of civility.

When I think back, I wonder how I survived those days of constant provocation from the fastidious and often unjust commandant. I could have been degraded to the ranks, but my good fortune prevailed. I think that the captain must have had some good points, for he certainly had patience when I least expected it. He could not have been a bad man, for he had the opportunity to secure my demise. He knew I was friendly with Doctor Weightman, but it may have been that he did not want an inquiry, as he behaved childishly on occasion. Sometimes I imagined his dislike for me was because I was English, for he annoyed a young man named Harris from Bedfordshire in a similar manner. It had a sad effect upon Harris who took to drinking in order to alleviate the effects of the captain's behavior.

The following letter was the last I received from my Father:

Long Bennington,
February 8th, 1835

Dear John,

You find by what Joe says in your last letter that it gave me great consolation to find that you have better health. By reading his letter you find he has given a glowing account of Old England, which I sincerely hope you may find to be the case, when you arrive amongst us please God. My opinion is different upon that subject, but I must allow that I never saw the land so full of plenty. Corn in the most abundance and fat sheep and beasts and pigs innumerable. Still two thirds of the people can't buy as cheap as provisions are and I must allow so far the country is beautiful. Though it is but February and moreover we have had the most plentiful years that ever I knew, the seasons being so much milder, than what they are generally. Dear John, as to anything as news, I have very little to say, things being much the same as when I last wrote. I can inform you, we are all in the best of health, which I know you will think that is the best of news. You find by Joe's letter, that William is farming with Robert Green and works pretty hard too I understand. But he let me to know that farming would never do and he had quite given up the idea of it, which gave me great satisfaction. For I was always sure it would not provide till there is a great alteration in the affairs of the Nation. I also have to inform you that Mary Anne Bemrose is married to Mr. Rogers, a merchant of Dublin. This happened a few weeks back and a very great match it is for her, as the talk goes. I have not seen any of the parties since it happened, therefore know no particulars farther than she is living in Dublin at this time.

And I remain your most affectionate Father,
J. Bemrose.

P.S. Dear John I can give you the place your relations the Sibsey's live at. It is William Dobbs, Milton Township, Richland County, State of Ohio.

Notice that he writes of good health and hopes of soon seeing me again in England. The last part of the letter refers to Mary Anne Bemrose, the daughter of Joseph Bemrose, my Father's cousin. He was the only son of Robert Bemrose, our grandfather's only brother, to whom I referred at the beginning of my story, when they were both living together at Stubton. Robert Bemrose had accumulated a great deal of money, about £10,000, and had purchased an estate at Bottesford. Afterwards the family built a beautiful home for their descendants, which never occurred. The only daughter, Mary Anne, a sweet and loving creature, died soon after she married Mr. Rogers, leaving an only child. Although they had great wealth, they did not appear to have enjoyed much prosperity.

When I reread my Father's letter I noticed his reference to my improved health. During the first two or three years that I lived in St. Augustine, I periodically suffered from intermittent country fevers that were common to the climate. I recall how debilitating such attacks were, particularly one that was most severe. I became ill with typhus and lay at death's door for nearly two months. Doctor Porcher believed that I would succumb, and I heard him whisper this thought to Captain Gardiner. I rallied soon after and was able to get up and out to view the beauties of nature with revived feelings of gratitude and delight. The sunlit morning and wholesome sea breezes put new life back into my exhausted and emaciated body.

I developed a habit of walking in the evenings, which began when I grew interested in listening at and eventually looking through the door of a Negro hut. Inside a black man would occasionally hold a scripture reading with some of his brethren. Though I saw in them the joy and peace of believing in God, I felt sorry for them. Though they expressed thankfulness, the life of the slave remained wretched. Christianity did not remove the bonds of slavery, yet their faith relieved the weight of the chains of their ungodly masters.

These Baptist men and women were the only really happy people I met since leaving Mrs. Lowth's in England. They listened to their Savior's teaching throughout their hardship and suffering. "Come to me ye that are weary and heavy laden." They found true meaning in those blessed words, which were as balm to their weary souls and miserable condition. Having looked around for succor from every quarter, they only found their hope and comfort in God. I could not ridicule their wonderful love and simplicity, which appeared to me as a foretaste of Heaven when at times they seemed to be in a state of ecstasy. Their brotherhood was so well known and believed by those around them that it affected people in various ways, and I now believe that through His words, the

Lord filled their hearts with His great and unbounded love. My long illness forced me to reflect upon these matters, and brought my soul nearer to God and produced in me a clearer conscience.

McLaughlin, a former hospital steward, was a Catholic who believed in the power of saints. He had such faith in the sainthood of Granny Tiara, the most ancient Negress of the community, that he gave her an occasional dollar. He believed that this good old woman was so befriended by Heaven that he would win money in his gambling transactions. This Christian woman even received reward and praise when McLaughlin lost, blaming his loss when he failed to offer her charity.

Just before our preparations for our march to Fort Drane, I received the following letter from my dear old Uncle Horspool:

23 July 1835.

7, James Street,
Camden Town,
London.

My Dear John,

Your letter of the 6th June to your father came to me yesterday and I have been requested to write to you to make you acquainted with the loss of your best friend. He to whom you wrote that letter was no more when you penned it. He had been a good deal out of order for some time, partly occasioned by irregular living. On the 19th of May, early in the morning on attempting to come downstairs he fell and slipped to the bottom and never spoke more. Medical aid was immediately procured, but in vain, he was dead a few hours afterwards. It appears that very little injury was sustained by the fall, scarcely any bruise and no outward injury to cause death. An inquest sat on the body and their verdict was "died by the visitation of God." As they wrote to ask me, I immediately went down to do any little service I was able on so melancholy an occasion.

There is reason to believe your father intended making a will, but was prevented by being called away so suddenly, as there is no will to be found.

Your brother William, who has been living for some time with Mr. Green of Fluitham, came home when it happened and when I returned to London he came with me to administer to the effects, he being the eldest son. After staying a fortnight with us he went down. Your father has left a considerable property of between six and seven thousand pounds. This will be equally divided amongst his children, except the house and homestead where Mrs. Rowbotham lives, which being copyhold goes to the youngest son, in addition to the share he takes with you all. This is the law of the case. In order that the property may be taken care of and properly distributed, your brother Joseph and your sister Jane have each appointed a trustee to take care of their interest. I think they could not have appointed better men in Mr. John Kenyon and Edin Rowbotham.

As soon as your time expires it will be advisable to come over immediately in order to claim and take your share. Then you can choose what you will afterwards pursue. You mention something about your late mistress claiming you. This is quite out of the question for no apprentice can be detained a single day after he has attained the age of 21 years. Under no circumstances could that woman come forward with any claim upon you. I think she has more reason to fear seeing you than you can have to dread her. When your time is complete, you are not likely to be provided with funds to bring you over. You must say when you again write and if you cannot suggest a better way to get it than was adopted last time, we must do as before. I am thinking whether you might not have credit enough to draw a bill upon me, if you please for £20 or £30, or what you might need and I would pay it. Perhaps it would be better to draw on Godfrey Halton & Co. Bankers, at Newark and give notice to Rowbotham and he would cause it to be paid. But ask your Doctor about it that is in case you want money.

About ten days ago Rowbotham brought your sister Jane, who is now with us on a visit, after the severe shock she has had. I am glad to say she is very well. Your brother Joseph appears to be a steady well disposed young man. I had some conversation with Fisher and Fillingham who spoke of him very well. They have just given up their business and Joseph remains with their successor as Shopman at a salary. They have given him his Indentures and he is no longer an Apprentice. Jane Gregory and your brother William still live in the House at Bennington. I think they will not continue to remain together long. It is said William contemplates marrying. I fear he is not very likely to succeed in any business (how prophetic). Your Uncle William who is still in the Guards was at Bennington at the time I was. I perceive by your letter, that you have to endure some severe hardships. Have a good heart and you will get over it all and I hope return once more and that we shall have the pleasure of seeing you in London. Above all things, stick to your determination to avoid drink and you will have a fair prospect after your difficulties to live an honorable and happy life. I have written the above as requested by Mrs. Rowbotham and am rather surprised to learn that no one has written to acquaint you with these particulars. Your sister sends her love and I would have her write a few lines to you, but she begs to be excused at this time and will take another opportunity to do so. Your Aunt and my two daughters, who are at home, desire their best respects. I shall be happy to hear from you and remain my dear John.

Your Affectionate Uncle,
R. Horspool.

I was stunned upon receiving this letter and began to grieve the loss of my Father. The realization that I would never see my loving Father again was at times more than I could bear. At night I wandered about determined that my selfish behavior was the cause of his death, which created regrets that piled up and left me desolate. To this day I am unable to forgive myself, a guilt which I will carry to my grave.

My evening walks continued, ending at Granny Tiara's hut where I stood outside to listen to her teachings. I found more comfort in her words than anywhere else, and grew to appreciate the link of fellowship that existed between us. Many of my countrymen believed that slaves were of an inferior race, but I knew differently. I knew that God looked upon all mankind as His children and that our differences are selfishly manmade, based upon stupidity, ignorance, and greed.

Granny Tiara was over one hundred years old and the matriarch among her ebony kin. Her life was an example to others, with every action and expression showing that she was living in a state of grace. She never sought her own good, but bestowed her favor on others while patiently waiting to be called to her eternal Father. It was as if the Lord had left a part of Himself in her and her band of worshippers to be like salt in an almost Godless city. If those forlorn souls were the chosen few of His St. Augustine fold, surely it was incumbent upon us whites to have acted toward them as brothers and not as if they were cattle.

Prelude to War

Many in England judged America harshly for the practice of driving their aborigines into reservations, but the truth was that this was the only reasonable solution. In Florida, the whites who settled on land adjoining the Indians were known as borderers, who were a Godless, reckless, and selfish people who degraded the land and decimated the game. The Indians, by comparison, were more civilized and keeping them side by side with the borderers threatened their existence. The government was aware of the situation and was anxious to civilize the Indians by isolating them from their white brothers and by placing them on reservations and exposing them to Christian evangelization, which the Indians rejected outright.

President Jackson had a long history of fighting the Indians even before the United States purchased Florida. The previous Seminole War ended with several treaties, but none was satisfactory to all the tribes, who did not trust the dictates of their white father. In the end they accepted their annuities and the government stipulations, but when the time came for their removal, they broke their word and embarked upon a campaign to murder all the whites they could meet, which included women and children. This was the primitive type of war the Indians knew, but I do not think posterity will look upon them kindly for their deceit and savage cruelty.

The government held a poor opinion of the fighting capabilities of the Seminoles, judging the situation from previous wars with the Indians. They did not consider the difficulties the thickets, swamps, and arid pine barrens of the Florida countryside presented against established warfare. These became insurmountable obstacles to a modern army and an asset to the natives. Florida was to become a killing ground against the army, and the Indians' greatest protection.

On June 27, 1835, an express arrived at St. Augustine from Fort King with dispatches from the commanding officer conveying information of an incident that took place on June 19 between Indians and whites at Hog Town Settlement, a village that lay about four miles west of Micanopy. An Indian was caught in the act of stealing and the whites took the law into their own hands, bound the native to a tree and flogged him. His cries brought some of his companions from the forest, who fired upon the settlers, wounding three of them. The whites returned fire, killing one Indian and wounding another before the Indians left the scene. This altercation was the start of the second Seminole Indian War.

On August 27 another express arrived from Fort King with dispatches from General Thompson, the agent. It told about a Private Dalton of the third artillery, who was murdered while carrying the mail from Fort King to Fort Brooke in Tampa Bay. From information obtained from an Indian, a party of Miccasuky Indians stopped him on the evening of August 6. He approached them without suspicion, when one of them seized the bridle of his mule, while another shot, scalped, and disemboweled him before throwing him into a nearby pond. The mule was also shot, and the mail, saddle, and bridle were taken by the murderers. When the commanding officer at Fort Brooke learned of the facts, he sent a detachment of soldiers in pursuit of the murderers, but after several days they returned without success. The information was then sent to Lieutenant Colonel Fannin, the commanding officer at Fort King, which resulted in the chiefs being summoned by General Thompson. Further attempts were made to find the murderers, but after fruitless searches of several Indian villages, the troops returned to their quarters. The reason given for the murder was that the Indian who had been wounded in the Hog Town incident died upon his return to his relatives. Dalton was the first white man the Indians found in order to seek revenge.

I knew Paul Dalton from the time I stayed at Fort King when he brought the express from Tampa. It always resulted in an excited group of men gathering to ask for the latest news. He was a jovial young man of slight build, but one who preferred the freedom of the wilds to barrack life. Dalton, a town in south Georgia, was named after him.

Late the following month we learned of the murder of Charlie Omathla. While the chief was returning to his village from Fort King with his two daughters, he was fired upon and killed. His daughters returned to the fort and informed the commanding officer, who immediately dispatched a company of soldiers to retrieve the remains of the old man and to search for his murderers. After a fruitless search they returned to the fort. It appeared the act was deliberate, sanctioned by the chiefs of the Nation, who invoked Indian law. Any Indian who forsakes his people to help the whites was subject to death at the hand of the first Indian he met.

The Indian raids continued through October, so it became apparent that war was inevitable. Brigadier General Clinch then assembled a force of seven hundred regulars and about one hundred and fifty Florida light horse.

At the beginning of November I received orders to purchase medicines and pack up hospital stores to carry with us into the Nation. We departed St. Augustine on November 8 and marched west for the Picolata Ferry on the St. Johns River, a distance of about eighteen miles. Our route took us through marshes with water sometimes reaching up to the middle of our thighs. Such hiking was laborious and took hours. During the march we came across a skunk, a pretty little animal with a bushy tail. It ran ahead chased by two or three men and occasionally stopped to view the advancing troops. When it found itself in danger of capture, it quickly turned upon its pursuers and sent them a battery of stench that drove them back grinning and laughing.

The vegetation by the St. Johns and Black Creek Rivers was mostly live oak and impenetrable scrub. Occasionally there were open glades, with plantations so beautifully laid out that they brought back memories of a noble Englishman's park. The water of the St. Johns and Black Creek was of a chocolate color due to decayed vegetable matter. The St. Johns had a brackish, bitter taste, but the Black Creek water was delicious, crystal clear and abounding in beautiful water lilies. Marching in autumn was not so exhausting as the temperature was quite pleasant, but it was cold and uncomfortable to get up in the morning covered with night dew. Our blankets became saturated as if it had rained, which increased the weight for the men to carry. With a complete kit, each man carried from thirty to fifty pounds.

We continued west from Picolata through wilderness towards Micanopy. Though we marched in cool autumn weather the men still suffered from various forms of sickness. This meant that I marched during the day and filled my evenings looking after men suffering from fevers. I woke up lacking my usual energy and went to rest exhausted. Those days were made more difficult with pain from the spinal injury I received the previous winter at Fort King, compounded with annoying visits from Captain Drane, who was full of energy and seemed to delight in questioning my responsibilities. It may have been due to his belief that I was too young to be in charge of so much government property that included wine, rum, tea, chocolate, drugs, clothing, and bedding. Though his visits were a constant annoyance, they kept me out of trouble.

His 2nd lieutenant, Smith, and orderly, Sergeant Scofield, were the opposite of the captain, being tall and slender men of delicate build. When we halted on the banks of a pond, I saw them both totally exhausted. The captain then took pity upon them and carried his sergeant's musket and his lieutenant's sword. I was impressed by this behavior as it showed how much he cared for his men, especially those who were not as strong as himself and who did not abuse themselves or his authority.

The march took us through hammocks of almost impervious thickets, so it became necessary to send out a dozen pioneers each morning, two hours in advance, to cut away the undergrowth. Every morning before sunrise the men would be up cooking in the dusk, preparing a breakfast of coffee, biscuit, and salt pork, which was the main meal for the day. By starting out after breakfast we were able to cover between fourteen and twenty miles before encamping by a large round pond or stream.

Our midday meal was taken reclining in the shade of the woods and usually consisted of a slice of cold pork, a biscuit, and a drink of water from a nearby pond. The scenery was limited to the shore of the pond and was normally quite picturesque, consisting of an extensive margin of green grassland that spread out as much as 100 to 200 yards from the water's edge. These grasslands had been used by ancient tribes and many were still the sites of Indian villages. Such sites gave birth to the title of Pond Governor for the village chief and of Great Pond Governor for their king, or head chief, as Micanopy was called.

I can still visualize groups of soldiers with stacked arms, busily engaged in preparing their evening meal. Some would roast coffee in their frying pans or knead dough in a bucket, while others would bake bread in a most primitive way. They would wrap strips of dough around a stake which was then inserted into the ground near a fire. To bake it evenly the stick was turned at intervals. Some owned a Dutch oven, which was used for baking hominy cakes, stewing pork, or preparing beans to make soup. This became my favorite meal for the march.

Our officers had servants who cooked for them, preparing grilled fowl and other dishes, usually accompanied by a small bottle of liquor. Occasionally I was invited by Doctor Weightman to share a meal with him, but I was also fortunate to have access to the best and most generous supply of stores assigned to the sick. Frequently young officers requested some of our supplies.

Company D marched unprepared to engage the enemy and did not practice any tactics until just before reaching Micanopy. At that point, the captain drew our company into line and ordered the men to throw off their knapsacks, load with powder and ball. and to charge a hammock. We could have been annihilated at any one of countless hammocks that we had passed, for our men had never even loaded their muskets.

As we neared our destination the land began to undulate and became very beautiful, with drooping ash and weeping willow intermingled with hickory, cedar, and bay. Underneath, palmettos, huckleberry, prickly pears, and cactus plants abounded. It was no surprise that the natives did not want to leave, for they would never see the same again. As the name of the Territory indicated, Florida is the land of flowers. The flora is magnificent and gigantic compared with colder climates. Occasionally there was a round pond, with pellucid waters and beautiful marginal verdure that spread out like a carpet.

General Clinch was already at Micanopy when we arrived so we were ordered southwest to his plantation, which was twenty-six miles northwest of Fort King. We reached the plantation on the fourteenth and found it to be a large holding of about four miles square. There were large works for making sugar and other buildings where cotton was processed and prepared for exportation. Upon arrival we passed the Negro huts and then found one company of troops billeted in some very dilapidated buildings, which were in no condition to protect the men from the weather, let alone the enemy. It was a desolate place and not a welcome sight for a band of weary soldiers. The open freedom of the woods was more inviting, for if we camped somewhere unsuitable, we knew that the following day brought the opportunity of arriving at somewhere more comfortable.

Not satisfied, I wandered about and found a long, low building situated on higher ground. It was the driver's residence, which was the only habitable building on the estate. It was aptly named, for he was the man responsible for managing, or persecuting, the slaves on the plantation. It was a shingle-roofed log house consisting of four rooms, two in the front and two smaller ones in the back. Each had a window, but no glass or latticework to keep out the mosquitoes or flies. The wooden floorboards were spaced so far apart that they could accommodate a walking stick or a table leg. The only redeeming quality of the building was a small porch in the front, upon which I placed my medicine chest.

A plank was fastened between two wooden supports of the veranda, which was probably used by the driver as a table to place his legs or a glass of liquor when he relaxed. It became my table on which I mixed my medicines and spread my bandages. I lined up the patients in front of this balustrade and attended to each one in turn. Immediately behind me and close to my medicine chest was the doorway, which became the entrance to the general's quarters and the headquarters of the Army of Florida. That room, not much better than a pigsty, served as the sleeping quarters and office of General Clinch, followed by Major General Gaines and finally General Scott, the victor of the Battle of Plattsburg, who afterwards became the hero who commanded and won many decorations on the Mexican battlefields.

The driver on this plantation was a tall, muscular Yankee blacksmith, who had used his whip to become the object of dread and hate by the blacks under his supervision. Power had transformed him into a tyrant who behaved like our Yankee mate on the ship *Constellation*. For a few weeks, his vulgar behavior and muscular power were on daily display. I gave him a wide berth as he strode around the camp cracking his whip in an effort to show his authority. Since the soldiers gave him little regard, he began to make himself scarce and eventually gave up visiting us altogether.

The path to our new quarters was via a row of Negro huts that were in abominable condition and uninhabitable. There were no windows, floors of mud, an open, wood-burning fireplace, and roofs thatched with reeds. The interiors were dark and dreary, even with large spaces between log walls which allowed snakes and other reptiles to enter at will. These were the conditions under which Southerners' cattle were kept. I found such conditions and policies disgusting and disgraceful. I believe that raising the standard of living would have produced more willing laborers and a corresponding increase in production.

The Negro village was situated at the edge of a hammock pond, about one mile in circumference, but it was an indefinite border that consisted of marshes and considerable undergrowth with large trees. It was also an ideal place for Indians to hide, and since it was only fifty to eighty yards from the driver's residence, it was too close for our safety. A bullock road, which passed through the centre of the plantation, ran from the driver's house for about two miles and ended at the sugar works that were located atop a rise in the land. The sugar mill consisted of a house built above a treacle warehouse and a rum distillery. The plantation was about four miles across and two miles from the edge of the woods. About one hundred and fifty yards to the left of the driver's home was the blacksmith's shop, situated at the only other entrance to the estate.

When the plantation was in production, sugar cane was brought in by bullock carts to the top of the incline from where it was thrown into the jaws of rollers and crushed. The juice fell into a reservoir below from where it was carried by spouts to boiling vats. All the refuse and dirty juice were taken via troughs to the rum distillery, which was located about one hundred yards down the incline. It was from that dirty mixture that the spiritous liquor called rum was distilled. The man in charge of refining the sugar, or "sugar boiler," was an Englishman who lived on the island of Jamaica. He told me that he came every year and spent three months at the plantation, making sugar for the general.

My first night was spent rolled up in my blanket on the floor at the entrance of the driver's house, but I was chilled from the air drawn through the passageway. The following night I slept in the open air near the cook's fire, among the cooks, bakers, and hospital assistants at the northern end of the building. Each morning, if there was no rain the previous night, we arose like a bunch of ash cats, covered with wood ashes from the many campfires.

We slept there for about two weeks, until cooler winter temperatures drove us into the corn sheds, which were miserable dark places with neither a door nor window, with the only entrance being a picking hole through which the corn was thrown. You could not stand, nor see your hand in front of you. Our beds were formed from corn husks intermingled with corncobs, which were not pleasant to sleep upon. Though I dreaded those nights I was so exhausted from my daily duties that my weariness allowed instant sleep in almost any position. The structure was a horrible place in which to work, for the only way the husks could be stacked was if the slave were in a recumbent posture. To work in a corn shed in the heat of a Florida summer was a sentence that heaped more persecution upon the slaves.

The quarters for General Clinch and his staff were scarcely any better as they only had rugs to lay upon bare boards. Nobody could complain and the conditions prepared us for the ensuing campaign. We all slept in our clothing and I always buckled my forage cap strap under my chin, as did others, to prevent earwigs, centipedes, and cockroaches from entering our ears.

General Clinch was very knowledgeable about the Indians, having lived amongst them in peacetime and fought against them in the previous war, but he and his officers held them in low esteem, treating them contemptuously and regarding them as a nation of thieves and cattle rustlers. They spoke of them with pity or disdain and seriously underrated their natural skills, as they had not yet learned to respect their zeal and fighting abilities. During the march Captain Drane bragged of taking his company of sixty men through the Nation and while on parade, a Captain Belton at Tampa Bay used to make jokes with his brother officers. He would take off his cap and, stroking his hair, would exclaim, "Gentlemen, look, I still have my scalp!" A few months after, over one hundred of his men were the first to fall victim and be left unburied, leaving their bones to be bleached in the Florida woodlands. The countryside was more favorable for the Indian and gave him a distinct advantage over our troops, who were not accustomed to the wilderness. The natives were born and bred in the wilds, knew the country to perfection, and instinctively took advantage of the geography and landscape.

As soon as the general realized the possibility of an Indian revolt, he informed the government of the military weakness in Florida due to the few troops scattered across the peninsula. At the time there were five companies at Fort King, one at Fort Marion in St. Augustine, two at Key West, six at Fort Brooke in Tampa Bay, and the Florida Horsemen at Jacksonville. Such a small number of men under arms made concentration difficult and impractical. The government response was predictably inadequate, adding a couple of artillery companies from Savannah and Charleston that amounted to 150 men, while ordering Florida to provide a military force of 600 and Georgia to provide a 500-man militia.

With insufficient trained troops it was impossible for us to crush the native forces in all sectors simultaneously. The militia and volunteers were undisciplined and unreliable, and arrived too late to avoid damage to the campaign, which eventually resulted in disaster.

The thickets were dense on the road from Micanopy to Fort King, which was a further sixteen miles from his plantation. This presented difficulties and great risk in supplying provisional trains to the garrison. The general therefore decided to make the plantation his headquarters for the army during the campaign. On our first visit, Captain Drane was given orders to fortify the fort and he immediately set his men to work to build a longitudinal picket fort. This work pleased the captain, who preferred active soldiering instead of parade duties. Every day they were busy with their ox team, bringing in large pine trees to construct a twelve-foot-high fence, one hundred and fifty yards long and eighty yards wide. It was loopholed to enable riflemen to shoot through the fence. At the eastern end, a square blockhouse was erected, upon which a large howitzer was mounted so that shells could be fired into the woods. Since it was designed and constructed by our captain, the general named the work Fort Drane.

Later in November, news arrived about a marauding party of Indians in the neighborhood. The general immediately gave orders for Captain William Graham to take thirty men to intercept them, and if they tried to escape, he had orders to fire upon them. The party laid an ambush that night along the trail that the savages had taken during the day. About one hour before sunrise one of the outer sentinels came in to the main body saying that an Indian was approaching. The captain gave orders to be still and not to fire until ordered. They allowed the first Indian to pass, when immediately there were two more following him. The officer took these to be a scouting party and gave the word "make ready," which so startled the nearest Indian that he ran past the ambush. One soldier fired at him, whereupon the Indian dropped his pack and continued running at great speed. Half the party fired, wounding him, and he fell two or three times, but eventually was able to escape. The other two Indians took to their heels without sustaining any damage. The troop returned to the garrison, bringing with them the pack the Indian dropped, which contained stolen property from deserted homes that belonged to some citizens. The action was considered rash by the general who thought that the Indian should have been taken alive. As it was, he had been mortally wounded, for his body was found in an adjoining hammock by some Florida Light Horse the following week.

On November 30, 1835, a public notice was sent from General Wiley Thompson, the agent to all the inhabitants throughout Florida, warning them about the Indians. This resulted in the forts and fortified villages throughout Florida becoming crowded by settlers and their families. We received about one hundred and fifty at Fort Drane, who were without food and had very little clothing. The agent then gave notice to the quartermasters at the different stations to issue the refugees with rations and blankets until they could be removed to St. Augustine.

At the beginning of the following month, an express arrived with information that Colonel Warren, with a force of 150 men, had arrived at Micanopy from Jacksonville. There he separated his troops and sent us half his men with wagons that contained commissary stores. The convoy was ambushed by a party of Indians at Micanopy Pond about two miles from the village. The colonel lost three men killed and six wounded, and two of his wagons were burnt. When the firing was heard at the fort, the other half of his troop joined the fight and they succeeded in beating back the enemy to the hammocks. The Indian losses were not known.

On the following day General Call, commanding the West Florida militia force of 650 men, departed St. Marks, Florida, for Fort Drane. His men were enlisted from Tallahassee and the neighboring counties of Gadsden, Leon, Jefferson, and Madison. Gadsden was named after Colonel Gadsden, a noted explorer and United States surveyor, Leon was named after the Spanish explorer, and the other two were named after the presidents of those names. The West Florida Horse comprised planters and farmers who were well dressed and equipped. It was a splendid company, the finest Southerners I ever saw. Each man was armed with a rifle and their officers carried swords as a distinction of their rank, as all were dressed alike in the plain settlers' dress. When they were within four miles of reaching Micanopy, they were attacked. They killed four Indians but lost one man killed and two wounded. They arrived at the fort on December 14.

December 20, 1835: Colonel Warren and his party were directed to be stationed at Witumpky, about ten miles along the Fort King Road from Fort Drane. About the same time Major Smythe, an aide to General Clinch, was called to Charleston, South Carolina, on duties related to his office as paymaster to the troops in the South. In his absence I was chosen by the general to act as his secretary to write his dispatches as he dictated them to the various posts and commands throughout Florida. When the general asked me to assume these duties along with my stewardship, I pleaded unsuitability, which he perfunctorily waived, telling me that I would suit him well, provided I had sufficient free time. I thus found myself for two or three hours each day sitting at an unsteady table opposite the general. What a change from the time of my first arrival at the city of St. Augustine. I now had the ear and companionship of a general of the United States Army. He was most kind to me while at Fort Drane and placed great confidence in me, though I was a mere private soldier. I am sure that my character reference must have been obtained from Doctor Weightman, as he and the general were bosom pals. Both came from the state of Old Virginia, (nebber tire) according to the Negroes' phraseology. He treated me with a father's consideration, always with great frankness and civility. He was so genuinely kind to me that I soon felt at home with him and began to love him like a parent, and to show how much I appreciated his great kindness, I used all my energies to please him. I write this not to indulge my vanity but to show that good conduct and attention to duty are invariably noticed by our superiors.

It was Doctor Weightman's greatest pleasure to praise me to all newcomers, especially if they were of high rank. Having had considerable leisure time at the St. Augustine city hospital, I made myself well acquainted with all army regulations and became quite expert in making out reports, payrolls, returns, and requisitions. Doctor Weightman knew this, so it became his custom to magnify these skills, and he often instructed various officers who required information, "Go to my steward, he will manage it for you." In this manner he made me many friends, and some of them scarcely knew how to thank me sufficiently.

I recall making out the pay papers for an assistant surgeon who had been advised to contact me by the doctor. He was a generous person, which was not uncommon amongst the American commissioned officers. For my performing less than an hour's work, he gave me a dollar and a bottle of brandy. The latter was an invaluable acquisition at Fort Drane, especially for me, as it was a great treat for John, a Frenchman whom I had the good fortune to hire as the head of our culinary department. Each morning I offered him a glass until the bottle was finished.

Unlike my countrymen, I feel it my duty to champion our French neighbors. They deserve my respect and even affection for I found them to be most friendly and of a loving disposition. John was with me at Fort Drane for about six months, and I was happy to keep him from his company for his services at my hospital. He was an accomplished cook and greatly prized by the officers whenever they had a party or anything extra to serve. His delight was in producing dishes to suit our gastronomic fantasies. You might have thought that his intentions were to make us like him for his culinary accomplishments, but in reality, he was so kind, considerate, and industrious that you simply had to love the man. When we parted, he presented me with a pretty, white-handled pocket comb as a memento, which for years I have prized and carried with me. John was a rawboned man of six feet in height, very handy, always ready, no grumbler, and a genuine lover of his art. I have met many Frenchmen and always found them to have a great love of their country, without being overbearing, which is so common among the English and Americans. The French are clever people, not sensual or groveling, and have the knack of confining their desires to their capabilities. They are generally satisfied with little and are evidently taught the habit of delayed gratification.

December 27, 1835: An express arrived from Fort King regarding the massacre of General Wiley Thompson, the agent; Rogers, the sutler; Lieutenant O. Smythe, and four others, which had occurred at Mr. Rogers's house, situated about half a mile from the fort, on the preceding day at noon. The murdered party was seated at dinner when the Indians poured a volley through the windows. They ran for the fort but were all slain except for one young man, an assistant of the sutler's, and his servant, an old Negress. The young man succeeded in reaching the fort, while the Negress saved her life by hiding inside an empty barrel that stood in the house. The old woman informed the commandant that Osceola was one of the party who came into the house with some of the savages. She spoke the Indian language and overheard that he was the chief in command of the bloody deed. It is probable that General Thompson was killed by this treacherous Indian to whom he had shown kindness and trust. His body was pierced by sixteen balls and all the party were scalped. What seemed odd was that the sutler's body was not found at the scene. It was first supposed that the Indians had spared his life since he had been such a great friend, but it was not to be. After a few days, his body was found lying beside the hammock near the fort. I knew Rogers well. He was a kind and sensible man respected by all, and a man full of faith, always seeking the welfare of others.

When Lieutenant Smythe arrived the previous winter at Fort King with a squad of eight men, I could hardly suppress my laughter at the way he marshaled his small command into camp. With an air of absolute authority, he commanded his fatigued troop, "Halt, shoulder arms, ground arms, stand at ease." All was done with such aplomb as to seem totally ridiculous for his squad of dirt-stained veterans. He soon picked me out from the group of idlers as a fellow countryman and invited me to his quarters for a chat of old times. During our stay at St. Augustine, we had many conversations about Ireland, where he was born. I received numerous favors from him and permission to pass through his quarters to suit my convenience.

At times he could be a quick-tempered Irishman, and on one occasion at a family reunion ball, he received a black eye. He was very upset and came to me for help, whereupon I mixed him up a rather strong solution of potassium liquid to eradicate the blackness. It was too strong and destroyed his cuticle. He then called Doctor Weightman, who tasted my solution and immediately emptied it into a small jug of barley water, at the same time saying, "Smythe, apply that." The unfortunate affair severed our relationship for a time, but it caused me to be much more careful with my prescriptions in the future.

On another occasion Lieutenant Smythe sent a card to Doctor Weightman and invited him to fight a duel, but the doctor's reputation for bravery was so beyond question by all that the Irishman withdrew the challenge and averted a catastrophe. He was a medium-sized, pug-nosed, ugly man with a permanent smirk. He was the best dressed lieutenant of Company D, with every limb and his most prominent chest padded with cotton wool. Unfortunately, he was excessively vain and prided himself on his origin (the Smythes of Ireland) and his position as an officer. Yet one small bullet from our Indian foe put all his aspirations to rest, forever halting all his desires for renown and greatness.

The Battle of The Withlacoochee

From the time we arrived at Fort Drane, we knew that plans were afoot for us to mount a military solution to move the Indians out of Florida. Every general wants to have a vastly superior force in order to overwhelm the enemy, save lives, and shorten the campaign. Though General Clinch sought more troops he was confident that what he had available was sufficient for the task. In December he was now prepared to take the fight to the enemy. About the middle of December, General Clinch had ordered Captain Belton, the commander of the post at Tampa, to dispatch Number Two Company to join up with us and form a junction at the Withlacooche River.

We learned a few weeks later that Captain Belton delayed the departure from Tampa to await the arrival of additional troops, who were joined by yet a further company of fifty bayonets under the command of Captain Gardiner, whom I knew from the time he was my captain of D Company, upon my arrival in St. Augustine. Though his wife was extremely ill he was prepared to leave, and at reveille on the morning of December 23 he mounted his horse in front of his detachment. At the point of starting out from the fort, a Major Dade made a proposition to Captain Belton to take Captain Gardiner's place on account of the critical state of his wife. The captain acceded to the request and the company left the fort under the command of Major Dade.

In the meantime Captain Gardiner learned that the United States schooner *Motto* was about to sail for Key West to pick up two twelve-pounders with ammunition. Captain Gardiner's children and their grandfather, Major Worth, afterwards distinguished as

General Worth in the Mexican War, were already at Key West. He decided to send his wife to Key West in the *Motto*, which enabled him to satisfy his strong desire to be with his men. Thus, he was able to rejoin his company and place himself under the command of Major Dade.

Meanwhile Fort Drane became a hive of activity as we prepared for our own departure. I was responsible for packing all the commissary and hospital stores while other men were busy loading Indian corn and other rations, supplies, and forage into twenty-seven wagons. When I recall the energy and excitement required to provision an army of one thousand men, I wonder how they manage to supply the immense armies of Grant and Sherman.

Late in the evening of December 27, while I was busy getting all my medicines and instruments placed in my medicine chest, Lieutenant Colonel Fannin arrived from Fort King with four companies of artillery. Wondering whether I had remembered everything, I finally retired to sleep. We rose early the following morning, when all the troops obtained and placed three days' rations in their haversacks. Thus prepared, we began our march upon the Indian Nation.

Fighting is not the only quality that distinguishes a veteran. Together with courage a soldier must show eagerness that he is prepared to participate in any upcoming event. That eagerness was shown in those three stirring days of preparation. To be successful, a good general will be thorough in selecting well-trained and efficient officers as heads for all his departments. A general may plan a good campaign and have his men fight well, but if his army is deficient in clothing, food, weapons, or ammunition, then the entire army could become a rabble, vulnerable to defeat.

The total number of troops for the campaign consisted of 650 mounted men under General Call, the governor of Florida; 150 horsemen under Colonel Warren, an Englishman; and six companies of regulars, amounting to 250 men, under Colonel

Fannin. One company of regulars was left to guard Fort King and about 120 men, those unfit for the march, were left at Fort Drane. We departed the fort at eight o'clock in the morning. The artillery and infantry regulars occupied the center, and they were flanked on the right and left about one hundred yards apart by the horsemen. General Clinch, the commanding general, with his staff took up the right, with the regulars about fifty yards from the rear. The march was two abreast, both for foot and horse, as this was the easiest mode to progress through the almost impassable country. The wagons followed immediately behind the advance guard, but had great difficulty maintaining speed due to the unevenness and softness of the ground, when at times they sank into the mud up to their axle trees. Even the troops occasionally had to wade through boggy ground, which slowed our advance so that by nightfall we had progressed only twelve miles.

On that first day we passed Charley Omathla's village, which consisted of about fifty empty dwellings, as all the tribesmen had joined the enemy following their chief's murder. The homes were constructed with reeds and reminded me of my father's sheep pen, except that the latter was made of stubble. The walls appeared to be about one yard thick, which made them impervious to the heavy rains as well as the sweltering heat of summer. The only opening and entrance was at the end of the building and was covered by a hanging cloth. There was no window nor chimney, yet they appeared prettier homes than the log cabins of the poor whites.

At dusk I took a stroll through our camp and was captivated by the scene of hundreds of campfires that lit up a space half a mile square, in an otherwise dark forest. The Florida Horsemen were quite at home in the wilderness, but their officers and men were kept equally busy tethering seven hundred horses.

There were no running streams so we drew water from large round ponds, which were a common sight on the Indian lands. The horses were the first to drink and they made the margins of the pond very muddy. This caused a routine during the march for the men to wade in some distance, and those who were last had to wade some fifty yards or more to obtain clear water. The ponds were very shallow for a distance of a hundred yards from the edge and were full of weeds and covered with decayed vegetable matter, except for the center where the water was clear. If we had possessed boats, we would have obtained pure clean water, as these natural reservoirs were fed by springs. The ponds usually contained alligators and water snakes, which sounds frightening, but our experience showed that both were harmless, especially the snakes. A large hungry alligator, when given the opportunity, would drown and eat a stray calf or dog, but I seldom heard of their attacking a human.

The forests appeared more ancient here than at any other part of Florida that I had seen, and the thickets were more numerous. When approaching a thicket, it became normal for the horsemen to ride through singly and then halt on the other side. The pioneers then followed and made a trail sufficiently wide for the wagons. The regular troops then brought up the rear. We covered twenty miles on the second day, as the country became almost one continuous pine barren where there were fewer, or no, thickets. At one stage we crossed twelve miles of flat, sandy ground upon which the pines were stunted and in poor condition. As we marched, we choked on the dust and were burned by the reflected rays of the sun. I could not imagine how much worse it would have been in the summer. I yearned to see a thicket, for even though they were difficult to pass through they almost always provided some water to quench our thirst.

On the 30th we covered similar country as on our first day, except it was more hilly and the soil appeared to be very black on the surface. When we passed a large Indian village about noon, a number of our horsemen rode into it and brought out some ornaments the Indians had left behind. I noticed a couple of small turtle shells that had peas inside. The Indians wore these fixed to their heels while they danced to create some considerable clatter.

As we marched we made fun of the Indians, whom we had yet to encounter. An Irishman exclaimed, "Are we not going to have a rap at them for our pains? By the Holy Spoor, are we not to have some diversion for the honor of auld Ireland, boys?" Then Johnny Crappeau would say, "Ah, le pauvre Indian. He be one grand coward, he non like le disciplinare." Our little army consisted of a very cosmopolitan group of soldiers, each with a distinctive manner of speaking. Georgian and Floridian Crackers were country farmers who spoke with a nasal twang. They would answer questions with "I reckon so." The Yankee favorites were "good nows," "guepes it taint," and "it twas." There were many Germans and some Dutch and French who were always "parlez-vous"-ing. The Irish were always swearing by Cromwell, the Holy Spoor, and all the saints, with their patron, St. Patrick, taking the lead. The Scotch praised their haggis and "the land o' cakes." Here and there was a John Bull (Englishman), who would drop the letter "h," and all their conversations included their "I knows" and "you knows." We also had Spanish, Minorcans, Poles, Swedes, Canadians, Nova Scotians, with here and there a South American. If that assembly of nationalities were advantageous, surely the poor Indians could not escape destruction.

Our bivouacs were particularly pleasant, as well as exciting. The nights were balmy like an Indian summer, bright and nearly as light as day. One night I had snugly ensconced myself in the long grass and for a little while listened to the music of a whip-poor-will that had perched himself aloft in one of the nearby pines. The sweet notes gradually lulled me to partial sleep, when I was awoken by the noise of our dog who was making a bed for himself nearby. I had forgotten about the dog, so imagined it was a rattlesnake. But for the dangerous reptiles, camping in Florida would be a most relaxing experience for the footsore, or over-weary, ride-stained traveler.

Then the men began to jeer our Negro guide, but he answered "Wait e bit Massa, you find yet, you no hab your walk and tote for notting." There were all kinds of wisecracks and jokes regarding the coming contest with the Indians. A tall Yankee soldier asked

Tweedy, a little Irishman who had served under General O'Hara in the British army, what he thought about the forthcoming fight. "By Jesus," said he, "the Battle of Waterloo will not be a cockfight to it." We had three friendly Indians with us and, when asked the same question, they would stretch their mouths wide in a broad grin, almost from ear to ear, while indicating that the Indians would fight the "big knives," the term they used to refer to the regulars.

We halted about three miles from the Amatura, or Withlacoochee, River. The general gave strict orders to be quiet and not to light any fires in the camp, as he hoped to surprise the Indians the following day. The Withlacoochee swamp was the place our spies had said we should meet the enemy, but up to that time we had not seen the slightest trace of them. It was an extensive inundated district, formed by the junction of several tributaries of the Withlacoochee River. It was spotted with islands, many of which were cultivated by Negroes who belonged to Chief Sitachey, who maintained a settlement on the archipelago in 1824. We believed that the Indians developed the area as a stronghold as soon as they knew they would have to fight a war.

I still remember that night clearly as I shared a tent with Fisher, the wardmaster, and Boz, the hospital steward from Fort King. Boz had a fine physique and took great pride in his large bushy whiskers, which he oiled and brushed up in the best style. This characterized him as a whiskerando and gave him his nickname. He had an amusing way of displaying his authority with humor, at times bursting into a peculiar grotesque laughter. But he was a man of peace, kind to the sick and much loved by them for he was a good and very useful soldier. Without a fire we ate our pork and biscuit cold and felt quite lonely, although surrounded by many comrades. Then Boz spoke freely about how he was frightened of the Indians. He anticipated that we would reach the river on the following day and believed that the enemy would be waiting for us. He had passed sleepless nights and had grown terrified that he would not see his home in New York again even though his term of service had almost expired

On the last day of the year we arose early and were allowed to make a small campfire so we could boil water for the sick. General Clinch expected to meet the enemy on that day, but he thought that they would have come to meet us. Suddenly one of the militia buglers blew the morning call, which infuriated the general for the grievous breach of his orders. The bugler could thank his stars that there was no time to give him a whipping, as that certainly would have been his fate. Dr. Weightman then instructed me to remain with the wagons and I asked if Fisher could remain with me. He answered firmly that he was taking Fisher and that I must attend to the sick. And so, five men with intermittent fever kept me from seeing the battle of the Withlacoochee. Lieutenant Dancy, who was acting commissary, was left in command of myself, the sick, the wagons, and four noncommissioned officers, a total of less than fifty men.

The army departed about five a.m., and at daybreak Lieutenant Dancy gave orders to his men to cut down the adjacent pine trees in order to erect breastworks. The wagons were placed next to one another opposite and south of the woods on the northern perimeter of an impenetrable bog. On the right and left of the wagons' fronts were erected two blockhouses, constructed most expeditiously as only Americans can, with large pine timbers, the tops of which filled up the spaces between the wagons fronting the woods. The horses were picketed in the center. This made up what we forever ever after called Camp Dancy. While the fortifications were under construction, I was busy administering emetics and other medications that would induce sweating, in order to counteract the chill of the night. Experience showed this to be the most efficient remedy for the intermittent fevers so common to Florida. The same treatment relieved the system of excessive bile, which was also very common in this climate.

Between the hours of twelve and one, a scout reported that he noticed a party of mounted horse coming toward us from the river. Lieutenant Dancy gave orders that each man with a loaded musket should assume his station, whilst he and another endeavored to learn the strength of the advancing enemy. Upon drawing nearer to our camp, they were found to be a party of General Call's Florida Horsemen. Their objective was to obtain rations for several days. Further interrogation by our little commandant revealed that they had no authority to make such demand, and thus became suspect of desertion. Accordingly, they were refused rations unless they could show a proper order from the officers in command on the Withlacoochee. Their officer then tried bullying and said he would take the rations by force if we did not deliver them to him. This was sufficient reason to put the back up of our spunky little lieutenant, who immediately gave the order, "Men, fall in! Attennnnnshun! Shoulderrrrr Arms! Orderrrrr Arms!" With his troop facing the Horsemen, he said, "Now then, sir," addressing their officer. "Come and take anything from my camp at your peril." This was sufficient reason for the militia officer to change his mind. He saw in the determination of our courageous little commander that blood would be spilt if he made good his threat. He wisely wheeled around and rode off with his company, taking the direction of home. As soon as the whole matter was understood, our men, in their anger, were so eager to fire upon the retrogrades that Lieutenant Dancy had some difficulty in preventing them. One man, more rash than the others, fired off his musket after their retreating steps, which caused them to scamper off all the faster.

Shortly after, a single horseman came galloping toward us from the river at full speed. He was a youth from one of General Call's Florida Light Horse. He arrived out of breath and speechless for a while due to his exertion. After pausing he exclaimed excitedly, "They're fighting, they're fighting!" "Who? What? Speak plainly to the point," was Lieutenant Dancy's reply. "And what do you want in such a hurry?" "Ammunition, the regulars are fighting the Indians on the other side of the river. They have been fighting half an hour and are out of cartridges. I was to ride for life and death, or they will all be massacred." At once I jumped into an ammunition wagon and handed out as many cartridges as he could carry, then he instantly rode back to the scene of conflict.

The incident made us realize our vulnerability and we saw how easily the Indians could make a circuit from the river and cut us off. We immediately began making preparations to strengthen our position for the night. Large fires were made about one hundred yards outside our works, on our front, and also on our right and left flanks. Our foe was very ingenious and used tactics assuming the appearance of a wild pig. If he came in force, the light of the fires gave us a good view of his proceedings. While this did not make us feel any safer, since the cunning enemy could see our fires as a sign of weakness.

Lieutenant Dancy predicted that if the enemy learned of our position, they were sure to come at night. He also considered that our circumstances were desperate, as our small force was inadequate to cover our large front of breastworks, as well as man the blockhouses on our right and left flanks. For the remainder of the day we heard nothing from the army, which we accepted as good news since defeat would have brought us stragglers. We prepared to sell our lives dearly, as we knew that no quarter was given in such cases. Even if we had cowards in our ranks, they could act bravely when their backs were against a wall. As darkness descended, the lieutenant placed our scouts outside our watch fires, and called upon every man of his little band, sick or not, to take a position at the breastworks at such intervals as to man our front as well as our right and left flanks. The swamp to our rear was considered sufficient protection as we had proved that day that it was impassable. Our orders were to stand firm and still at our posts, as any movement was a sure aim for the unerring marksmanship of the savage. If we were to be attacked, our orders were to immediately divide our forces equally and man the blockhouses.

It was common practice in England to sit out the old year, but that night we all had to stand our watch. Up to that time the nights had been beautiful, calm and mild, but all that changed suddenly on the last day of 1835, when Florida was hit with a rimy frost. We watched through the long and dismal night, hoping not to see John Indian. By constantly staring, my eyes grew tired and, combined with an over-vivid imagination, created false images, turning stumps and logs into the stealthy foe. The flickering flames of the fires gave everything the appearance of movement, imparting life into inanimate objects. This happened so frequently that now and then one or two of our men received permission to search the gloom, but the sightings turned out to be either a clump of scrub, a log, or a stump of some large pine.

Of all the men in our little band, none failed in their duty except for myself. I became very weary following another almost sleepless night talking with Boz and incessant duties with the sick. It was very cold, and my musket clung to my hands from the hoar frost. I found myself nodding and eventually crawled beneath a wagon tarpaulin and was soon asleep. I do not know how long I was asleep, but it was our commander who discovered my disgraceful conduct. He awoke me by asking, "Who's this asleep?" When I sprang to my feet I found myself confronted by the officer whom I greatly respected, which caused me even greater shame, vexation, and disgrace. My own emotions were the more poignant as Lieutenant Dancy addressed me. "Steward! I did not expect this of you. What an example you are setting for the others." I felt dumb and did not offer excuses; neither would I account for my dereliction of duty, although I knew it was the result of my being unused to night guard duty.

On the morning of December 31, while we were constructing our camp, the army departed camp early in the morning and reached the river at about 10 a.m., where they found many fresh Indian footprints, which indicated that the enemy was not far off. The regular troops crossed the river in a small canoe, which could only accommodate eight at a time. By the time all the regulars had crossed it was nearly noon. As soon as General Clinch and his staff had crossed, the troops were formed and ordered to "stack arms," whereupon many fell prostrate to the ground to rest. Some others formed circular squads or squatting groups and amused themselves with playing cards. All were waiting for the horsemen to cross. The troops were resting about one hundred and fifty yards from the bank of the river. To their right and about eighty yards distant was a large hammock where the outlying scouts were stationed. Doctors Weightman and Hamilton, with four militia surgeons, were stationed about one hundred yards to the rear and left of the battalion. They had not rested more than an hour when suddenly one of the scouts came running in and cried the alarm, "Indians! Indians!"

Immediately the men were formed into double order, which was a mistake, but such was the effect of discipline. They were joined by about sixty militia who had succeeded in crossing the river. Captain Mellon was the first to recognize an Indian skulking in the thicket and obtained permission of his battalion colonel to fire. No sooner had he done so than it was answered by the peeling sound of one thousand rifles firing into our troops, accompanied by yelling which was intended to frighten us. It began with a low growling noise, which finally burst into a yelling screech that rang through the forest. The suddenness of the attack, and the terrible cry of the Indians, struck terror and a degree of panic amongst the soldiers who retreated to the surgeons' position, leaving about twenty of their comrades soaking in their blood. The retreating troops had drawn about two hundred of the enemy from their cover. Seeing this, they were soon rallied and ordered to fire a volley amongst the advancing Indians, which was done with great effect. The savages then skulked back into the hammock dragging their fallen comrades with them. When the troops had regained their former position, both sides maintained a steady fire at each other. The troops continued to suffer severely, and many wounded were brought to the rear. Officers predominated, which indicated that the Indians had made them their main targets according to their tactics. "Pick off the big bravos, then massacre the big knives at close fight with the tomahawk."

The soldiers continued to form a line according to order, making a constant target for the unseen enemy. Losing their officers, their ranks gradually thinned so that eventually they lost discipline and reformed into groups, a situation that probably would have ended in wholesale butchery. This brought the commanding general to his senses just in time to see the futility of such valor against a treacherous and cunning enemy. He had already had one horse killed under him and had been shot through his clothing, but all of that meant nothing but pleasurable excitement to the brave old officer, who could have afforded to bask on his laurels of former days when he had fought against the British and Spanish.

His battalion officer, Colonel Fannin, was a man of a different quality, equally brave like himself, but with more tact. Even during peacetime his word of command almost spoke of battle, with a voice so earnest and thrilling that it went right through you. His every action spoke of war and not drill, and he maintained his troops in a state of readiness and good discipline at all times. Noticing his position was untenable, and seeing his men falling continuously, he asked the general for permission to charge the hammock but was ordered back to the head of his troops. Shortly after, he made the same request and again was ordered back to his duty. But when he found he had lost all control over his men, he made yet another appeal and with tears in his eyes went to the general, saying, "My men will all be cut down. Oh, let me charge and I swear on my life they will run." This time General Clinch gave in to his persistence and gave his approval for the order to charge. With his one arm, a diminutive figure, and his own peculiar shrill ring of a voice that went through you with its decisional energy, "Men," said this little hero, "fix bayonets, charge and follow me." No sooner had he uttered the words than they burst out and, dashing into the thicket, drove the Indians from tree to tree, from shrub to bush and scrub palmetto, till the battle was almost won, but to their left was a small thick scrub, wherein a party of the enemy were still firing upon our men with unerring accuracy. It was common practice for our soldiers to aim at the flash of the Indians' fire, so they developed a method to confound our soldiers. After each shot the warrior would yell and cast themselves to lie on their left side. In that position they would reload their rifles and then position themselves for another shot at their enemy.

The skirmish in the hammock was severe and bloody and lasted just a few minutes, but when the enemy retired they left behind about thirty dead. If this charge had been made after the first fusillade, it would have saved many wounded. We subsequently found that the best tactic was to rush the Indians and fight in extended order, each man taking a tree for cover, copying the enemy in his mode of warfare. Discipline and close-order formations were stupid strategies for Indian warfare and inevitably ended in defeat, as in "Braddock's Defeat." This was written about in the colonists' war against the French and Indians, in which Washington, the "young buckskin," did excellent work by helping to save the remnant of the British Army. The Indian position was eventually charged by Captain Gates and Captain Mellon's companies, which was completed so efficiently that they dislodged the enemy, who retreated making loud groans and yells which our Indian scouts interpreted as signals of defeat. Although we maintained our ground, I was unable to say what side had suffered the most. The Indians lost the most killed, while we had lost only six. Yet every third man had been wounded and some very severely, with many having two and three wounds. During the battle, which lasted three-quarters of an hour, our general had two horses killed, three balls through his clothing, and one through his cap. Truthfully the bullets came so thickly, those who escaped bodily injury had ball holes through their clothing or accessories. I believe it was a miracle that we escaped a massacre.

Had the bore of the Indian rifle been larger the story may have been different. In lieu of six we might have had sixty killed, as many of the wounds were dangerous and located in vital areas such as the lungs, head, face, and abdomen. Owing to the smallness of the balls, only one out of one hundred or more cases ended in death.

As soon as the fight began the West Floridian Horse made no further effort to cross the stream, making the dishonest excuse that the Indians would also cross and outflank them. Surely they could have sent at least four out of eight hundred of their number? General Call, their commander, was very annoyed, but found his reproaches at their cowardliness useless. He left them and crossed the river with some of his officers, determined to assist our men to the last. Those who did cross were the Jacksonville Horse commanded by Colonel Warren, an Englishman, and they fought gallantly. That was their second encounter with the enemy, having fought with them at the Micanopy ponds. When General Clinch became aware of the cowardliness of the militia, he addressed his men and made an impassioned plea that a positive outcome of the day depended upon their bravery.

When the battle was over it was as if our men were like targets for the Indians. One soldier named Woods of Company D, 2nd Artillery, was shot in the head, with the ball lodging above the ear in the temporal bone. He fell, apparently dead, but was only stunned and, on regaining consciousness, he wrapped his handkerchief around his head and joined his company. Another soldier named Davis of the same company got shot in the neck and, although covered with blood, stood his ground until he received a second shot to the groin, when he was removed. Lieutenant John Graham, commanding Company H, 2nd Artillery, was shot in each leg and in the mouth, carrying away the teeth of the lower jaw. Captain William Graham, his brother, commanding Company D, 4th Infantry, was shot in the shoulder and hip yet stood his ground. This small band of five hundred officers and men fought bravely and were equally harmed.

Lieutenant John Graham was the tallest in the company and the most likely to be shot, but he was protected by his friendship with Osceola, the Seminole chief who commanded the Indians at the Withlacoochee. All of us knew of the friendship that existed between them, so it was no surprise that wherever the lieutenant was stationed the balls flew less thickly. At a later time Osceola had a meeting at General Gaines's camp and he particularly asked after Graham. He was very pleased to learn that his friend was unhurt in the battle even though he, Osceola, received a shot through the hand.

The above account of the Battle of Withlacoochee I deduced from various versions I heard from the wounded under my care. I also include the following, which was produced from extracts of General Clinch's dispatch to Washington.

Head Quarters,
Territory of Florida,
Fort Drane,

May 4th, l836

Sir.

On the 24th ultimo, Brigadier General Call, commanding the volunteers, called into service by the order of the Governor of Florida, formed a junction with the regular troops at this Post. Lieutenant Colonel Fannin with three companies from Fort King arrived on the 27th. The Brigade of mounted volunteers composed of 1st and 2nd Regiments, commanded by Brigadier General Call and a Battalion of regular troops, commanded by Lieutenant Col. Fannin took up the line of march for a point on the Withlacoochee River, which was represented by our guides as being a good ford. About four o'clock on the morning of the 31st after leaving all our baggage and provisions, protected by a guard commanded by Lieutenant Dancy, we pushed on with a view of carrying the ford and of surprising the main body of Indians, supposed to be concentrated on the West Bank.

On reaching the Withlacoochee at daylight we found instead of a good ford, a deep and rapid stream and no means of crossing, except in an old and damaged canoe. Lieutenant Col. Fannin however soon succeeded in crossing the regular troops and took up a position in advance, while Brig. General Call was engaged in crossing his Brigade and in having their horses swum over the river. But before half of the troops had crossed, the battalion of Regulars, consisting of about two hundred men, were attacked by the enemy, who were strongly positioned in the scrub that extended from the river bank. A small band, aided by Col. Warren, Major Cooper, and Lieutenant Yeoman, with twenty seven Volunteers, met the attack of a savage enemy nearly three times their number, headed by the chief Osceola. With Spartan valor they fought an action that lasted nearly an hour, during which time the troops made three brilliant charges into the swamp and scrub and drove the enemy in every direction. After the third charge, although nearly one third their number had been cut down, they were found sufficiently firm and steady to fortify the formation of a new line of battle, which gave protection to the entire flanks, as well as to the position selected for re-crossing the troops.

Brig. General Call, after using every effort to induce the Volunteers remaining on the East bank, when the action commenced to cross the river and in arranging the troops still remaining on that bank, crossed over and rendered important service, by his coolness and judgment in arranging part of his corps on the right of the Regulars, which gave much strength and security to that flank. Lieutenant Colonel Fannin displayed the greatest firmness throughout the action and added much to the high reputation long since established. Captains Drane and Mellon exhibited the greatest bravery and judgment and likewise added to the character they acquired in the late war. Captain William Graham, 4th Infantry, was fearlessly brave and although severely wounded early in the engagement, continued to head his company in the most gallant manner, until he received another severe wound, when he was taken from the field. His brother Lieutenant John Graham, commanding adjacent company, was likewise severely wounded early in the fight, but continued with his men, till another wound forced him from loss of blood to retire. When almost every noncommissioned officer and private exhibited such firmness, it was almost impossible to discriminate between them, but the Commanding General cannot withhold his high approbation of the judgment and courage displayed by Sergeant Johnson of H Company, 3rd Artillery, on whom the command of the company devolved after Lieutenant Graham was removed from the field. He, although severely wounded, continued at the head of the Company till the action was over. Also of Sergeants Kenton and Loffcon and Corporal Paget, 4th Infantry, Sergeants Scofield and Potter of D Company, 2nd Artillery, (my friends), Sergeant Smith, C Company, 1st Artillery and Corporal Chapin, C Company, 3rd Artillery, (another of my friends). Much credit is also due to the medical department, composed of Drs. Weightman, Hamilton, Randolph and Bradon, for their activity and attention to the wounded.

As soon as the enemy had retreated, and being unable to follow them, the general recrossed the river. He positioned his main body of forces in the hammock, so they were ready if the enemy returned with a greater force. Then he gave Colonel Fannin and Doctor Weightman orders to recross the river with the wounded, a slow process due to the severity of the wounds and the great pain the soldiers endured during transportation. The wounded were all removed from immediate danger before nightfall, and they were followed by the main body.

The troops had barely constructed a breastwork for the night, when the enemy returned in greater numbers. Their yelling indicated a readiness to continue the fight, but when they found that all the troops had recrossed the river, they came down to the riverbank sending yells of defiance. They did not like the appearance of the breastwork camp and soon retired to plan a more opportune time to continue their attack.

The last night of December 1835 was miserable and very cold. The wounded suffered the most since they had not eaten since the previous day. I recall how Corporal O'Brien, my former attendant in hospital at St. Augustine for three years, had broken his right arm immediately below the elbow. O'Brien had thrust his arm into his haversack for support, his blood running down onto and being soaked up by a piece of bread. When Sergeant Potter attended to him, he removed the bread from the haversack, whereupon it was greedily requested by some of the wounded. Potter divided it into small portions and gave it to the men, who ate it readily.

Before dawn on the first day of 1836, we buried the dead in shallow graves under the bivouac fires of the preceding night. The loose sand was removed with tin cups, then the graves were trampled by mules and horses so as to leave no trace of their existence to the prying eyes of the cunning enemy. The precaution was useless, for when General Scott's troops were to pass the same place, the skeletons lay bleaching in the sun. About fifty dangerously wounded were brought back on horse litters, which consisted of a blanket stretched between two long pieces of pine so placed as to allow two horses to be yoked before and behind. The militia, who had no stomach for fighting, enthusiastically helped to prepare comfortable coverings for the wounded. We filled the wagons with more wounded and left those less grievously harmed to ride horses.

At dawn we rested from our extra duties and made breakfast, which reinvigorated our weary bodies. Then the sun rose, beautifying and brightening the day. About 10 a.m. the advance guard of the army returned from the river, followed by the dreadful sight of litters filled with the wounded. We claimed that we had won the battle, but our wounded were so many that we were obliged to retreat back to the fort. Among those cut and swollen bodies I saw poor Fisher, the ward master, whose eyes were almost out of their sockets, and as cadaverous-looking as the others. I ran up to him, shook his hand, and asked him where he was hurt. I was agreeably surprised to learn that he was not touched but was exhausted from working the whole of the previous night washing and dressing wounds. I then asked him about my friends, Sergeants Scofield, Potter, and Caull, and my doctor. I was happy to learn that they had survived without a scratch. Boz related the bad news about our Company D. "It was a terrible fight, we lost one killed and 15 wounded." Only thirty-six went into battle. This statistic showed that Company D suffered proportionally greater than the British Army at Waterloo, which made Tweedy's jeering remarks of the previous day no longer a joke. I then attended to my friend, Ambrose Mackay, and was glad to find only his clothing and canteen had been riddled with balls.

Later I asked how Fisher had fared in the battle and was informed that he presented himself well, for he was seen to be in the front of those who dashed into the hammock. My informant said, "I knew him well from having a tin wash-hand basin dangling from the back of his knapsack." I had tied the utensil to his knapsack myself just before he left the commissariat camp. Sometime afterward, when I congratulated Fisher for his bravery and dash, he described his feelings as being quite different than what they appeared to others. "Why?" he said. "I did not know what I was doing. My orders were to remain with the surgeons, but I was amongst the men as an aid to the wounded when the charge was given. I suppose through my excited feelings of fear and horror I unwittingly went with the rest."

My workload soon increased so I ordered my attendants to brew enough coffee to give each of the wounded a cupful. After refreshments our camp was struck, and I took charge of the long cavalcade of groaning men. Major Cooper and another officer were in such bad shape that they were hand-carried in litters by fresh relays of eight men detailed from the battalion every half hour. In this manner we began our return from the commissariat camp to Fort Drane.

We retreated via the shortest route, and on that first day we managed to cross twenty-two miles of difficult and dangerous country. It was heart-rending to witness the great suffering in the long cavalcade of the wounded. The constant groans and cries for water, water, water, which could only be provided at long intervals. Evening was welcomed by all, but especially the wounded who had been jolted in the wagons all day. Upon arrival we unloaded the wagons and the litters and suddenly I and my assistants were busy making fires, cooking, boiling coffee, and clearing away the undergrowth to form resting sites for the wounded.

Providing comfort was more important than tending to the wounds. I remember the exhaustion and anxiety of that night, but also saw a selfish side of human nature. While my own feelings were to do my duty, six of my extra attendants abandoned their responsibilities and hid themselves for the night. Then General Clinch came to visit the wounded before he went to rest. When he saw what little help I had, he ordered a search for the delinquents, which proved fruitless. Though he was angry at the conduct of my missing help he then willingly offered his own, and together we covered the various groups of wounded with wagon tarpaulins, which kept them from the cold and frost. This first encounter with the Indians showed me a character of the general I had not seen before. As a youth he chose the army, but I knew him when he was way past his prime. Over the years he had nurtured his mind to control his body and always performed in excess of his duty. I saw him act with bravery, confidence, and high moral principles, no matter how difficult or dangerous. During conflict he was calm, not impulsive nor excitable, but steadfast, well suited to command, and a credit to his rank. This kind and brave soldier was not forgotten, for years later his name was honored at Fort Clinch on Amelia Island in Florida and the Clinch River and mountains of Tennessee.

It was about two a.m. before I was able to rest and, though surrounded by groaning men, I was asleep at once. I slept for only two hours as I had to rise at four to prepare for the day's march. The general was eager to reach the fort by the following day and the wounded had to be fed and arranged in the wagons and the litters. Their wounds had stiffened, causing the men to feel their pains more acutely. Their cries were constant and all just wanted to arrive at a place of safety, which we tried to do as quickly as possible.

It was essential that we maintained our guard since our return journey crossed the lands of an aroused enemy. Our progress was slow, and the men were thoroughly worn out, but still we expected to be attacked. The disheveled militia horsemen instilled little confidence due to their previous behavior but did prove themselves to be useful. Occasionally they closed in on our right and left flanks, which gave us the appearance of a ragtag band, rather than a proper, disciplined army expecting an enemy attack. Even in winter, when the Florida sun was high in the sky, the heat was fierce. This, and the dust raised by the horses, caused considerable discomfort for the already overheated men.

At about four p.m. we came upon an Indian village situated on higher ground that was enveloped in flames. Rumor spread of an imminent attack and every man imagined Indians in the smoke and fading light. There was so much fear that I was sure that if we had met the enemy, we would have been defeated. Lieutenant Dancy, who was mounted, rode up to me and hinted at his lack of faith in the militia, saying, "Steward, if yonder are Indians, those fellows won't stand." As they were nearly all mounted, they would have ridden off and left us to become easy prey to the savages and their scalping knives. But there were no Indians. All the panic was created by our Negro guide who hated the chief of the deserted village. He was responsible to lead from in front, but upon reaching the village he set fire to the whole place. When the general heard what our guide had done, he ordered him to be put under guard with a warning that "if he again caused a false alarm, he was to be shot."

Due to exhaustion, we made little progress on the following day and called an early halt so everyone would receive a few hours' extra sleep. Once more I was busy overseeing and helping my assistants. Some made bread in a frying pan and others prepared coffee, tea, or chocolate for the wounded who lay around large fires with their feet to the blaze. I assisted with the cooking and made temporary coverings for my charges out of wagon cloths. Once again, I went to rest at two in the morning and was interrupted so we could begin early. Having had so little rest on the three preceding nights I was totally exhausted and unable to stay awake. As we moved along, I clung to the hospital wagon where I found myself periodically sleeping and walking. This was all I knew until our midday halt, when I fell asleep in the long grass. I did not hear the commotion when the march resumed and may have slept all day had not General Clinch almost ridden over me. He woke me and instructed others to lay me in the hospital wagon, where I concluded that blissful siesta, which was so delicious, I remember it to this day. I slept soundly till evening, unaware of the cries of the wounded or the rattling of the wagons, and awoke close to our destination. We had lost none of our wounded on a difficult march.

Some soldiers, anxious for news, came to meet us from the fort and were shocked to see the long train of litters and wagons filled with wounded that stretched for nearly a mile. It was a sight of ghastly pale men with broken arms and legs, some shot through the body and some in the head. Many were so swollen that it was impossible to distinguish even those I knew well.

Those who witnessed our departure for the Indian Nation just two weeks previous expected a victorious outcome. To them the sight and smell of blood, wounds, and pine smoke and our travel-stained weary bodies was overwhelming. Our shattered remnant of a hitherto vigorous fighting force graphically showed that our prospects for an easy campaign had dimmed. We had learned a valuable lesson, "never to despise an enemy," however simple or childish he may seem. The primitive savage was able to fight and defend his own ground, even though we outnumbered him three to one. General Clinch and his regulars behaved with great gallantry. Our men were fearless, but ignorant of Indian tactics.

When we lived with the Indians at Fort King and competed with them physically, we invariably found them to be the weaker party, for in all trials of strength they succumbed to the whites. As a result, our men did not give them credit for their daring, courage, and bloodthirsty characteristics. Once hostilities were declared they exhibited the true nature of a savage whose back was against a wall.

I found the Indians to be metaphorical talkers. They could not describe either their own people, or strangers, except in analogical terms, but their characteristics were uncannily accurate. For example, Osceola, known as the Rising Sun, proved himself to be a capable commander and warrior; Black Dirt was the chief of 150 warriors and his characteristics were those of a supine, dirty, and lazy Indian; Jumper, the son of an Old Warrior, had fought energetically in the Jackson campaigns; Deerfoot was swift; Eagle was an ambitious chief of mixed blood. And so on throughout the whole Nation, all had a *nom de plume*, given according to each man's peculiar life and habits. Thus, our men of the Withlacoochee battle were dubbed by these Indians as Clinch's Bull Dogs. The reason was doubtless their bullheaded stand and tenacious hold of their unsheltered position. They stood for half an hour as targets to be shot at. Eventually, after being roused, or to save their own scalps they, ignoring the bullets, tomahawks, and scalping knives, dashed headlong into their enemy, hurling destruction right and left, stubbornly maintaining possession of the hammock until the Indians retreated.

There were others, like Lieutenant Talbot, physically strong who charged out spewing fire, but that was all. Captain Mellon and Captain Drane had gained fine reputations fighting with valor against the British but were not up to the task of fighting Indians and were both seen developing their courage through a liberal use of whisky. It upset me to question his character for it could seem that I was acting out of revenge for the discipline he meted out to me some years before. He gained his lieutenancy legitimately at a time when he was a hot-blooded young man full of life, vigor, hope, and ambition, looking forward to reward and promotion. Such acts accomplished during an emergency show character beyond the norm. But during the intervening years he lost his youth, become a man of power and wealth, and married a lady whom he greatly loved. His hopes had changed, and his desires were for peace and tranquility. He no longer saw the honor or any purpose in dying at the hands of a savage foe and this new outlook prevented him from behaving like a man of principle.

As soon as we halted outside the picket fence of the fort, I began to receive help to move the wounded and get them settled. The officers filled the three rooms of the driver's house, while the soldiers were placed in a long row of tents which reached across the interior of the fort. Afterwards Doctor Weightman and I rolled ourselves in our cloaks and blankets and slept soundly upon the floor of the driver's house. It was very uncomfortable, but we were so weary that we neither knew nor cared.

The wounded had not had their wounds dressed from the time they were staunched on the night of the battle. On the morning after our return, we began at six a.m. and completed our work shortly before midnight. Doctor Weightman extracted balls continuously, beginning with those that had nearly gone through the body or limb and were showing their coagulant marks. The balls clung tenaciously to their snug sites and required constant cutting and tugging by the thumb and forefinger. It was physically demanding work, and I was initially repelled by the sound of the surgical knife slicing through living flesh. The men withstood their surgery heroically, except for one, a German, who had a ball deeply seated in one of the gluteus muscles. He was most obstreperous, yelling so desperately that he prolonged his ordeal, which took treble the amount of time than would otherwise have been required.

While the operations were taking place, my duties were to stand by with the surgical instruments, plinths, and needles, and then to finish by staunching the blood and applying bandages under the doctor's supervision. When all the operations were completed, I followed the doctor to the general's quarters, where he pulled out of his vest pocket all the lead shot extracted that morning. He counted them in the palm of his hand and exclaimed: "General, here are nineteen, not a bad morning's work." For the following three days I was fully occupied in washing the wounds or applying poultices to reduce inflammation. All my patients were put on a reduced diet of gruel, which we called the battle of water gruel. Experience showed that it was sound treatment as we saved all the soldiers except one, which was a huge success, for many were dangerously wounded.

During this period I had little rest either by night or day, taking my meals hurriedly while standing. Many times, I saw the general overseeing my work with such interest that an observer would have thought he was the chief surgeon. His quarters were close to the hospital and his interest was to see that none were neglected. He never passed me without saying a kind word and treated us all like family. This helped to spur us on to do our best, which was successful for no one gave up while under his surveillance.

When I lived at St. Augustine, I was taught to regard General Clinch as a strict, unfeeling disciplinarian but I learned how good men are often maligned. To me he was most fatherly, always available to others and full of kindness. The private soldier who was shot in his side suffered greatly before he died of his wounds. But his most constant visitor was the old gray-haired man of 5 feet 10 inches and 250 pounds, who sat upon the dirt floor to give him counsel and comfort. "My poor man, bear your sufferings like a soldier as you must now become a soldier of Christ. Put your trust in Him, He is your commander, He is your only salvation." Finally, both were rewarded when the soldier had a peaceful death. That was the true General Duncan L. Clinch that I knew.

He was called the Spartan General by his peers as his ways were plain and simple, living in a tent like all the other soldiers, except he had a bed and mattress to sleep upon. His food was plain and many times I saw him dining with his staff on pork and beans, occasionally getting a beef day like the rest of us. Now and then he would have an extra dish of Indian corn. He only drank water, which I fetched for him in a pitcher from the spring outside the camp.

I virtually lived with the general in the driver's house. My medicine chest was close to his door; I was the first person he saw in the morning and the last at night. When we were in the field, my hospital tent was immediately in front of the general's. His habits were so plain that he was no burden on the army, only requisitioning a campstool when we were on the move. Other generals like Scott required a band of music, with a company of professional cooks and servants to attend him.

Those of us assigned to the medical department worked night and day. Though my duties were particularly heavy, I was in my element, taking great delight in them and learning something new every day. By then I was in overall charge of the wounded regulars as well as a few of the militia officers such as Major Cooper, Colonel Warren, Lieutenant Yeoman, and Lieutenant Ridgley of D Company, 2nd Artillery, who was an old friend of Dr. Weightman's. All of these were dressed by me. The other officers of the regulars were under the immediate care of Doctors Weightman and Hamilton. I arose at four and used the early morning hours to prepare my dressings, which after the third day generally consisted of adhesive plaster cut into squares with a small portion of resinic ointment placed in the center of each. The bandages were fastened so they would cover the opening where the ball had entered. This was no easy task when there were as many as three, four, or even five dressings for the same patient.

The wounded displayed varying personalities, idiosyncrasies, and behavioral characteristics during their suffering. One would become irritable, another quiet, while another displayed revenge and yet another fear. The following account describes individual cases:

Captain William Graham of the 4th Infantry was a calm, brave, and friendly man, who quietly bore the effects of his wounds. One day while I was dressing Lieutenant Ridgley's wound, a soldier brought in an Indian's scalp for him to gloat over. I thought the captain was losing his mind when he displayed extreme antics of delight over the small portion of flesh belonging to a dead Indian, whom one of the men had shot and then scalped.

His brother John, who lay in the same bed, had his teeth and part of his lower jaw shot away, plus two other dangerous wounds. He was calm and the sight of the scalp conveyed in him a look of compassion and forgiveness.

Major Cooper was a brave and gentlemanly soldier from St. Marys in Georgia. He was in a most critical condition having been shot through his chest. The ball had pierced his lungs and for many days his life flickered close to death. He possessed a childlike good nature and through his suffering was calm and easy to nurse, whether undergoing surgery or while moving him in his bed. Through it all he never once complained. I still think of him as a martyr and hero and remember how glad we all were to see him go home to his family, to be once again reinstated as the head of his household.

Jeremiah Eskridge was a private of D Company who had been shot through the lungs, similar to the major. For whatever reason he lacked the self-control so wonderfully exemplified by the major. For days he lay consumed by a morbid fear of death. Yet upon his recovery and after joining his company, he showed uncommon bravery by volunteering to ride express through the wilds. It was an almost suicidal occupation while surrounded by Indians.

Daniel Daley was from Northern Ireland. His jaw was broken from a shot in the mouth, but he was a quiet patient, very good-natured, who was a pleasure to nurse.

Corporal O'Brien of Company D was so irritated by his suffering from his broken arm that at one point during the battle he was actually on the point of severing the dangling limb with his jackknife.

There are many more cases worth mentioning, which would have been tedious for me to record and for you to read, but the following clinical reports are worth mentioning:

William Pagis: He was twenty-five years old when he received two wounds in action, one of which was a rifle ball in the abdomen, about two inches to the left and three below the navel. We presumed that it followed a lateral direction and lodged in the os ileum. The case would have been hopeless if the intestines were cut. Treatment: The patient was put on a low diet of soups and the wound dressed daily with resinic ointment, which was held in place with straps. After dressing for one week, he complained of increased pain and began to suffer from clammy sweats. Poultices were applied, which relieved the symptoms, but after a few applications the peritoneum membrane protruded from the wound for about two inches. After removal of the dressing the stench was intolerable, followed by about a pint of thin pus, resembling water colored with milk. Eight days after the membrane appeared, I removed it altogether, as it began to look gangrenous and nothing like the normal delicate tissue viewed on dissection. The following morning when I removed the dressing, I saw two gangrenous marks the size of a pea, one above the other below the wound. I was directed to immediately apply a poultice of Jerusalem oak (chenapodium). After two poultices I noticed two openings into the abdomen, both with healthy margins and no appearance of the gangrene. The patient was then allowed a more generous diet and his wound was dressed daily with simplex ointment, until it was completely healed. His situation was a peculiar one, which brought the officers and men to see the peristaltic motion of the intestines, which was plainly visible when looking through the wound as he lay on his back.

Thomas Cagwell: This man was shot with a rifle and the ball penetrated the upper part of the pectoralis major muscle of the upper chest and was treated in the usual manner. After a period of three weeks, he was seized with severe paralysis of the whole body, preceded by the most agonizing pain. After making inquiries, I found he had eaten a large quantity of onions with animal food. Treatment: We commenced by cleansing the intestinal tract with an emetic to induce vomiting, which was followed by doses of ricinine, or castor oil, which tended to relieve the spasms. After eight hours I administered a grain of morphine acetate. During the night, after the effects of the morphine opiate had worn off, I was awoken by the cries and hisses of the poor man, who I found suffering with trismus, or lockjaw, which added to his other miseries. I immediately prepared an anal injection of soap oil and salt and found that after several evacuations of undigested onions he was greatly relieved. I then injected a lineament with an ossification tincture and left him for the night still suffering with the lockjaw.

In the morning I found him in much the same condition, with severe paralysis and almost total loss of expression. The surgeon then directed me to apply poultices to his wound, which had become fistulous, and to administer one grain of morphine every two hours, together with three injections daily. This treatment was followed for a week, when it was found paralysis had extended farther. All his limbs and muscles, even of his face, were rigid and emaciated, he not being able to eat except through suction via a quill. The poor man's frame and all the external muscles were in such a contracted and frozen state that he seemed like a manikin. We began to inject spirits and water daily into his wound in order to commence the healing process, and the dose of morphine was increased to one grain each hour in order to abate the spasms. After a time, we found the suppuration was becoming thicker and slightly tinged with blood, prior to which it was watery. The injection was continued to the wound and the dose of morphine increased to two grains. Then I found that when I gave him an enormous dose of ten grains of morphine in the space of five hours, it did not appear to improve his situation significantly any better than the previous smaller doses, showing the habit of anodynes. On the other hand, the increased pain may have required an equal increase of morphine to subdue it. He was also allowed to take spirits and water, or wine and water, to support his urinary tract. After using the above treatment for a period of three weeks, the spasms gradually abated and the ball forced a passage to the glutei muscles from which it was extracted.

His appearance improved soon after the trismus abated and there followed a gradual restoration of the use of his limbs and faculties. He remained partially crippled owing to an ankylosis of the hip joint, which restricted the movement of his leg. When I made his bed, I realized that his body had elongated an extra two inches because of the spasms. His case caused us much trouble and he required the consistent attention of two nurses. Though he was given great care and sympathy, he proved to be very ungrateful, which reminded me not to expect gratitude, but to welcome it with humility when it was offered. "Put not your trust in Princes." We mortals so easily forget our benefits, yet let not our virtues wane, for there is One who is pleased by our sincere intentions and keeps an account of the matter.

McCawly: He was shot in the linea alba, or stomach muscle, but the trajectory of the ball was unknown. He was in great pain and producing bloody stools that had a fetid odor. Though there were occasional bowel movements he was generally constipated. Treatment: The bowels were aided with injections of warm water, which was also applied to the abdomen to keep up a proper dilatation. On the seventh day the scab was removed, and gentle suppuration was initiated to excrete all the pus until a new scab formed to close the wound. There was scarcely any bruising apparent and granulations on the wound were of a healthy appearance during the whole healing process. This was a merciful and extraordinary escape from death, as we thought that the intestines had been breached.

Private Pockenburg: This young man was shot through both lungs, with the ball entering that part of the pectoral muscle near to the serratus anterior and cutting through the lower portion of the teres major, exiting the back through the latissimus dorsi. (The ball entered the left side of the chest below the heart and departed through the back just below the ribcage.) Treatment: This case was extremely tedious with the lung occasionally discharging a bloody pus. After the scab fell off, the flow of pus increased greatly and the patient grew subdued. His stomach became irritable and his skin jaundiced. Poultices were applied to the wound and purgatives composed of hydrated submer and pulverized silver were prescribed in minute doses. His diet consisted of soups and occasionally a little panada (a thick sauce or paste made with breadcrumbs, milk, and seasonings). This mode of treatment continued for three months. At all times he displayed a calm demeanor and good temper until he recovered and returned to normal duty.

Case of Urbain Stoll: He was shot by a ball that entered the muscular part of the thigh and came to rest by the upper thigh bone. The wound healed over, but the area began to swell due to infection. Poultices were applied to assist in reducing the inflammation but the thigh kept on swelling until, after nine days, it looked frightful. An incision of three inches was then made at the highest point of the swelling and about two quarts of pus was removed. During the procedure he held his leg, smiled, and never complained, except for the following curse against his comrade: "Twas all along for Broadt, de dam cowart, who got behind me, dis ball belong to him." The wound was repoulticed and, when removed after two days, another pint was pressed from the cavity. The festering gradually reduced and by the fourteenth day the ball made its appearance in the center of the wound just below the skin, when it was cut out. Afterwards he quickly recovered.

These clinical reports about a few of our wounded describe the sort of work that was our daily experience at Fort Drane, when at one stage we had over one hundred cases. It is impossible for me to imagine what the daily life must have been like in the military hospitals during the civil war, when the wounded were in the tens of thousands.

Following our encounter at the Withlacoochee, the Indians reacted swiftly and increased their raids. They were daring, vengeful, and treacherous, filled with a ravenous bloodthirst that even included women and children.

Because Fort Drane was the military headquarters it became a refuge for civilians from the surrounding country, such as farmers, who left their homes and came with their families. These and others filled the fort with noncombatants, who included their share of the daily sick. Wagon trains and express riders also brought in their quota of sick and wounded. As the hospital filled, all were served with rations and medications supplied by the government. The normal monotony and stagnation of camp life also added to our list, so that my dispensing duties steadily became more arduous. Yet we managed and the hospital ran smoothly. Even my health improved due to the extra exertion. We did not have sufficient tent accommodations due to the extra patients, so I and my attendants had to lodge among the wounded. Unfortunately, many times their groans and cries went unheeded owing to our state of fatigue.

January 6, 1836: General Call and the militia left Fort Drane for home. These troops were entered into service for just six weeks and their departure was seen as a blessing. Though they added to our number they were in reality a weakness. They were generally insubordinate, tended to be cowardly in the field, and consumed much attention and valuable supplies.

January 7, 1836: Advices were received regarding the murder of Mr. Woodruff of Spring Gardens, which took place on Christmas Day 1835, and also of the murders of Messrs. Lenovar and Hatch at Picolata. Every day we received tales of murder and scalping from all directions throughout the Territory, which indicated a very active enemy. After one week at Fort Drane we began to wonder why Major Dade and his force had not arrived. As we grew more anxious, we came to realize the hornets' nest we had stirred and being far from either coast made us feel less secure.

General Clinch then gave orders to increase discipline in the fort, as it was evident the enemy sought our total destruction. The Indians instilled a fear that made us imagine they were in every animal that approached the pickets. The Indian was very cautious and seldom crept up to our night guards alone. Three would advance in a creeping posture, one direct for the sentinel and the others on either side. When sufficiently near, the center Indian would fire. If his shot took effect, he would advance to scalp the fallen man, having his aides ready to secure a safe retreat. It was so common for us to lose men in this manner that a new order called for all sentinels to wear dark belts and to keep guard in a standing position.

Almost nightly the guards sounded the alarm, only to reveal a grunter or stray dog prowling outside the camp. Additional guards were posted and placed closer to one another to prevent any Indian from creeping into a position from where they could do harm. The guards had to remain stationary at their post for long hours, for if they moved, they ran the risk of becoming a target for any Indian with a rifle. They were stressful nights surrounded by croaking bullfrogs and the yelling of what sounded like ten thousand wolves. Every night the animals came and filled the forest with their incessant yells. Continuous howling indicated great hunger and I used to wonder why they never attacked the sentinels. I suppose the campfires deterred them as they had a great dread of fire. From General Clinch downward all the soldiers wore forage clothing. Belts were blackened and officers were dressed like privates, the only distinction being a small lace shoulder strap. The one exception was our venturesome Dr. Weightman, with whom I had no patience as I knew whenever he was out with the troops, the Indians would mark him as our Great Chief.

Then I began to put our hospital department into proper working order. First, we received a large-fly marquee tent, which was erected at the northern end of the driver's house in a cotton field which was breaking out of pod and looked like a field of snow, a most beautiful sight for an Englishman. I was allowed two nurses to each wooden building and attendants in the ratio of one to ten sick or wounded men. I had a total of twenty aides plus a dozen cooks to prepare all the various kinds of diet ordered by the surgeons. My hospital tent comfortably held about twenty sick persons and also had space for the medicine chest, a table, and four campstools. Although the floor of the tent was earthen, we were able to make a tolerably comfortable hospital.

Our old tent was used as a warehouse for food and stores, which we had in such abundance that we filled the requisitions from the hospitals at the smaller forts of Micanopy, Witumpky, Fort King, and Mackintosh's Oakland. This added to my duties and I began to act as a quartermaster, having to pack up medicines and stores for the surgeons of the neighboring stations. I felt quite at home in this business, which reminded me of my apprenticeship in England. There was only one occasion when I was unable to satisfy a requisition. It occurred when one of our junior assistant surgeons came to select his own stores. He was very hard to please and I was glad when he had to return to his own little command. His self-indulgent behavior made me realize how fortunate I was to have Doctor Weightman as my supervisor.

I became fond of the peace of the surrounding woods and frequently went outside to obtain relief from the innumerable requests of our increasing medical officers, on top of continuous necessities of duty. Except for these breaks I believe I could not have borne the stress. Consider the surgeries, teeth extractions, cupping and dressing of wounds, and dosing of over two hundred patients and you will have an idea of the magnitude of the work that had to be completed daily. When I think about it now, I know that the Almighty blessed me with a healthy body. I took my daily half-hour stroll at about three in the afternoon, when all were taking their siesta. I found the cool promenade in the beautiful and silent woods under the shade of immense pines was more invigorating and refreshing than the midday sleep of the heated camp. I realized that a prowling Indian could be near, but I felt it a necessity to have the daily interlude.

Before we responded to hostilities the majority of us anticipated meeting the enemy as a welcome change to our duties. A few, whose term of service had nearly expired, were naturally looking forward to returning home to family and friends. So it was with one German soldier in our company, who was killed at the Withlacoochee. Before the campaign he had received a letter from home advising him that he was a beneficiary of considerable wealth. His loss was met with great sympathy by the men of his company, which was rare. My experience showed that soldiers were mostly thoughtless. It was also the opinion of officers that men made better soldiers fighting as machines, and such men were highly prized by their officers, who told them that they were paid to think for them.

I asked myself why we were willing to spill the blood of the armies of a great Nation and a small tribe of Indians, located in an almost inaccessible wilderness. The only reason I could think of was the insatiable appetite of man for more. The government of the United States was usually not to blame. It was the ever-encroaching white squatters who inevitably incited the Indians and afterward called upon their government for protection. Consequently, the government, to please its citizens, arranged to purchase land from the natives. Paid agents were sent to negotiate with a simple people. Negotiations normally began with the offering of gifts followed by much talk. Treaties were agreed to where annuities were to be paid per head of population according to rank. In this manner the tribes were integrated into the United States and made subject to the laws of the land, but the Indians did not understand all these matters. The natives were very amenable to receiving all the gifts and tithes of the governing power, but did not associate that the receiving of them obliged them to barter away not only their freedoms, but their homes, their lands, and even their lives.

Yet I was hardly any different, for I had bartered away my own suffering, hunger, thirst, and liberty to become an American mercenary. In addition, I was an ungodly man. Of the five thousand soldiers I saw and knew in Florida, there was just one man who admitted to being a Christian, and that was our commander, General Duncan E. Clinch. All the others, as far as I knew, were heathens like myself. We never spoke about religion, and battle with all its bloodshed and death never produced any Christian feelings amongst any of us. I believe that where God is absent, even the greatest calamities tend to harden, rather than soften, men.

The Dade Massacre

From the time we arrived at the Withlacoochee we wondered about the whereabouts of Major Dade and his Number Two Company of artillery. Nobody thought they were lost. After three anxious weeks, an express arrived via Jacksonville that brought dreaded news of the massacre of the major and his command while they were on route to Fort King. His command had consisted of one cannon troop plus rank and file soldiers and officers that amounted to one hundred and twelve souls. They were attacked at daybreak on the 28th of December, 1835, the same day we had left Fort Drane for the river.

Their first halt was at Hillsborough Bridge where Major Dade wrote to Captain Belton urging him by all means to forward the six-pounder cannon, which had been left four miles behind when the team of horses pulling the cannon failed. A six-pounder had been brought along in the belief that it would produce panic among the savages. Three horses, with the necessary harness, were dispatched, which enabled the cannon to rejoin the column the same night. On the following morning the whole detachment pushed on, but no more was heard from it until the 29th of December, when two of the company's surviving soldiers turned up. John Thomas became one of my attendants and Rawson Clarke made his way back to Tampa. From their statements it appeared that the Indians were harassing them every night they were on the march. Clarke also brought with him a letter from Captain Frazer to Major Mountford, which had been fastened in a cleft stick and stuck in a creek. It urged him to push on, as they were surrounded by Indians every night and were forced to make entrenchments for their own protection.

On the morning of the 28th, after the company had marched about four hours from their previous camp, they were attacked by a large number of Indians as they were crossing an open pine barren. The enemy were concealed in the high grass and cut down nearly the whole advance guard in the first volley. When Major Dade rode forward to determine the cause of the firing, he was shot from his horse, a shot that was attributed to Micanopy himself. Captain Frazer, the next to ride forward, was also shot off his horse. It was an Indian warfare tactic to attempt to kill the officers first. The remainder of the troop immediately broke formation and each man took cover behind a tree. The cannon then commenced firing canister shot, and this, with a fusillade from the soldiers, caused the enemy to retire. It was said that the interpreter, Louis, fell in the first fire, but we have since learned that he shammed death and that his life was spared through the intercession of Chief Jumper, because he was an educated Negro. Afterwards he worked for the Indians and read all the dispatches and letters that were found on their victims. Captain Gardiner was the surviving commander and after making an assessment found that about half their number had already been killed or disabled. He then ordered all the able-bodied men to cut down trees and erect a triangular breastwork.

Captain Gardiner, who stood no more than five feet tall, was a mean-looking man who looked almost as wide as he was tall. He was a man's man with a determined character, but also a perfect gentleman with such sound judgment that those whom he led could not ask for a finer leader. His short stature was an advantage which preserved him for a longer command. The cannon was brought inside the breastworks and the captain counted his men. There were sixty-five remaining, and many of them wounded. Those who were not severely disabled were anxious to sell their lives dearly. After an hour the breastworks was nearly completed, and the Indians began another advance. The men had orders to lie down within the breastwork, except for a few who were required to man the six-pounder. The fight was so unequal it lasted for just another half hour. They were hemmed in on all sides but fought until nearly every man was either killed or wounded. When the enemy eventually rushed in and overwhelmed them, of one hundred and twelve men, only three escaped.

Rawson Clarke, the last to be saved, reached Tampa after heroically walking forty-five miles while suffering with five wounds. He was a man devoid of principle and conscience and turned his misfortunes into a joke. This experience failed to alter his character, he remaining thankless and swearing throughout his surgery. When broken bones were removed from his lacerated shoulder he asked if they would make good soup. When I think of him, I cannot help but wonder at the mercy of God. Better men were taken, yet this thoughtless wretch escaped to tell the following tale of butchery:

It was 8 o'clock when suddenly I heard a rifle shot in the direction of the advance guard and this was immediately followed by a musket shot from the same direction. Captain Frazer had rode by me a moment before, but I never saw him again. I had no time to think of the meaning of those shots, before a volley as if from a thousand rifles was poured in upon us from the front and all along our left flank. I looked around me and it seemed as if I was the only one standing in the right wing. I could not see an enemy until several other volleys had been fired at us, and when I did I could only see their heads and arms peering out from the long grass far and near and from behind the pine trees.

The ground seemed to be an open pine barren with no hammock. On our right and a little to our rear at some distance, was a large pond of water. All around us was high grass among the pine trees, very open, particularly towards the left. The first fusillade from the Indians was the most destructive and seemed to kill or disable about half our men. We promptly threw ourselves behind trees, and opened fire with our muskets. I, for one, never fired without seeing my man, that is, his head and shoulders. The Indians chiefly fired lying or squatting in the grass. Lieutenant Bassinger then fired five or six rounds of canister from the cannon, which appeared to frighten the Indians. He kept on firing and after twelve to fifteen rounds they retreated over a little hill to our left, about one half to three-quarters of a mile off. Immediately we began to fell trees and erect a little triangular breastwork. Some of us went forward to gather the cartridge boxes from the dead, and to assist the wounded. I had seen Major Dade fall to the ground by the first fire and his horse dashed into the midst of the enemy. While gathering the cartridges, I saw Lieutenant Mudge sitting with his back reclining against a tree, his head fallen and evidently dying. I spoke to him, but he did not answer.

We had barely raised our breastwork knee high, when we again saw the Indians advancing in great numbers over the hill to our left. They came on boldly until they were within range of a long musket shot. Then they spread themselves out from tree to tree to surround us. We immediately extended as light infantry, covering ourselves by the trees and opening a brisk fire from cannon and musketry. The cannon was not as effective, as the Indians were so scattered. Captain Gardiner, Lieutenant Bassinger, and Dr. Gatlin were the only officers left unhurt by the volley, which killed Major Dade. Lieutenant Henderson had his left arm broken, but resting on the stump he continued to load his musket and to fire it, until he was finally shot down towards the close of the second attack. Lieutenant Keyes had both arms broken in the first attack. They were bound up and slung in a handkerchief and so he sat reclining against the breastwork for the remainder of the battle, keeping up his spirits and cheering the men, regardless of everything that was passing around him, until he was killed.

One by one our men were cut down. We had maintained a steady fight for over five hours, from 8 a.m. until 2 p.m., allowing three-quarters of an hour's interval between the first and second attack. Lieutenant Bassinger was the only officer left alive and he, too, was severely wounded. As the Indians approached he told me to lay down and pretend to be dead. I looked through the logs and saw the savages approaching in great numbers. A heavyset Indian of medium stature, painted down to the waist, (corresponding in description to Micanopy) seemed to be the chief. He made a speech, frequently pointing to the breastwork. Eventually they charged into the work but there were none to offer resistance and they did not seem to suspect the wounded as being alive. Offering no indignity, but stepping about carefully, they quietly stripped off our accoutrements and carried away our arms. They then retired in a body in the direction from which they came.

Immediately upon their retreat, forty or fifty Negroes on horseback galloped up and alighted, tied their horses and commenced with horrid shouts and yells butchering the wounded and indiscriminately stripping the dead of their clothing, watches and money. All who showed the least signs of life had their heads split open with their axes. Their bloody work was accompanied with obscene and taunting ridicule and with frequent cries of "What have you got to sell?" Lieutenant Bassinger, hearing the Negroes butchering the wounded, sprang up and asked them to spare his life. They responded with blows from their axes and their fiendish laughter. Having two scratches on my head and five wounds in different places, I was pretty well covered with blood. This gave me the appearance of having been shot through the brain, for the Negroes, after grabbing me by the heels, threw me down again, saying, "Damn him, he's dead enough." They then stripped me of my clothes, shoes, and hat, and left me. After stripping all the dead in this manner, they trundled off the cannon in the direction the Indians had gone and, after shooting the oxen in their gears and burning the wagon, they went away. Another soldier who escaped said they threw the cannon into the pond and burned its carriage.

Shortly after the Negroes departed, Private Wilson of Captain Gardiner's company crept from under some dead bodies and hardly seemed to be hurt at all. He asked me to go with him back to the fort and I would follow him, but as he jumped over the breastwork an Indian sprang from behind a tree and shot him down. I then lay quiet until nine o'clock that night, when D. Courtney, an Englishman, the only living soul beside myself, and I started upon our journey. We knew we were closer to Fort King, but we did not know the way and we had seen the enemy retreat in that direction. As I came out of the breastwork I saw Doctor Gatlin lying stripped amongst the dead. The last I had seen him alive, he was kneeling behind the breastwork with two double-barrel guns by him, and he said "Well, I have got four barrels for them." Captain Gardiner, after being severely wounded, cried out: "I can give you no more orders, my lads, do your best." I last saw a Negro urinating on his body, saying with an oath, "That's one of their officers."

Courtney and I got along quite well until the next day when we met an Indian on horseback with a rifle, coming up the road. Our only course was to separate and we did so. I took the right and he took the left of the road. The Indian pursued him and shortly afterwards I heard a rifle shot. A short while later I heard another shot and concealed myself among some scrub and saw palmetto. Soon after I saw the Indian pass, while looking for me. Suddenly, he dug his heels into his horse's ribs and went off at a gallop towards the road. To ensure I was not followed I made a detour before returning to the beaten track. That night I was forced to continue my march while I was continuously pestered by wolves who had scented my blood and came very close to me. The following day, December 30, I reached the Fort.

Clarke was mistaken with regard to the dead being stripped, as will be seen by the report of Captain Hitchcock, which stated:

General Gaines's Army encamped on the ground occupied by Major Dade on the night of 27 December. On the morning of the 28th our advance guard passed the site of the massacre without seeing it, but when the general and his staff advanced about four miles they came upon the most appalling scene. First they saw some broken and scattered bones, then a cart, the two oxen of which were lying dead, as if they had fallen asleep, their yokes still upon them. A little to the right, one or two horses were seen. Then we came to a small enclosure, made by felling trees in such a manner as to form a triangular breastwork for defense within the triangle. Along the north and west face of it were about 30 bodies, mostly skeletons, although much of the clothing was left upon them. These were lying, every one of them, in precisely the same position they must have occupied during the fight, their heads next to the logs over which they had delivered their fire and their bodies stretched with striking regularity parallel to each other. They had evidently been shot dead at their posts and the Indians had not disturbed them, except by taking the scalps off most of them.

Passing this little breastwork we found other bodies along the road and by the side of the road, generally behind trees, which had been resorted to for cover from the enemy fire. Continuing about another two hundred yards further we found a cluster of bodies in the middle of the road. They were evidently the advance guard, in the rear of which was the body of Major Dade and to the right that of Captain Frazer, who must however have fallen very early in the fight. Those were all doubtless shot down by the first fire. Those in the road and by the trees fell during the first attack. It was during a cessation of the fire that the little band still remaining, about 30 in number, threw up the triangular breastwork, which from the haste with which it was constructed, was necessarily defective and could not protect the men in the second attack.

We had with us many of the personal friends of the officers of Major Dade's command. It is gratifying to be able to state that every officer was positively identified. All were buried and the cannon, a six-pounder that the Indians had thrown into a pond, was recovered and placed vertically at the head of the grave, where it is hoped it will long remain. The bodies of the noncommissioned officers and privates were buried in two graves and it was found that every man was accounted for. The command was composed of eight officers and one hundred and two noncommissioned officers and privates. The bodies of eight officers and ninety-eight men were interred, four men having escaped, three of whom reached Tampa Bay. The fourth was killed the day after the battle.

Such is the account of Captain E. A. Hitchcock, then acting inspector seal for the army of General Gaines. He later became a general and an influential person in Washington.

A Negro who had been captured by the Indians, and subsequently escaped and came to St. Augustine, stated that he was at Powell's camp when riders arrived with news of the Dade Massacre. The Indians stated that they had been fighting all day, had killed 200 whites, taken a big gun, and lost 100 men themselves. After the first attack, when they retreated, it was difficult for the chiefs to induce them to renew the assault. Jumper and Alligator upbraided them for their timidity and tauntingly asked if they were drunk, sick, or women, to be afraid of a few white men. Many wondered why the Indians had attacked the soldiers in the open, when there were many swamps and hammocks along the route. We concluded that it was to ensure that none escaped, as the Indians were sufficiently numerous to surround them. If they had attacked in or near swamps or hammocks, many men could have hidden themselves and thus have escaped. The Indians probably did not plunder the dead because Osceola fully expected to encounter General Clinch on the Withlacoochee to secure the crossing. As we have seen, he was too late to do this, as Clinch had already crossed during his absence.

We received information from another Negro who was sent into the Micanopy camp as a spy. He stated that Micanopy was present at the massacre and that he shot Major Dade, telling his warriors, "We've killed their chief, now you can destroy the long-knives." General Gaines also made a statement about his viewing the scene of the massacre with his army. He noted that many of the men had money on them and that one sergeant had $800. Some of the officers had rings upon their fingers and others had watches. It seemed strange that the Negroes would have left the jewelry and watches, especially considering their great penchant for finery. Because the money was in paper dollars, it would account for its not being taken, as the Indians and Negroes did not use it. The fact that the dead were not scalped was more strange, but this may have been owing to the Negroes being left to plunder, for they did not practice such a barbarous custom of mutilating the dead.

Thus, Major Dade and his command perished at the hands of a canny and savage enemy in a massacre that caused us great distress. Though they were mourned by us, their graves are remote, lying in the solitude of a dangerous forest. I hope they are still remembered by their countrymen, although I know that their leader was shortly afterward honored by the Legislative Council, when they created a new county in southern Florida called Dade's County.

Sixteen of the men who were slain were comrades of mine. We served together in New York and survived the hurricane on our voyage to Charleston. At Sullivan's Island we separated when they moved on to the Augusta Arsenal in Georgia, while I continued on to St. Augustine. Captain Gardiner had been a good friend to me in St. Augustine. He died fulfilling his duty, leaving a young wife and family to mourn his untimely fate.

It is natural for men to mourn the loss of their comrades during warfare. Some may imagine the terror or agony they may have endured during their final moments when death seemed assured. Those are lonely moments, far from family and dear friends who would never be seen again. One fine Scot, who had belonged to the Scotch Greys, sold his life dearly. They said he killed seven of the enemy and, when he saw all hope was gone, while using his musket as a club and fighting to his death, he exclaimed in his last agony, "O, God, whoever thought I should come here to be killed by these red devils."

John Thomas was another survivor of the Dade Massacre, and some time after became my hospital attendant. Though his arm had been broken, he never spoke about the massacre. He and his younger, good-looking brother were on board the *Amelia*, the vessel that originally brought us from Charleston to St. Augustine. The two of them were inseparable; when you saw one, the other was nearby. John was thirty-five years old and looked more like a father than an older brother to the youth at a time when it was considered very uncommon for two brothers to enlist together. The younger had rashly joined the army on an impulse, as I knew well. John was a steady, quiet man who never wanted the life of a soldier, but he was so close to his brother that he could not bear to be away from him and wanted to take care of him.

Unfortunately, John was overcome by the loss and retired into a lonely world of sadness that no longer held any meaning. He never spoke of the sad affair and went about his work mechanically. Yet I never doubted that under his quiet demeanor, there existed the ferocity of a tiger where Indians were concerned. I once asked him whether he would reenlist and he calmly said, "Yes." "Why?" I asked. "Did you not have enough of Indian fighting in the massacre?" "Oh," said he, "I shall stay as long as the war lasts." "What for?" "To have my revenge."

John was an excellent help to me, but I always felt that there was something else, something he could not communicate. It may have been a dread to go home without his brother and break other hearts. Who can imagine the daily or hourly sufferings of a person in grief, unless you have been in that place yourself?

The Second Seminole War

While these incidents were taking place west of the St. Johns, Indians to the east under the direction of Chief Philip were systematically and ruthlessly attacking settlements from Cape Florida to the gates of St. Augustine. King Philip, as he was called, resided on the largest island in Lake Tohopekaliga. This island was surrounded by water so deep that it could not be forded, except in one place. Nor could it be approached from any direction without discovery. Here he resided, with his women, children, old men, and Negroes who cultivated his crops. The blacks were compelled to work under the supervision of armed guards and were shot if they attempted to escape. King Philip's tribe numbered about 500 warriors and perhaps as many Negroes.

The war had opened up an avenue of escape, which the slaves used to their advantage. A great number of Negroes escaped to join the Indians and increased the number of the enemy from an estimated 1,500 warriors to over 5,000. It showed how the slaves hated the southern slaveocracy. Even though they knew they would suffer great hardships, including disease and death, they preferred to join the savages than to remain in bondage. The exodus was so prevalent that planters around St. Augustine confined them on Anastasia Island.

Mr. M. Cohen, author of the "Florida Campaigns," a Charleston lawyer, tried to explain it differently. He wrote, "They are attached to their owners from motives of gratitude and affection and neither ask nor seek for any interference, which can do them no possible good." In another quote he stated that "Colonel Rees alone lost about one hundred and sixty carried off." It was an absurd argument that slaves were carried off by marauding Indians since they were ready to leave and motivated by Abraham Black, who had infiltrated the plantations.

I remember Abraham from Fort King. He was adept at wheedling and I still picture him with his peculiar gait. I am sure he was the man who enticed many of his ethnic brothers to forego the lash and paltry allowance of a peck of corn per week. Dr. Cohen's beliefs must surely have depended upon the human behavior of tolerating a life of hardship when confronted with an unknown alternative.

We received reports of attacks in quick succession from all directions, which meant that the plantations were destroyed by Indian gangs of thirty to fifty. This enabled them to strike throughout the country simultaneously. All whites were doomed, as men, women, and children were systematically slaughtered. None escaped, not even the infant at the breast.

January 23, 1836: An express arrived with details of the murder of Mr. Cooley's family on January 6. While Mr. Cooley was away from home, a party of about thirty Indians attacked his family at New River, which was about twelve miles north of Cape Florida. The children were sitting in the hall attending their lessons when the Indians crept up upon them and shot them. Flinton, their teacher, whom I knew from visits to St. Augustine, was killed on the threshold and the little girl of about eleven was found dead with her book in her hand. When the firing began, Mrs. Cooley snatched up her infant and attempted an escape by a back door. She was shot about 150 yards from the house; the ball entered her body between the shoulders and, passing through, broke the arm of the child which was cradled on her bosom. The little boy of about nine years old was found in the yard with his skull and arm fractured. Having killed all the white inhabitants, they shot the cattle, plundered the house of property worth from one thousand to twelve hundred dollars, and took away two Negroes and all the horses. Then they set fire to the house.

Mr. Cooley had lived among the Indians for many years, spoke their language, and treated them with uniform kindness and hospitality. Such was his friendship that he named two of his sons after their chiefs, Ainomock and Montezuma. His wife, who had once been a captive among them, was esteemed as a great favorite. Because of the close relationship, Cooley had lulled himself into a false security and left his home unguarded. I can only imagine the sorrow and desolation that accompanied him to the end of his days. The savages, fearing the jibes of their comrades and squaws, did not have the courage to take the scalps of Mrs. Cooley and her children, for the Indian could not bear the taunts of his kith and kin. The unfortunate schoolmaster, who was not known to the tribe, was the only one to lose his scalp in their savage triumph.

The families living nearby fled to Cape Florida. Mrs. Rigby, her two daughters, and son ran through the bushes and mangrove swamps for twelve miles. They arrived at the Cape without shoes and almost naked as their clothes had been torn to pieces by the bushes. About sixty men, women, and children received shelter at the lighthouse on Key Biscayne. When their provisions were consumed, they moved to Indian Key, accompanied by Mr. Dubose, the keeper of the light, and his family.

Within one week the Indians had visited all the plantations extending from Cape Florida to St. Augustine. Along the way they destroyed buildings, sugar mills, and property worth over $200,000. Nothing was left except the storehouses containing corn and provisions, which the Indians used as a reserve for their campaign. Over five hundred Negroes were carried off, with Colonel Rees alone losing one hundred and fifty.

Then we heard that a body of Indians under a Negro, John Caesar, had burned the splendid Dunham mansion at Mosquito, the same building I saw when I went on the expedition to the Indian River. Judge Dunham was a friend of Doctor Weightman. General Hernandez, who commanded the militia of East Florida, then gave orders for Major Putman to take the fight against this band of marauders, wherever they could be found.

By mid-January news of the Dade Massacre and other savage deeds had begun to resonate throughout the country, which aroused a patriotic spirit among the citizens to support their brothers in Florida. By the end of the month, we heard that Brevet Major General Scott was appointed the commanding general of the army in Florida.

In the meantime, South Carolina sent a strong body of volunteers to St. Augustine, while Georgia also offered to give aid. On January 26 an express arrived from General Hernandez in St Augustine, with information that troops south of the city had been engaged with the Indians at a skirmish dubbed the "Battle of Dunlawton," where the company of eighty men were obliged to retreat before an enemy of over three hundred. They lost four killed and sixteen wounded, while the Indians lost ten killed and many wounded. Domingo Martinelli, a friend of mine who grew up in St. Augustine, was a casualty. He was a young clerk in Mr. Hansom's store. Our matron at the hospital also lost Charles Flora, a fine young grandson. On the following day 170 of the Augusta Troop of Blues arrived at Fort Drane.

During the month of February troops arrived almost daily. They were principally volunteers from Georgia and Carolina. On the 29th an express arrived from General Gaines stating that the enemy had been found in force, and requesting General Clinch to form a pincer with him at the Withlacoochee. But General Clinch could not respond due to orders he had already received from General Scott at Picolata.

Immediately after receiving the express, a convoy arrived with provisions and the body of a dragoon who was picked off during the march. This soldier had been warned by his commanding officer to stay close to the main body of men for his own safety, but he ignored the advice and dismounted at a pond only seven miles from our fort to get a drink. Upon remounting, three shots were fired from a thicket and one found its mark. He only had the time and strength to regain his command, whereupon he fell from his horse, exclaiming, "The damn rascal's killed me."

The outnumbered Indians typically waited on the outskirts for a chance to ambush a stray or lagging soldier, who generally paid for his error with his life. Such cases occurred almost daily, and the losses became so great that the men were not allowed to lag behind on any account. The one exception were the express carriers who were well mounted and picked for daring.

When the dragoon was brought in, he was carelessly left lying on his back on the loose sand where men congregated about him, examining the wound and gossiping. The heat was oppressive, and the flies soon settled upon the body, but we were so full of wounded and sick that I could not find a space for the dead soldier. There he lay awaiting an evening burial in a shingled coffin, which was already under construction. After a while the general came by and seeing the situation called out to me: "Sergeant, have the poor fellow taken out of the sun." "General," I queried, "where can I place him, my hospital tents are full to overflowing." "Take him to my tent," which was immediately done. Once more I was witness to the kind, humane, and decent character of our commander.

Our tents and buildings were uncomfortably full, with over one hundred and fifty wounded and one hundred sick men. It was also the general hospital for the sick and wounded for one hundred miles around. Dr. Weightman was still the senior staff member, with a good many assistant surgeons, but even with so many masters, I was invariably met with kindness from all. With so many patients I was almost worn out with fatigue, and there was every probability of an increase as the hot season approached.

There were volunteers under General Smith and regulars under Lieutenant Colonel Twiggs of the 4th Infantry encamped about four miles from Fort Drane. The colonel was the examining officer at Bedloe's Island who passed my physical to join the army, upon the solicitation of Doctor Moore, the inspecting surgeon of New York. He had treated me very kindly and considerately during my examination. I came across him accidentally one day as I was walking through the fort and it gave me great pleasure to see him in Florida. I knew him at once and felt the urge to address him and let him know that the once fragile recruit who stood before him was grateful for his past kindness. But discipline got the better of me and we passed one another as if we had never met.

On the 14th of March there was a skirmish about four miles from the fort between volunteers and Indians. The Indians suffered some losses but killed one volunteer and wounded two.

On the following day General Clinch received a letter from Osceola stating that he was prepared to continue the war for another five years. The following is an extract: "You have guns, so have we, you have powder and lead, so have we, your men will fight and so will ours, till the last drop of the Seminole's blood has moistened the dust of his hunting ground." This was not an idle boast, as it was well known that the Indians were well stocked with powder and lead. History has shown that he held his ground for ten more years, well after my return to England.

By mid-March the number of men under arms at Fort Drane consisted of 1,500 artillery, 340 of the 4th Infantry, 800 Louisiana Volunteers, 370 Georgia Volunteers under Major Cooper, 180 Florida Rangers under Colonel Warren, 110 of the Darien Troop, 170 Augusta Troop of Blues, and two companies of U.S. Dragoons comprising 94 soldiers; a total of 3,364 men. These servicemen, with the exception of the Louisiana troops and 4th Infantry, camped outside the pickets. It was a beautiful sight from the fort at night, from where we could see the campfires. Their temporary sheds, or huts, were covered with branches lopped off from the surrounding forest trees and gave it the appearance of an immense thicket swarming with a multitude of noisy inhabitants. Occasionally we heard the sounds of martial music which enlivened the entire scene.

General Gaines's Campaign

General Gaines commanded the Western Department of the Army. He and General Scott were both brevetted on the same day and eligible to assume the supreme command of the U.S. Army.

It was well known at the time that the two of them were jealous of one another, so the government selected General Macomb, their junior, to be the commander-in-chief. Even men of high stature and nobility found it difficult to be self-disciplined and to act humbly in the service of each other, but when the interests of these two men clashed, all gentility was cast to the winds and they became like lesser men.

When General Gaines received the news of the Dade Massacre he immediately left for New Orleans, where he urged Louisianans to volunteer for the Florida campaign. This resulted in over eight hundred men joining the Louisiana troops under the command of General Smith of New Orleans. Since he believed it was necessary to provide aid to Florida in a timely manner, he then accepted the responsibility to bring the regular infantry stationed in Louisiana to Florida as quickly as possible.

He arrived in Tampa Bay from New Orleans on the 9th of February with one thousand three hundred men in three steamboats and by the 15th they were already in the field. He first marched southeast toward the Haffia River, but after two days reconnoitering the country, he was satisfied that the Indians were not in that vicinity. Then with only ten days' rations he changed direction for Fort King, where he thought there was a large supply of stores. More than halfway along his route he passed Dade's battleground, where his troops moved to solemn music around the little breaswork. After interring the bodies, the march continued for a short distance before calling it a day.

Gaines arrived at Fort King on February 22, where he surprised and delighted the garrison of one company of artillery that was stationed there. He found the camp very short of supplies and departed to Fort Drane the following morning with a detachment of 200 mounted men to obtain additional stores, with a few provisions of their own. Two days later he was back at Fort King after a round trip of forty-four miles with all that they could procure. It was only seven days' rations, which was added to the two days' that remained at the fort.

On the 26th he departed Fort King for the Withlacoochee and arrived on the right bank of the river the following day at the very same point where General Clinch had crossed on December 31. The army was divided into three columns, a right, center, and left, being about 100 yards distant from each other, with a strong advance and rearguard; the baggage was in the rear of the center column. The army struck the river in this order at five points, with the advanced being at the usual crossing place. The men exposed themselves while sounding the stream and suddenly were fired upon by war-whooping savages. The exchange lasted for half an hour, after which the troops encamped for the night. One man was killed and eight wounded.

The next day the army moved down the river about two miles, where the bank was more open and less covered with thickets. The advanced guard was again fired upon and Lieutenant Gizzard of the U.S. Dragoons was mortally wounded. He fell, but partially recovered himself to command his men, with the utmost composure, to keep their positions and lie close. After five days of suffering, he died on March 5 and was buried on the bank of the river. They continued the fight with little or no intermission until 1 p.m., when the army encamped. This time the Indians kept up a continuous yell, but the losses were small. At one point General Gaines recommended that some troops should cross the river some distance above the enemy and take them in the rear. On the 29th they were attacked from 9 a.m. until 11 a.m. One man was killed and three officers and fifty men wounded. The general himself was shot in the mouth. On the following two days the skirmishing continued at intervals, preventing them from leaving the breastworks on this side of the river.

Meanwhile at Fort Drane we heard the booming sound of General Gaines's artillery every day at 10 a.m. Though about thirty miles from the river as the crow flies, the great stillness of the woods allowed us to distinctly hear the firing. We congregated outside the fort, away from the din of the camp, to better hear the cannon. Some placed an ear to the ground to hear the thundering more distinctly. The daily occurrence informed us that the general had his hands full, otherwise the cannons would have ceased. This daily sound of cannon also caused anxiety among the men in anticipation of any possible consequences.

His troops were gradually being destroyed by hunger and began to subsist upon horse and dog flesh. Gaines sent word to General Clinch requesting a relief force to assist him in a retreat from the river. When their ammunition was nearly exhausted, they used broken vessels and chains to fire from the cannon. On March 1 General Clinch sent a convoy with provisions to relieve the beleaguered army.

On March 5 Osceola requested a parley, promising not to molest the troops if General Gaines would give his people the river as the boundary between the settlers and the Indians. Osceola probably suspected that the soldiers were starving and, by arranging a parley, he would have confirmed his suspicions. The Indians were consistently cunning and deceitful in an effort to take advantage of their enemy. The general could not agree to those terms since he was under no direction of the government. He told Osceola that his only option was his unconditional surrender. Earlier that same day General Clinch left for the Withlacoochee with 500 men to relieve Gaines. When they arrived at Camp Izzard the advance party saw a body of Indians standing around within view of the breastworks. They immediately fired upon the Indians, killing two, not knowing that they were in parley at the time.

By March 8 both Generals Gaines and Clinch arrived back at Fort Drane with their respective forces. The emaciated men under General Gaines were so starved that they looked like living skeletons. The relieving troops said that upon their arrival the state of famine was so advanced that many of the men could hardly stand and they leaned over the breastwork crying for food. Every man from the relief party reached into his haversack and threw in biscuits, which were voraciously devoured. Some men were seen picking through the horse feed for single grains of maize from the sacks the wagoners had spilt. Many of General Gaines's men were sick and wounded and brought back in wagons, filling the hospital to capacity. It is difficult to describe the filth I saw, as the starved sick were not strong enough to clean themselves. It was my duty to bear the burden until the men were whole again.

Upon his arrival General Gaines took the driver's house as his quarters. Because my medicine chest was close to the entrance door, and as I had to frequent it for my supplies almost hourly, I had the privilege to overhear many of the conversations between the officers.

I remember how General Gaines laughed at the loss of his only upper incisor, which was removed by an Indian bullet. He was always in a good mood, very sociable, and a great favorite amongst the officers. From the first time I met him I knew I had to love the man. Completely unpretentious, with a warm heart for his fellow man, he was gracious, refined, and gentlemanly. He was a scholar of military tactics and was looked up to as an authority on the U.S. Army military code. It was obvious that he was a man of superior intellect who found it unnecessary to use the power of his rank to lead his men. He was the opposite to General Scott in manners, appearance, and character and very easy to approach.

During the short time General Gaines was with us, he gave us all good reports and consequently he was loved and greatly respected. He never seemed annoyed by my presence nor bothered about the chance of my hearing his unrestrained conversation. It was easy to distinguish his superior intellect, minus an air of authority. I formed the impression that he was a brave, dependable man and a formidable foe to his enemies. Unfortunately, he was not allowed to prove himself in Florida. When General Gaines and General Scott first met at Ft. Drane, I noticed there was no friendship between them, which indicated to me that two of the same rank seldom agreed. Three days later, on the 9th of March, General Gaines addressed the troops and handed over his command to General Clinch, stating that he was retiring from Florida and moving to his station on the western frontier. The total loss of his troops was eleven killed and forty-six wounded.

One day after the convalescence of the wounded of the Withlacoochee battle, I was coming out from the picket square toward my hospital tent when General Clinch called me to him. He was surrounded by his staff and a group of officers including Captain Drane, my company commander, and Doctor Weightman. Evidently the matter was prearranged to do me honor and to have proper witnesses to the general's instructions. "Sergeant," (he always called me sergeant though I was a mere private) "I now have great pleasure in thanking you for your industry and attention to the wounded, and as proof of my appreciation of your services, I now grant you the last three months of the term of your enlistment, so that you may be able to return home before winter sets in. When that period arrives, you are to apply to me directly." The general knew my term of five years expired on the 1st of November, 1836, so this kind gesture was indeed special, for it showed how others cared for my personal welfare. I had often thought of the general and Dr. Weightman as substitute fathers, and this kind act was further evidence. I thanked the general with all my heart for he could not have granted me a greater gift or given me anything that would have pleased me more. Immediately my hopes of seeing home and England began to be realized. It was a proud day for me, never realizing that I had been working for such a reward. I loved the men and they loved me, and I felt I could not neglect any. The self-esteem that I received from General Clinch's eulogy, his praise and kindness, lifted my spirits then, and I still find them to be gratifying when I am feeling low or cast down, to help raise my spirits.

Toward the end of March I was busy making preparations for another march into the Nation. During this period Generals Scott and Clinch paid joint visits to the hospital, when both of them were very kind and good-natured to the men. General Scott gave orders to Doctor Weightman to send home all the disabled by the wagon trains. He also issued orders to have their certificates made out for full pensions, as it was his opinion that half pensions were too small for their sufferings and hardships. He also took great pleasure to question the men, asking about their wounds and how they obtained them. He particularly enjoyed visiting those men who had acted well in danger or had borne their sufferings with fortitude.

About the same time I had a serious disagreement with one of the assistant surgeons, who always found fault in my work. He was a youngster and a newcomer, with duties that frequently clashed with mine. Each morning began with some disapproval of my work, an opinion I shared about his. This struggle continued until I told him I would no longer serve under him and I would prefer to carry a musket. Soon after the exchange I met Captain Drane and requested to rejoin my company. This suited the captain and he told me he would obtain my release. This was not easily accomplished as he had to apply to General Clinch for approval. I did not obtain my release and the matter reached a climax the morning of General Scott's departure, when I presented myself to Doctor Weightman and told him that I wanted to join my company that was departing with General Scott. Dr. Weightman knew all about the war between the young doctor and myself and immediately resolved the issue by saying: "Steward, I know what is best for you and you are to tend to your duties as usual. You will not be troubled by the young doctor as you will remain here with me." I found out later that the assistant surgeon was stationed at Witumpky, with a small company of soldiers to keep open the route for Fort King.

It was a beautiful sight to witness the departure of the army on March 26. General Scott, four aides, his staff, his band of 2,930 men, four howitzers, and six pieces of artillery made an imposing appearance. A young lieutenant, Joseph Johnson, one of his aides, was to become the famous General Joe Johnson of the Confederate Army. They left behind 227 sick and wounded, and fifty men to work the convoy that kept the fort provisioned. Dr. Weightman and a young Virginian assistant surgeon were left in charge of the hospital and Captain Lendrum was the commander of the fort. That night a quartermaster sergeant returned with a wound. He had been accidentally shot in the shoulder by one of the officer's fowling shotguns. I extracted nine small buckshot from the deltoid muscle.

With the army away, my duties became lighter due to the decrease in the sick and wounded. We had no communication with anyplace other than Black Creek, where we received our provisions. Each time we sent out a wagon train to collect provisions we also returned a number of disabled and wounded to St. Augustine via the steamboat. On March 29, following orders, we also sent about thirty of the approximately eighty of the Louisiana Troop of volunteers.

Less than two weeks later we learned that General Scott was handing over his command to his baffled junior, General D. Clinch.

General Scott Campaign

General Winfield Scott, the newly appointed commanding general, and his staff arrived at Fort Drane on March 15 and took command. All of General Clinch's regulars, including myself with the wounded from the Withlacoochee battle, were marched across the parade ground. Then we were addressed by the general who read the thanks of Congress and President Andrew Jackson for their bravery on the river. I forget the words, but the meaning was quite flattering to the poor men who had suffered. I suppose it was designed to raise the spirits of the depressed and wounded soldiers to hear that their services were not forgotten by the government. The document was signed by General Lewis Cass, who was then the secretary of war.

Then General Scott addressed the problem of animosity between the regulars and volunteers, stating that there was no prospect of success unless all joined together as one group to overcome the enemy. He sought to strengthen discipline, hoping that the volunteers would pay the proper respect due to their officers.

The general was a fine specimen of a man, standing six feet four inches, and was well proportioned. There was a slight drop of one shoulder due to a wound he had received at the Battle of Plattsburgh, where he was the hero of the day after taking command of the American army after General Brown was carried off the field. He was well aware and proud of the grandeur of his towering form, but he was not a favorite with his countrymen, who criticized him for being too regal, proud, and ambitious.

On his journey from Washington he stopped in Savannah, where he leisurely walked the city, purchasing furniture and luxuries. The *Southern Press* was not amused, and wrote: "General Scott has called at Savannah on his route to Florida and is showing his plumes to the crowd of civilians. Why is he not in Florida fighting the Seminoles?" Much of the dislike was prejudice, for my personal experience showed him to be a clever, patriotic, and brave general, attributes that endeared him to his soldiers. He was a daily visitor to the hospital where he showed kindness and consideration to the sick and wounded. His custom was to ask me to point out which men bore their sufferings bravely. To them he spoke paternally and offered them fruits and other sweets.

Three large wagons laden with fine furniture, wines, and other luxuries accompanied the general to Florida. He also travelled with a band of selected musicians, complete with all their trappings. He always made a grand appearance decked out in the panoply of his rank, which was most unsuitable for Indian bush fighting. Such opulence had never been seen in a roadless wilderness and was completely out of place in a war against a primitive and savage enemy. It was starkly different to the spartan necessities of Generals Clinch and Gaines, who lived rough and ready to meet the enemy.

His plan was for all the troops to act simultaneously, making the Withlacoochee River the center or focus of their converging routes. General Scott was to command the right wing, marching south from Fort Drane. General Eustis was to command the left wing, marching west from Volusia, and Colonel Lindsay was to march north from Tampa Bay. He formulated this plan as if he had drawn it upon his living room carpet, believing the countryside was open plain instead of almost impassable terrain. It showed a conspicuous lack of local knowledge or any appreciation of the bush-fighting tactics of the Indians.

On March 24, the day after departing the fort, a detachment of twenty-seven men confronted a band of about sixteen Indians in an open pine barren, killing two and wounding one. Two days later, on March 26, a wagon broke down and the Negro driver was killed before he could rejoin his troops. That same night the army encamped at Omathla's Town, ten miles from Fort Drane.

On March 29 four savages were seen near the forks of the Ocklawaha River and were pursued by the advance guard. General Tosh Shelton dashed ahead and, when about twenty-five yards from his quarry, leveled his gun just as the Indian about-faced and aimed at the general. Shelton fired first and put a ball in the Seminole's neck. Finding no cap on the nipple of the undischarged barrel, Shelton dropped his gun and drew a pistol. He approached within six feet of the savage where he pointed his weapon at the Indian's chest, but the gun snapped. The Indian then brought his rifle up to his shoulder and shot the general in the hip. Another soldier ran up and fired, killing the Indian. It was Mad Wolf (Yahahadgo), an Indian chief. After proceeding another five miles they came across a few Indian lodges nearby where they found a handful of small pine sticks. At the top of each was a tassel and a portion of a human scalp cut into strips. From the softness of the hair, they must have been women's scalps.

On the same day they arrived at the river without further incident. At nightfall, his forces encamped on the bank of the river and his band played during the evening meal. The Indians listened from the opposite bank and obviously did not approve of the music. They opened fire and shot two men, which caused the troops to move camp from the bank of the river.

On the following day the army crossed the river and were fired upon without loss, after which they fired the signal guns. The troops were then attacked on the left bank by about 200 Indians.

Colonel Bankhead, commanding the artillery, was ordered to charge the hammock. The men were formed in extended order, each taking a tree. They dispersed the enemy so quickly that they left their meat still cooking at their campfires. On entering the forest, the Indians turned and opened fire on the Louisiana volunteers, who returned fire with volleys of grape, which caused the Indians to retreat into the open. The Indians then regained a narrow strip of forest, from where they kept up a running fire, but were finally driven into another hammock from which they succeeded in regaining the river, their chosen battleground. Our troops lost two killed and fifteen wounded, while the Indian losses were unknown.

On April 1, our troops moved against an Indian town located about five miles from the river, which they torched. It was the General's policy to starve out the savages in order to force them to capitulate, but the Indians became even more tenacious, desperate, and bloodthirsty. It was an unchristian policy that should have never been used by a civilized society against a primitive enemy, whose passions were all too easily aroused.

On the following day, having heard nothing from Generals Lindsay and Eustis, Scott decided to proceed directly to Tampa Bay. For the sake of speed, the sick and wounded were left on the Holathlikaha Lake in the care of the Georgian Battalion under the command of Major Cooper. They had eighteen days of supplies and a promise of being relieved in nine days.

On April 6, General Scott arrived at Tampa realizing his plans had proved a complete failure, with his army of 2,930 losing seven hundred sick or disabled. Lindsay and Eustis were already there. Each had about the same distance to cover in order to meet and form a junction on the river, and all should have started out about the same time, even though the different routes presented their own difficulties. When he realized the difficulties associated with finding the enemy and engaging him in battle, Scott decided to relinquish his command.

Ten days later General Scott and General Eustis departed Tampa for their return march to St. Augustine. They took a route striking east forty miles before turning northeast, passing Tohopekaliga Lake. Then they marched north about fifty miles to Spring Gardens (about present-day DeLand) which was twelve miles southeast of Volusia, arriving there on April 22. Upon reaching Volusia, General Eustis embarked aboard a steamboat on the St. Johns River and sailed south.

General Scott arrived at Picolata by water on May 1. He had been detained by a court of inquiry at Volusia, regarding an alleged act of cowardice by Major Gates. Though Major Gates was cashiered, General Scott took much of the blame for acting with undue harshness. The inquiry related to an incident when a soldier was being interred outside the pickets. The burial party was fired upon by Indians concealed in a nearby hammock and two of the men were killed. The major prevented his men from attempting a rescue as he thought that his losses would be greater. Unfortunately, he was overcautious and his actions were construed as cowardice.

Colonel Lindsay was a gray-haired officer with the same portly figure as General Clinch, but was well appreciated by the men of all the armies. He commanded the 2nd Artillery, which was the smallest command, and departed Fort Brooke, Tampa, on March 10. He followed the Hillsborough River for about twenty miles then curved northeast for about fifteen miles, remaining within fifteen miles of the Clinch and Gaines route. On reaching the Big Hillsborough he established Fort Alabama (now Fort Foster), where he left Captain Marks and a garrison of eighty men. That fort was attacked on the 27th by about two hundred Indians who caught a soldier outside the pickets, where they killed and scalped him. A steady fire was kept up by both sides but made no impression on the fort. Then the daring Indians mounted the trees that overlooked the fort and wounded several men. One of the Indians was seen by a rifleman, who fired and hit him. The wound was so severe that blood was seen to trickle down the tree trunk. The savage still descended the tree and made off successfully with his rifle, which showed how difficult it was to catch a wild Indian under any circumstances. About twenty Indians were killed, including a notable chief, as indicated by three different colored plumes which he wore in his headdress. When Lindsay arrived at the Chicuchatty settlements he halted to learn the whereabouts of Scott. Upon receiving no news, and with his provisions becoming scarce, he was obliged to retrace his march to Tampa. During this march there was no formal engagement with the enemy, although small parties of Indians followed them at a distance and were able to kill and wound several men.

General Eustis was the commandant at St. Augustine. On his departure for Volusia, he left Major Gates (my commander at St. Augustine) as the commandant of the fort, with a force of 180 men representing the left wing of the army.

Eustis was a just and fearless leader who carried the nickname Black Jack for his strict discipline, showing no favor and treating all ranks the same. Consequently, he was not a favorite among officers and was hated by the volunteers, who burnt his effigy at St. Augustine. Southern volunteers consisted of the elite men of Georgia, South Carolina, Louisiana, and Florida. It was well known that General Shelton of the South Carolina Militia became a private like many others to fight in Florida. They lay aside their ranks or civilian stations, such as planters, merchants, and physicians, and were usually treated with special consideration and courtesy by their officers. General Eustis sought no popularity and would not offer any extra kindness or recognition, treating all the same, allowing no liberties or restraint. On the other hand, he was loved by the men of the artillery who felt that their commander would always do right by them. He was probably an abolitionist, for I knew that in later years during the great rebellion his son stood out in favor of anti-slavery.

On one occasion, when he was commandant at Point Comfort, Virginia, a certain captain had two lady visitors. With one on each arm the trio promenaded up and down the barrack square, passing and repassing the sentinel who, on each instance, according to etiquette, came to attention and saluted. The distracted officer never returned the salute. All of this was observed by the general, who counted the number of times the officer failed to recognize the salute. Afterwards the general sent his orderly to summon the captain. "Captain, how many times have you passed the sentinel this last hour?" "I really don't know, General." "Well, I have counted," said the general, at the same time telling him the number. "And you never returned the salute. You are therefore to go and pass that sentinel the same number of times and give him the acknowledgments of his salutes, as I cannot allow my soldiers that do their duty to be treated so carelessly." It was done as requested after the sentinel was instructed not to come to attention during the whole time the Captain carried out his penance. The behavior was typical for the general.

On March 10, while he was encamped at Camp McCrea in Volusia, about sixty Indians attacked some of the Charleston volunteers. The Indians had been watching the unarmed soldiers from a nearby hammock as they strolled to the sugar millhouse to obtain firewood. When the soldiers, loaded with firewood, were within 200 yards of the fort the Indians ambushed them. Jumping, screaming, and thirsting for blood, the painted Indians, some half clad in hunting shirts and others totally naked, sprang on their prey. They shot three and scalped two, but a rescue party from the fort prevented them from obtaining a third scalp. An Indian lookout stationed on the wall of the mill noticed the rescue party and gave the signal to retreat.

Then, leaving the camp on March 22 and after crossing the St. Johns, two companies were attacked while bivouacking on the opposite bank of the river. The Indians had crept within twenty-five yards of the sentry before being discovered. As their arms were stacked, armed response was slow and consequently three soldiers were killed and seven wounded. Six Indians were also killed, including Chief Euchee Billy.

They arrived at Okihumpki, located twenty miles southwest from Volusia, on March 28 after another skirmish which the general dubbed the "battle à la distance," since the two parties were far apart. Continuing southwest he reached Pilathlicaha on March 31. This was where Micanopy had his village, which Eustis burnt. He was twenty-five miles south of Fort King and about midway between Volusia and Tampa Bay. On April 4 they arrived at the Withlacoochee and gave the signals, but hearing no reply they moved on to Big Hillsborough.

On the following day they arrived at the site of Dade's Massacre and established a breastwork they called Camp Shelton, where they remained a week, awaiting the commanding general. When their provisions were exhausted, they continued to Tampa and arrived there on April 12.

On the 16th, General Eustis departed Tampa with General Scott for St. Augustine. When he reached Volusia he separated from the rest of his force and, with an escort of seventeen men, embarked aboard a steamboat on the St. Johns River. They sailed south as far as practicable and then returned to Volusia. Without meeting any enemy they headed northeast to Picolata, where they arrived on April 26. By that time the men were very tired, and all were obliged to halt a few days before they could move on to St. Augustine, where they arrived on April 29.

A Major McElmore arrived at the Withlacoochee on March 29 with a supply of provisions from Tampa via the Suwannee River. He had previously advised General Scott that he had a suitable boat and could complete the trip without risk. The general accepted his offer, providing he reached the Withlacoochee by March 29 and waited no later than April 4, as he would move the army south. On returning to Tampa, he stopped at the blockhouse on April 5 and left half of his men under Captain Holleman. He continued to the Suwannee with the remainder of his troop but did not advise the commanding general. This oversight caused the men occupying the blockhouse to remain there until all the volunteers were disbanded and had returned home. This small band held off more than a thousand warriors for six weeks.

On April 12 the blockhouse was attacked at dawn by a large body of Indians. Eli Sealy and Captain Holleman were killed, while another five were wounded. From that time on they were continuously surrounded by Indians.

They were again attacked on the 15th, this time by four to five hundred in a battle that lasted nearly three hours. During the attack the savages gained possession of the flat, which they destroyed, while a chief who made himself conspicuous was brought down by a marksman. Four Indians sprang to assist him but they were also felled at once. The Indians suffered severely during this engagement but blamed their losses on witchcraft. The bravery shown by this beleaguered band was remarkable, as not a shot was fired unless at a specific target. Retreat was impossible since they were cut off by the loss of the flat, so they decided to send for relief. Three men were drawn by lot and embarked in a canoe at 11 o'clock at night. They heard Indians on both banks of the river trying to intercept them and they constantly had to bail the canoe. Finally, they were ambushed at the mouth of the Suwannee, but none were hit. As soon as they arrived, a volunteer company of eighty men was raised under Major Held. This corps proceeded to the blockhouse and brought off the noble, deserted band. Their mode of fighting clearly showed that such tactics should have been used from the beginning of the campaign.

I believe that after I left such methods were followed, as forts were built and manned throughout the Territory. The army learned to become masters of the wilderness without risking the lives of their soldiers. Fifty well-trained men in a fortified blockhouse were a match for 500 of the enemy. It became evident that the best plan was to man a chain of well-provisioned forts and to keep them supplied and garrisoned through relief trains in bodies of between three to five hundred men.

The War Continues

Reacting to the confession of a captured Indian, General Clinch once again took to the field. This Indian of mixed blood had been captured by friendly Spaniards near Charlotte Harbor and stated that Indian women, their children, all their plunder, and their Negroes, were concentrated at the head of Pease Creek. The general decided to make an example of them.

On April 5 he ordered the Louisiana troops to move down to Charlotte Harbor by water, while Colonel Goodwin's regiment of mounted men were to proceed by land to the head of the creek. Major Reed was sent with the Florida volunteers to the mouth of the Withlacoochee, with directions to explore that stream as far as practicable. Colonel Lindsay was ordered to move up, explore, and scour the fork of the Withlacoochee and then to meet General Clinch, who went by a different route, at a given point. No Indians were seen, but the army ended this escapade by burning a large Indian town called Toplapchopko.

On April 12 we received an express from the convoy that gave information of the murder of a regular army soldier named Davis, by Private Jackson of the Louisiana troops. When the troops halted for dinner on the 11th, Davis and Jackson got into an argument. Davis was on the point of striking the volunteer when Jackson immediately drew a pistol and shot him dead. Davis was buried in the wilderness and Jackson was put in irons and handed over to the civil authorities on arriving at the creek. I remembered Jackson from a time when he spent a long period in the hospital suffering from a burn. Because of a lack of medical attention, the burn became so ulcerous as to expose two large tendons of the leg. We had a very difficult time to save his leg, an effort that amounted to nothing since he used his regained strength to become a murderer.

Violence was common in the volunteer forces, where cases of stabbing were frequent. We found that soldiers from the South were quick-tempered. Growing up in the South lacked the same supervision, education, and discipline as in the North, where citizens were generally more religious and respectful. Records showed that there were fewer stabbings and less murder amongst the citizens of the northern states than in any other part of the world. It was sad to witness the prevailing ignorance amongst the poor whites of the South, who were so thin-skinned that the slightest provocation induced revenge, which frequently ended in a stabbing or worse.

Before Jackson's case I had only one other stabbing. An artilleryman who was insulted by a Southerner good-naturedly dared him to a fistfight. When the artilleryman raised his fists he was met by a knife that cut through his arm and severed the artery. The soldier had a mere fifty yards to run to the hospital, but as he entered the tent, he fell his full length before me. He would have died from the great loss of arterial blood in under one minute had I not applied a tourniquet. The officers of these Southern troops were also frequently wrangling. The slightest provocation brought on their evil natures, which showed them to be cruel, pugnacious, and revengeful. Though I knew many fine hospitable Southerners, these unfortunate traits were characteristic of the majority. I consider the revengeful passions of the poor whites of the South to be only one shade superior to the Indians to whom revenge was a virtue.

At about two in the morning of April 14, our fort was attacked by a party of Indians intent on stealing some of the quartermaster's horses from a pen outside the fort. The attack began when a group of Indians stationed about twenty yards to the right of the pen, and one hundred and fifty yards from the pickets, began to fire. They hoped to draw the attention of the defenders while another party carried off the horses. Captain Lendrum immediately raised about sixty men who were capable of bearing arms. After keeping up a continual fusillade for about an hour, the savages were driven off with some loss. But the attack was partly successful, for at daybreak we found the pen had been reduced by half, as the Indians had taken about fifteen horses.

When we examined the enemy's position we found great quantities of blood, as if several Indians had been shot. It was their custom to carry off their dead and wounded to save the dead bodies from being dishonored and mutilated by turkey buzzards. These birds were most useful as scavengers in the hot southern climate and protected by law. Killing one of them in South Carolina carried a fine of five dollars. Consequently, they were so tame that they would hop quite unconcernedly on the crowded pavements of Charleston.

I hope it was an error by General Scott to leave so many sick and wounded at the fort, almost at the mercy of the savages. We comprised a most unusual company of defenders. Some were minus the use of a leg, others an arm, some were on crutches, and the majority in a state of emaciation. If the enemy had known of our feebleness it would have been easy for him to have mounted the pickets and scalped us all. This was the first time I was under fire and made myself as small as possible as the balls whizzed past to the right and left. The attack was most frightening for the men in hospital, who could not get out of their beds while the balls tore through the tents and struck the walls of the wooden hospital buildings. All of this was accompanied by the shrill whoops of the savages, which were most terrifying and which made me go to reassure and pacify the men. The following day we found the site of the Indian firing party and noticed the signs that plainly indicated that, as each man fired, he fell on his left side to reload. Since we knew of these strategies, our men fired accordingly to the right of their muzzle flash. Here and there we found bloody fingermarks, but no bodies except for one large grunter, who was in the pen with the horses. On the same occasion we had a case of a very frightened though pugnacious artilleryman. He was a sentinel on duty outside the pickets who was taken by surprise and unable to flee. He lay in hiding in the blacksmith's shop as the balls of both parties flew around him. His fear of the bullets was so great that he soiled his britches. All of us had forgotten about him, thinking he was inside the stockade, but after the Indians retreated he came out of his hiding place and hailed the pickets for admittance. We received word that General Clinch departed Tampa and began his return to Fort Drane that same day.

On the 17th, General Clinch arrived at a friendly, deserted Indian village about four miles from Fort Cooper. The previous evening Nero, a Negro guide, and several men were sent to the fort, to be followed by a detachment of cavalry under the command of Colonel Bankhead the next morning. The additional forces were sent to advise Major Cooper of the arrival of the division, with instructions to abandon the fort and to have his battalion join the main body of the army. The detachment was also ordered to act as an escort for Major Cooper's wagons.

There was little fear of an attack and the men were riding along carelessly, but when they arrived within about a mile of the fort, they were fired upon from a hammock. The cavalry soon rallied at the command of their colonel and dismounted, made a breastwork of their horses, and fired into the hammock, which soon dispersed the Indians. Colonel Bankhead then scoured the hammock with his light infantry, but after a fruitless skirmish again resumed the march and reached the fort. Though they found the beleaguered men in terrible shape, with no provisions, they were met with warm and cordial greetings.

Unknown to General Clinch, the garrison at the fort had been under attack for thirteen consecutive days, while subsisting on two and a half ounces of meat and the same amount of flour per day. On one occasion the enemy, numbering about four hundred, made a daring but unsuccessful attack against the fort. They were led by four or five chiefs, who were distinguished by their white plumes and by the inspiration and directions they gave their men. During the attacks the garrison made sorties every other day, often advancing under heavy fire from tree to tree and sometimes coming to within thirty paces of the Indians. Losses were slight on both sides.

After proceeding two miles further south on the Tampa Road they turned east which, after a few miles, brought the army to the western bank of the Withlacoochee where a junction was formed with Colonel Lindsay, according to a previous arrangement. They followed the west bank northward for a few miles before encamping for the night.

A party of Indians was then seen on the opposite side of a pond with some draught oxen and cattle that had belonged to General Clinch, whom they presumed was in the camp. That night they came within hailing distance and called the general to come out and give them a fair fight. They promised him provisions and rum and said that he had killed their men and they sought satisfaction. They were then fired upon and immediately they dispersed. They were probably Negroes, having taunted our men by calling them "white sons of bitches." This was just one more example of Negroes venting themselves for all the injustices perpetrated against them prior to this period of liberty. On the following morning a party was sent to retrieve the cattle, with orders not to remain more than one hour. They exceeded the allotted time and delayed the march, which caused General Clinch to grow increasingly impatient while he awaited their arrival.

When the cattle arrived, the general in his haste forgot his sword and belt, which he had removed and placed against a tree. He did not realize his loss until they had proceeded about four miles. Major Holmes, one of his aides, then volunteered to take five horsemen from the Jefferson Troop to return and retrieve the sword. On arrival at the campsite they met six Indians, with one of them wearing the sword on the wrong side of his body. The horsemen fired on the Indians, who returned fire and wounded Private Bostwick's horse. They fled to a hammock, but during the pursuit they encountered another body of about twenty Indians who attempted to cut off their retreat. Assessing the danger, Major Holmes halted and returned without the general's sword.

General Clinch returned to Fort Drane on April 20 with 1,600 men from Scott's army. On a previous occasion he felt that he had been treated unfairly by the chief of the war department. He expressed a wish to leave the army and had put in his application, which was rejected, and he was given command of the Florida campaign. Later, when Scott was subsequently appointed as the commanding officer, General Clinch again made his application to resign. Upon his return to Fort Drane, he received notification from Washington that his resignation would be accepted. This brave and gallant officer was disgusted at the slight that had been put upon him without apparent cause, other than to give Scott another campaign to gather fresh laurels. Prior to leaving, the general handed over his command to Colonel Bankhead. It was a sad day for me as I considered him my best friend, next to Doctor Weightman. He had also given his word to release me from service three months early and I no longer felt that this promise would be fulfilled. I knew military discipline sufficiently well to understand that the word of a departed general was of no consequence to those who came after. He departed Ft. Drane on April 26 with a convoy of the Jacksonville troops.

On the same day, the Alabama volunteers of about 750 men, comprising several companies of the 4th Infantry and one company of artillery, with one field piece, left Tampa for Fort Alabama, which was reached on April 27. On the following day, after securing the provisions and stores, they evacuated the fort and brought out the sick and wounded. A quantity of powder was placed in the magazine to explode when the door was opened. Then they took up the line of march, but when they were about a mile and a half from the fort a loud report was heard, which was probably the explosion of the magazine. Proceeding about ten miles further they found the dead bodies of two men who went missing the previous day; one was horribly mangled while the other was untouched. When the men were looking upon the scene, they were fired upon by about 500 Indians from a hammock about thirty yards distant. A general action ensued with the enemy maintaining his ground until they had received several rounds of grape, and when the hammock was charged by the infantry the savages took flight. Several dead Indians were found, and numerous traces were seen of where they had dragged off the wounded. This was called the Battle of Clonoto Lassa, where five soldiers were killed and twenty-one wounded.

That night the Indians destroyed the sugar works on the plantation located about three miles from the fort. They set fire to them, and we saw them plainly dancing like demons in the light of the flames. Colonel Bankhead declined to send any men to attack them, as he considered the Indians intended an ambush. The decision was proved correct when the scene was examined the following day. The enemy had advanced in three strong bodies, one on the right, another on the left of the sugar house, and a third in the rear. This proved beyond any doubt that their intentions were to encircle an attacking force and cut them off from any retreat back to the fort. Colonel Bankhead enlarged the pickets by building a blockhouse at the northern extremity and mounting two cannon and two howitzers upon it. He also made the pickets sufficiently large to accommodate three hundred portholes.

My first exposure to army tactics was when General Clinch underrated the enemy by fighting in close order at the Withlacoochee. If he had fought them in extended order, as light infantry, with each man taking cover behind a tree, he would have saved several lives and probably vanquished his foe. General Scott capably demonstrated his abilities against a well-disciplined army at the Battle of Plattsburgh against the British, but he was not suited to fight the cunning and unchivalric Indians. It is evident that he thought they could be subdued through the great strength of his armies, but his methods were useless as they had the effect of scattering the enemy and creating a guerrilla war, where the Indians were superior. It is true that in 1832 he had defeated the Sak and Fox Indians at Bad Axe River and captured their chief, Black Hawk, but those Indians did not have the woods or swamps of central Florida to hide in. Clinch was a better man than Scott at Indian fighting, but to be fair, there were other good or better commanders. It is a pity that the almost untamable and brave Crackers of the wilds of Florida, Georgia, and Alabama were not asked to subdue the Seminoles.

Crackers were Indian-like in their habits and appearance, fine horsemen, good riflemen, trained to fire on horseback, full of tact, with great coolness and foresight. Their mode of attack when fired upon from thickets was to dismount and tie their horses to a tree. Then they would dash into the hammock in an extended line, covering themselves by trees and underbrush as best they could, taking special aim and never firing without seeing either the head or shoulders of their foe. Being truer shots and better armed than the Indians, they always succeeded in beating them off unless greatly outnumbered, when they steadily retreated and remounted, riding off to await a fairer field. They did this even when victorious, knowing that an Indian could be concealed nearby, ready to take a scalp. Crackers were accustomed to hardship, used to natural food, and able to ride long distances with nothing other than what each man carried in his saddlebags.

Major Heilman arrived at the fort on May 2 with a convoy of provisions. They had been attacked by about 300 Indians en route at Micanopy Ponds. He was stated in the dispatches to Washington to have acted gallantly and, as a result, received a promotion to Brevet Lieutenant Colonel. The report stated that Indians fired upon some stragglers near the fort at Micanopy, whereupon Major Heilman gave Lieutenant Andrew Humphreys orders to march out with seventy men to attack them. After firing a few cannon rounds of grape into the edge of the hammock, the men then charged in extended order and followed the retreating enemy for a distance of about one mile. During that time Lieutenant Humphreys, the actual hero of the day, continually exposed himself to encourage his little band, while Major Heilman returned to the fort once the cannon ceased firing. The young lieutenant later served and became prominent as a general during the Civil War in the Army of the Potomac.

Colonel Bankhead took a leave of absence and departed Fort Drane on May 8. He was accompanied by Major Cooper's Georgia Regiment of the Augusta and Darien troops in convoy to Black Creek, as their term of service had expired. Dr. Weightman also obtained a month's leave and accompanied them to the creek and afterwards to St. Augustine. Colonel Heilman was left in command of a small force, but sufficient owing to the strength of our fortifications. About that time I was taken ill with dysentery, which was a common complaint in the camp.

A convoy arrived on May 17, bringing information of the retirement of General Scott from St. Augustine to Washington. There was talk about his being superseded by General Jessup, who was engaged against the Creeks of Georgia. Also that Major General Macomb, the commanding general in the United States Army, had been on a visit to St. Augustine and Pensacola. There was also information of the disagreement between General Eustis and the volunteers, who burnt his effigy in the streets of St. Augustine when they returned to the city. General Eustis then left for Fort Monroe, Virginia, and the volunteers left for Charleston.

Life at Fort Drane

At that time there were about five hundred sick and wounded men at the fort who belonged to various detachments. All my staff came from the regulars, but few were available to me since guard duty required almost the entire available strength. With no available matrons, I had to detail men to wash the patients to avoid them being left in a filthy condition. I also supervised two dozen hospital cooks to bake and prepare soups and a team of attendants for each hospital. There were two men who were a great help to me in the dispensing of medications.

Andrew Mann, a druggist, was descended from a well-to-do Scottish family. His father was a British consul in India and his two brothers were surgeons. He was good-natured and gentle with the patients so that all appreciated his services. He was also humble and unpretentious and looked upon me like a son, so I called him Dada.

Joseph Lindsey was a young cockney from Manchester. One day when I was stepping around and over the sick as they lay on the hospital floor, a young man was brought in exhausted. He caught my attention, claiming he was my countryman and a druggist who had been apprenticed at a corner shop in Cateaton Street. At once I applied to Dr. Weightman to have his aid as a dispenser. Fortunately for him, my request was granted because he was too delicate for the arduous duties of a soldier. Marching through the swamps and sterile sands of Florida for another half a year would have killed him. This still left me undermanned.

I was always allowed the privilege of choosing my attendants, as Dr. Weightman well knew that such little matters helped make up the sum of all our happiness. If there are many duties to be completed, especially by others, you ought to have men both willing and useful.

Soon after General Clinch returned to Fort Drane there was a cry of "Indians! Indians!" throughout the camp, A band was seen in the distant woods making for the fort. I, like the rest, left the hospital to see and found that they were carrying white flags, showing a desire for peace. The news hurriedly passed from mouth to mouth and caused such a great stir that General Clinch came out onto the stoop of the driver's house to see what all the commotion was about. Immediately he ordered a company to fix bayonets and then called out to me. "Sergeant," he said, "you must take an unarmed man, one on your right and another on your left, and proceed to meet the Indians." I chose two men and, taking hold of their hands, we laughingly set off to meet the savages about twenty yards in advance of the soldiers. It was then I suddenly realized that I was the plenipotentiary, or potential hostage, on an errand of peace.

In one hand I carried a stick of succus glycyrrhiza, for at the time of the cry of "Indians" I was mixing Barton's mixture for catarrh and rushed out with the licorice in my hand. When we were about two hundred yards from the fort, we met about one hundred and fifty young Indians, many of whom were youths. When they saw our mood, they met us with the same good nature and walked past us in single file. At the pickets they were received by General Clinch and his staff. They turned out to be friendly Indians of Black Dirt's tribe from the Tampa neighborhood. As they camped outside the pickets, we found rations for them. It became common for soldiers to visit their camp and study the ways of Indian life. I noticed that they were very lazy and dirty, but as they were no threat to us, they were far more preferential than our deadly Seminole enemies who waited in the woods for our scalps.

Dr. Heiskill then became my immediate superior at the hospital. He was a tall, youthful, athletic Southerner who was usually absorbed by some great problem, which often rendered him unfit for duty. I only saw him in the mornings when he received the sick at the hospital marquee, where he attended to his cases in a perfunctory manner. Day by day we reviewed over one hundred and fifty cases and invariably he lost his temper, especially if a patient was too slow to answer his abrupt questioning. Frequently he would turn to me and exclaim: "Steward, place a good, thick stick ready for me tomorrow and I'll give these stupid mortals a drubbing." Morning after morning we repeated the same ritual and, as usual, he would turn to say, "Why don't you place a stick at my ready?" I was reluctant to fulfill his demands and it was not my place to reason with him. Due to his persistence and not wanting to be disobedient, I procured a stick. I thought to make such a cudgel that he would be ashamed to use it upon a sick man, so I fashioned a weapon that required two hands to operate. The following morning he came in, looked at the clumsy weapon, and made no remark. He never touched it and never again requested a stick to thrash a soldier. I was glad that my ruse succeeded, but anxious whether he would accept my rather forward behavior.

At the time, the rains came every morning at about ten, for about half an hour. My hospital then included wooden houses inside the pickets and a long lean-to shed on the southern side outside the fort. All were filled with soldiers in a miserable condition, suffering from intermittent and remittent fevers and dysentery. It was common for me to use one ounce of quinine every morning. The doctor had a great love for the lancet, claiming that his patients recovered quicker. From our list of daily patients, he would mark from fifteen to twenty of them with "V.S." next to their names.

Dr. Heiskill was always kind to me and never gave me a rough or angry response. I often wondered how I escaped his displeasure and eventually learned that he had left behind his young and newly married wife, as well as his valuable and faithful Negro manservant, who had died from malaria. Immediately I was sorry for his circumstances and tried to make things easier for him. I began to take his side when I heard him being maligned by those who had suffered the effects of his anger.

One morning while attending to cases outside the fort he came across a new arrival from Company D, 2nd Artillery, with a character similar to his own. This man was unable to get his tongue out, which some people have difficulty with. Some can lay it out of their mouths, almost like a mortarboard, while others, like this patient, will roll it up like a ball. The doctor instructed: "Man, put your tongue out," but there was nothing more to come. The doctor repeated the order, and the soldier answered savagely, "I do!" Doctor Heiskell then rushed at the man and, catching him by the throat, throttled him. The soldier vigorously resisted and threatened to report him to his captain. Subsequently he did report the matter to Captain Drane who, as a stickler for his soldiers, brought up the matter at the general's quarters. Shortly after, an orderly came for Doctor Heiskill and I learned later that he got a good drubbing by the general. He would have been court-martialed, if it were not for the fact that General Clinch had pity on him because of his troubled mind. Soon after this episode he was sent away, doubtless to a more congenial station. I could not say that I was sorry to see him go, as I had good relations with his substitutes, Doctor Hamilton and my kind friend, Dr. Leavensworth.

A swamp and thicket surrounded a large round pond where the plantation was located. The driver's house was about fifty yards from the pond. One night some Indians entered the swamp and made a surprise attack upon us. The balls flew thick all around, striking Doctor Weightman's marquee and the hospital tent, which caused much alarm and confusion. The general fled and Doctor Weightman ran behind him into the house with only his shirt on. I, of course, ran, too. The Crackers stationed outside, along with all the other men, women, and children, ran into the fort. The doctor, who was very fond of his bed, had undressed as usual, and came to me stockingless and asked, "Steward, dare you go to my tent and fetch my clothes, and if you feel under my pillow, you will get my gold watch." I soon returned with all of his essentials and received an approving smile. As for myself, I always slept in my clothes, even my forage cap.

By the time our soldiers scoured the hammock the Indians had fled. All night attacks were alarming, and this was no exception. Following the attack, the general ordered the hospital tent, his tent, and Dr. Weightman's marquee to be placed inside the fort, which was accomplished immediately. Once more the doctor was my nearest neighbor, being placed not more than ten yards away, but I felt no discomfort since I revered and respected him, and he remained my staunch friend under all circumstances.

Our new home was neither healthy nor pleasant, as we were shut up both day and night. I was instructed to receive the women and children of the Cracker community, which left me no room to lie down even though our marquee was the largest. The first night I slept on a couch, but afterwards I preferred to rest upon a bench at the guards' fire in the open air. My daily duties remained the same, but the longer we stayed at Fort Drane, the more patients we received. The hospital became impossibly overloaded and deaths began to increase. The induction shed, which lay on the edge of the swamp, was one hundred yards long and covered with bark that allowed the sun and rain easy access through innumerable openings. Our patients lay exposed to the fetid swamp air and began to contract dysentery and typhus. Only when stricken with a disease were they moved either to the hospital tent or another one of the hospital buildings inside the fort, where they were more carefully looked after.

The fort was not large enough to contain everyone. Seven large buildings and the hospital fly tent were filled with desperate cases, leaving temporary sheds outside until the fort could be enlarged. When I went through these sheds in the morning to check up and medicate the men, I felt disgraced and humbled to see such fine soldiers brought to such a state of misery, devastated by their ailments. One would call out to me: "Steward, for God's sake, get me out of this." Another would groan, saying, "I am wet through and I shall be steamed before the day's done."

Sand flies and mosquitoes were constant pests, as well as centipedes, cockroaches, scorpions, and huge spiders. At night we were surrounded by yelling wolves and the croaking of bullfrogs. The sand of the fort was full of chiggers, and a sort of black flea was the greatest torment of all. Dr. Leavensworth, an amiable, clever, and unpretentious man who regularly absentmindedly conducted his rounds with his trousers turned up to his knees, was a source of ridicule by the men. When I warned him, "Your trousers are turned up, Doctor," he replied, "Oh, ah! Those confounded fleas! Are the rascals laughing at me?" His brother, General Leavensworth, after whom they named Fort Leavensworth in Arkansas, commanded somewhere out west. I served under the doctor until my time expired, when we both departed the fort together. We parted company at Alachua Courthouse; I was on my way down to the creek and England and he for the West. His parting words were, "Be sure to return, and be sure you settle in Ohio."

In those days I worked very hard and am grateful that I did not flag, but rather seemed to have extra energy for the extra work. Then in the spring a great sickness, in the form of a fever, struck the fort when Lieutenant Colonel Heilman fell ill with country fever. It began with great fatigue and a fullness of the blood vessels. The patient developed a jaundiced appearance, which was generally accompanied by continual bleeding from the nose. The fifth day was critical as survival on that day usually led to the patient's recovery. Afterwards the brain was affected, producing delirium during the midday heat. Many of our men died from the fever, sometimes as many as five daily, but usually at least two or three.

Eventually I succumbed and, having observed that patients generally bled profusely from the nose before death, I requested Doctor Leavensworth to bleed me. He promised to do so, but I realized he never intended to and eventually bled myself. I removed an unusually large quantity and, as the blood flowed, I almost felt to cry out like the Indians, "Inclemais cha, inclemais char. Good, good!" Sometimes I still think that I did well through this act.

I was outside the pickets when the fever struck me unconscious. I was carried into the fort and was tended throughout my sickness by Andrew Mann and God, to whom I owe my life. About fifteen to twenty of the worst cases were with me in the hospital and we all suffered from delirium during the full heat of the day. My couch was near an open window and when I looked out everything seemed to be in flames. On one occasion I thought a troop of dragoons would all be consumed in a blaze. When I recovered from my delirium, I noticed some of my comrades were lying around dead. It was an awful sight, which few could imagine, and I wondered whether I would be next. The uncertainty of life in that climate, even for the fittest, left me with little hope of seeing my English family and friends once more. Yet such daily sights helped to take my mind off myself and to consider that we were all brothers suffering each other's misfortune.

We received visits from superior officers and from men of all the ranks. All showed great compassion and wanted to be of service to us. Once a patient began to recover, they made little niceties for him, from whatever was available in the camp. This made me believe that, when we find ourselves all suffering in the same boat of misfortune, it brings out the good in people. I firmly believe that human nature responds all the more the greater the need.

Colonel Heilman died on May 25 while I was still in a very precarious state. He was buried in the evening of the same day, as it was dangerous to keep a corpse over six hours. Captain Gates took command of the fort.

Dr. Weightman had been away on other duties and returned with the convoy on May 31, which brought me great comfort and hope for recovery. He was soon at my bedside to check my pulse and told me that my vital signs were low, but that good nursing, rather than medicine, "will bring you round." Most would say that I had been over-medicated, having received heavy doses for ten mornings in a row. At first I suffered greatly, everything was difficult, and my anxiety sapped my power to achieve my recovery, but I was anxious to get well. Hope of returning home to England brought me peace and my longing slowly confirmed the reality that I would be free in three months. If it were not for Doctor Weightman, I believe I would have died. For some time after, I walked with a stick and suffered great pain in my cheekbones from the effects of calomel.

Once I was back on my feet I gradually resumed my duties, but being surrounded by the dead and dying, it took me a while before my mind caught up with the reality of our situation. Fort Drane had become a place of misery where we all suffered from the consequences of disease, climate, and the war with the Indians. Our food deteriorated, we grew more filthy, and began to run short of clothing. Every day there were daily downpours and insects were a constant harassment, which made every hour of the day almost impossible to bear. To add to the discomfort the surrounding ponds generated mists every morning, which floated over us, making our situation even more gloomy.

One day we lost one of our first lieutenants when, out of despair, he fired his pistol into his mouth and blew out his brains. Another young man was brought in from his sentry post, scared out of his wits because his dread of the Indians was so great. Ultimately he died, shrieking "Indians! Indians!" The strength of our garrison steadily decreased due to the constant sickness of the troops. McIntosh's plantation had been garrisoned to provide a source of forage, sugar, and molasses for the army so we could be ready for the winter campaign. Eventually Captain Drane had to evacuate the post and return to Ft. Drane so his soldiers could help garrison our fort.

At the time there were about one hundred and fifty sick and wounded and the daily increase steadily sapped the vitality of the whole force. One man went while singing psalms, another gentle man died just like an infant falling asleep, while the majority seemed to pass away quite unperturbed. My nurses reported the death of a man so frequently that I scarcely thought of the person who had departed. I developed a callous attitude toward death and when someone died, I mechanically gave the order to "lay him out," and then went to the quartermaster for a coffin. Through it all I prayed to God that He would deliver us in His own good time.

Following my convalescence, I began a daily routine about 3:00 p.m. to stroll outside the fort to get a little fresh air and some peace and quiet from my hospital duties. It coincided with the time the men took their afternoon nap. My stroll took me along the back of the Negro huts beside a fence where there were huckleberry bushes. I plucked the fruit and sauntered along until I came to a beautiful green stretch of turf, about 300 to 400 yards beyond the extreme end of the Negro village. There was a clump of bushes to break the heat of the sun, and I would lie dormant and allow the breezes to fan my cheeks and revive my spirits. After resting for about half an hour, I would stroll back in front of the huts, along the pathway to the fort.

After passing the huts I formed a casual acquaintance with a huge black snake about eleven feet long and as thick as a man's leg. Its hole was on the opposite side of the pathway to the swamp, to which it wandered every day, and on its return journey it often crossed my path. We were mutually fearful of one another; it held its head erect and watched me the whole time, while I walked away in the opposite direction to give him, as the sailors say, "a wide berth."

One day something prevented me from my taking my stroll. About the same time two of our men who were walking around the pond were shot at by Indians from a hammock located about a quarter mile from the huts, but they were too far off to be hit. If I had taken my stroll it would have led me into an ambush, as I would have been between the Indians and the hammock, where escape would have been impossible. They had probably seen my daily walk and planned to secure my scalp.

Upon hearing the firing, the drums beat to arms and we mustered a body of more than fifty men who assembled with fixed bayonets. I had orders to muster as many men as possible, but when I called Davis, one of my attendants, he hung back out of fear, showing that men are not brave at all times. He had fought bravely at the battle of Withlacoochee where he had stood his ground even after receiving a ball in the neck. He fought on until a second shot disabled him. Afterwards, when I asked him about his reticence, he told me that his previous sufferings were so great that he felt very reluctant to sustain any more wounds.

We followed the Indians to the rear of the Negro huts where we saw them running swiftly for the hammock. They fired at us, but they were too far off and too flurried to take aim at our advancing force. Upon returning to the fort, I clearly saw that my escape from certain death could only have been through the grace of my Heavenly Father.

After that incident, an order was issued stating that the men should not stray farther than the pickets, yet there was always someone who would disobey. One day, a cavalry sergeant and his companion rode out on horseback to a watermelon patch about a mile from the fort and a half mile from the hammock. While they were busy selecting the cooling fruit they were suddenly fired upon by Indians, who hit the sergeant in the arm. This disabled him so that he was unable to remount his horse and was then shot through his chest and scalped. The other succeeded in getting mounted when a volley was fired at him. He was fortunate that he was not hit as he rode for the fort at top speed. His horse saved the soldier's life, but as it entered the fort it fell dead. The animal was hit, and the ball penetrated its abdomen. About eighty men were sent to retrieve the sergeant, who was drawing his last breath as they got to him. The savages had torn away the whole of his scalp leaving his skull bare.

The hospital was so full that there was no room to lay the sergeant to await his coffin, which would not be ready until the following morning. I was ordered to have him placed in our store tent, but I preferred to lay him in my small sleeping tent than to have him among our provisions, as the flies would flit from his bloody head and settle upon our food. I put him to lie alongside my couch, but that night my lively imagination created for me some ghastly images of the sergeant in my dreams.

He had suffered with depression and it was said that he purposely sought his doom. In a previous skirmish with Indians, he and ten of his men were ambushed by about fifty Indians. While five of his men rode off, he and five others dashed into the midst of the enemy. Two were instantly killed but he laid into the savages like a demon courting death. In the end two of his men took hold of his horse's bridle and retrieved him from the melee. It is possible that some men earn a reputation for bravery in combat when, in reality, they are suicidal.

As the hot season progressed it was obvious that the troops could not operate in the severe heat and humidity. Even garrison duty was too much, for we lost more from the climate than from the war. The Indians took advantage of the summer heat and became more active and venturesome. It was their home and the climate only made them more bloodthirsty. No party of men could pass through the woods without being ambushed, and without loss from the first fire of the savages. The detachments always took a six-pounder and a howitzer with them, for the enemy disliked those weapons and always retreated after a few discharges.

On the morning of June 6, Doctor Weightman departed for Black Creek with a convoy of sick and wounded. He wore his usual black dress coat and I remarked how foolish it was to present himself as a target. All the officers were dressed as privates so the Indians would suppose the doctor was the commander. When they were about seven miles from Fort Drane, they were attacked by a large force of Indians who killed three men and wounded the doctor. He was struck in the leg but did not complain. Soldiers who saw the blood running out of the top of his boot removed him from his horse and staunched the blood. The wound could have killed him, and I was sorry that he was carried to Micanopy instead of Fort Drane, where I could have looked after him.

The convoy returned on June 16. They had been attacked and ambushed twice on their way from Fort Drane to Micanopy. As they were encumbered with sick, they had great difficulty in beating off the enemy, who burned one wagon, killed two men, and wounded eight to ten others. Captain Gates (brother to the major), our commandant who was sent by the last train, also remained at Micanopy, where he died on June 22.

Returning Home

On June 24 a convoy arrived bringing the welcome news that by order of Colonel Ichabod Crane, commanding officer at St. Augustine, Fort Drane was to be evacuated. We were overjoyed at the thought of leaving. The news set in motion preparation to depart, which included the destruction of everything that was impracticable to take with us. Fort King was also evacuated and that command under Captain Lendrum was brought to Fort Drane. Capt. Lendrum, through seniority, took command of the fort. Over the next few days, we shipped out three detachments of sick servicemen by wagon train to Micanopy, which began their return to St. Augustine.

July 7, under the command of Captain Child, I departed on the last train from Ft. Drane. Dr. Hawkins, the senior surgeon, took command of the whole body of sick on the final move to St. Augustine. We left the fort as untenable as possible in a retreat brought about not only by the Indians, but by the natural difficulties of climate and country. We reached Micanopy about noon and I immediately looked after the accommodations of the sick and wounded. Then I reported to the commanding officer of the medical department at the post, who ordered me to be ready for duty the following morning. In the meantime, Dr. Weightman sent for me to come to his quarters inside the fort. After wringing my hand, he inquired about my health and invited me to his marquee, instructing his manservant to serve me some refreshments, which I badly needed. Since I had last seen the doctor, he had suffered much from a leg wound and intermittent fever, but he was well on the way to recovery. He informed me that he was also going on the wagon train to Black Creek and then to our old quarters at St. Augustine, where he planned to spend the winter. When I heard this, I decided to submit my claim for discharge, as I had a little over five months remaining until the expiration of my five years of service.

I reminded him of the promise General Clinch made to me at Fort Drane, whereupon he told me it was unfortunate that the general was gone, but that he would discuss the matter with Doctor Hawkins, the new senior surgeon, and the post commanding officer. He advised me not to worry, as he was sure that my wishes would be granted. This confirmation lifted a huge weight from my shoulders, as I knew I could depend upon the doctor, whose word was his bond. Early the following morning there was an order for me to present myself before my best friend, who had already spoken about me with the commanding officer. He informed me that I would accompany him to St. Augustine, where he thought I could make arrangements for my return home. He also raised the question again regarding my possible entry into the College of Surgeons, and was happy to make recommendations on my behalf to his medical friends in Philadelphia. I knew that I was not strong enough to begin medical studies and felt the outcome would not be in my best interest. Once more I declined, thanked him warmly, and told him that I was looking forward to returning to my homeland.

Then he referred to promises made when I began my service under him at the St. Augustine Hospital that "if I behaved myself, it would give him great pleasure to make me comfortable and do something special for me at the end of my term." He continued, "As your health will not permit me to do as I would wish, by getting you into college, I shall obtain your discharge and see you on your way to St. Augustine where your expenses shall be mine. What I have you will therefore claim also." What could I say in return? His kindness so filled my heart that I was unable to express myself, knowing how hard it was going to be to part from Doctor Weightman, my American parent. I was overjoyed at the prospects that he laid before me, which were beyond my expectations.

Afterwards I went to the hospital building where my sick comrades lay. In my joy, I told them of my good fortune that, on the following day, I was to begin my journey home. They all congratulated me, but many who were remaining behind cried how they would miss me. "Already we miss you, for since you have been away, we are starved of water, nobody cares for us. Please get us one drink of water before you go." I comforted them as well as I could under the circumstances, for there was a great shortage of medical supplies and hospital personnel at Micanopy. Soldiers came and went, and none cared for others. It seemed that every man was for himself.

The following morning Doctor Weightman's servant brought me a horse to ride down to the creek. Before I departed, I visited my patients once more and our parting was a scene I never forgot, for we were never to see each other in this world again. They lay all over the floor and, as I passed over and about them, they shed tears and actually clung to my legs as if they would not let me go. This moved me so much that I cherish the memory more than when General Clinch thanked me for my service before his staff officers. I cannot account for my good fortune but believe that my recognition from both my commanding general, as well as my fellow soldiers, may have been due to my honest and conscientious attitude toward my duties and with all whom I worked. It was difficult to leave but I went on my way most pleased, having received blessings from the sick and wounded, with whom I had shared so many days of horror and hardship. To this day, whenever I am feeling low, I recall these scenes at Micanopy Hospital to bring me comfort.

After I supervised the loading of the wagons with the sick, I rode up to Dr. Weightman's carriage. He gave me strict instructions to stay alongside his carriage and, due to my run-down condition, not to involve myself in any work. But Doctor Leavensworth, the medical officer, requested my assistance as a favor which I could not refuse. The wagon train was laden with one hundred and twenty sick and wounded and I found myself unequal to the task. I made sure that all received refreshments during the day, and at night I worked till late making and administering medicine. I was allowed four assistants to cook in the evenings, but they were so inept and careless that, had I not constantly watched over them, the helpless soldiers in the wagons would have gone without food. Doctor Leavensworth left us at the Alachua Courthouse, about halfway down to the river, and we bid each other goodbye.

I did not realize that I was issued a cavalry horse until the cavalry fell in as an advance guard to the convoy. My horse, in spite of my resistance, rushed toward them and joined the cavalcade. I found myself a prisoner in their midst and for a little while was unable to leave. He was a most stubborn animal. Frequently I had to ride ahead of the convoy to obtain clear, fresh running water before the horsemen got into the streams or ponds, and was never able to coax the animal to return to meet the train. Invariably I had to wait until the train caught up with us before I was able to pass out the water to the thirsty men. There was nothing so resuscitating to the weary men as a drink of that pure water.

One day during the march I was forward of the train, when I gave my mount his head to take a drink out of one of the round ponds so common in the country. All of a sudden, an alligator about eight to ten feet in length rose to the surface and came steadily toward us. The horse snorted and the alligator stopped. Just then we were joined by more horsemen and the alligator disappeared.

This was the first time I saw an alligator show signs of interest. My experience with much larger specimens was that they invariably hid themselves as soon as they were approached, which made me believe that they were generally harmless and timid until hunger forced them to be aggressive and dangerous. There were four or five playful black bears at Fort Drane who wrestled with the men, but they became dangerous when pressed by hunger. This made me believe that hunger was the chief cause of ferocity among wild animals.

Dr. Hawkins, the senior surgeon, was the only surgeon for the remainder of the journey to the river. He took little notice of the sick and seldom came near us during the march. After three days we arrived at the creek having survived a terrible tornado, intolerable heat, and acute thirst. The tornado occurred one evening about an hour before sundown. It was terrifying, as the rain came down in torrents and the trees crashed together breaking their limbs which were strewn all over the ground. We were soaked within minutes but fortunately for the sick, the storm lasted only half an hour, after which we halted and gathered around large pine fires to dry off.

On arriving at the creek I had barely housed the sick for the night before I was visited by the senior surgeon of the depot. Black Creek was the depot of the commissary and quartermaster department for the interior. He told me that his steward had met with an accident a few days previously and that he had requested Doctor Hawkins detain me in his place. It was a sudden damper to my hopes for discharge, but then I noticed the order of the day was everyone for himself. I decided I was not going to be used by anyone to suit their convenience, and replied that I was unfit for duty and was on my way to St. Augustine where, if necessary, I would seek redress from a higher authority. He immediately fell into a rage, accused me of feigning, and said that he would take the necessary steps to see that I was detained.

That same night I ate a piece of beef which was badly cooked on the point of a bayonet and when I arose in the morning, my body was covered with large wheals the thickness of rope. The post surgeon examined me, told me to get some bed rest, and then reported me as sick to Dr. Hawkins. The following morning the post surgeon again visited me to determine if I was fit for duty, but prescribed no medication. For two days I languished without care from a severe digestive fever. During that period, I received nothing but a cup of coffee from a soldier who took compassion upon me. I then requested Mr. George Clarke, a young surgeon I had known at Fort King, to come and examine me. He gave me medicine and promised to mention my case to Dr. Hawkins, which was done, and I saw no more of the selfish post surgeon.

I had ignored Doctor Weightman's advice to keep close to him, but during my sickness I was able to send him a note at the hotel where he was staying, about two miles away on the other side of the creek. On July 3, a soldier came with orders to bring me to the doctor. When he met me he gently reminded me, "I told you to stay close to me." Then he gave me his camp mattress and instructed the hotel to provide me with every comfort at his expense. I was directed to help myself to his demijohn of wine, which he claimed was the best medicine for me. I remained there a week or more and began to regain my strength. One day I took a row on the creek and filled my boat with clusters of grapes which hung over the stream. I also took short walks into the woods when, on one occasion, I came upon the home of one of the Crackers who knew me at Fort Drane.

With all the doctor's care and kindness I was still weak, but he told me that it would take time to regain my strength and renew my shattered constitution. Another guest at the hotel was a Captain Robert Lee, a Virginian who had been badly wounded. He was a jovial man of about forty years, but too old to be the celebrated general of the Civil War. Before he came to Florida he was living among a tribe of friendly Indians, somewhere in the Rocky Mountains. Since he was a man fond of adventure, he came to Florida as a volunteer and not a member of the regular army. Most days the captain, the landlord of the hotel, the doctor, and myself relaxed in the lobby of the hotel and chatted about Virginia. I was a patient listener and recall that the captain was also friendly toward me at all times.

We left Black Creek by steamboat on July 18 and passed into the St. Johns River, putting in at Jacksonville for half an hour, before moving out into the stream and anchoring for the night. On the following day we sailed down the broad river, which varied in width from two to four miles. Occasionally we passed huge alligators who evidently had little regard for steamboats, as they moved out of the way only just in time for us to pass. They were frequently fired at with ball cartridges that had little effect upon their armored hides. During the entire time I was in Florida I had never seen so many alligators as on this river, and estimate that I saw over one hundred of them. We passed out of the main stream at about 10 o'clock in the morning and coasted the rest of the way to St. Augustine, where we arrived about 5 p.m.

Most of the respectable families had forsaken St. Augustine at the commencement of hostilities, and the city had taken on a melancholy appearance. The principal buildings had been turned into hospitals, where there were now about 600 disabled men, and the streets were thronged with maimed and worn-out soldiers.

My Black Creek experience taught me not to report myself, but to take independent lodgings in the city. While there I completed my estimates of requisitions that were used in the hospital during the campaign, which took me about two weeks to complete. Afterwards I presented myself to Doctor Weightman who told me that Colonel Crane had a serious objection to giving me a discharge unless I was seriously disabled. He said I could remain where I was at my own disposal, as my term would shortly expire. This was more preferable for the colonel, who did not want to break the rules. I did not receive the information graciously and told my friend that if I could not have my discharge at once, I would go back to my company at Picolata and serve my time to the end. "Well, well," said the doctor. "I will see the colonel again, so return tomorrow." When I called upon him, he said he would give me a certificate of disability and asked that I complete a disease debility form, which he handed to me. I then made out my pay papers and arranged to receive my discharge. My papers showed that I was discharged by surgeon's certificate, having served four years and ten months in the service of the United States. Thus General Clinch's promise was nearly fulfilled, through the representations of my master and old friend, Dr. Weightman. The negotiations had lost me one month.

I still had to go to Picolata to obtain my papers so that on arrival in Charleston I would receive my pay. I travelled in a tilted express cart, which was constructed for swiftness and security against sudden attacks. Both I and the driver made it through without harm. On the following day I returned to St. Augustine after another five hours of express traveling to find the packet schooner ready for sea, only awaiting a fair wind.

Captain Drane was very friendly and helpful in arranging my departure. At the same time he asked me to carry a letter to his wife who was staying at one of the hotels in Charleston. He also was anxious that I should write to him upon my arrival in England. I delayed calling on Dr. Weightman for nearly a week. He gave me the money I had deposited with him for safety ever since my entering the hospital. Then we parted quietly, for we were both too emotional to have a conversation. I later wrote to him after my safe arrival in England. Finally, I said farewell to my tried and dear friends, Sergeants Scofield, Potter, and Caull. When Ambrose Mackay found out that I was likely to visit Oakham, he said, "For God's sake, don't mention me to Miss Mould or any of my friends, for if they write to me, I shall not answer them." He shed tears at our parting, doubtless feeling that I was the last link between him and his relations. When I finally arrived home I found his mother, blind with age, living with her son-in-law, the Reverend Laurent, the father of the grammar school at Alford, Lincolnshire.

Before we set sail for Charleston I was introduced to Henry Deane, a discharged soldier and native of Ireland. He had received a classical education, and I found that he was one of those uncontrollable people that even the army could not tame. We arrived in Charleston after being at sea three days, only to find that cholera was raging in the city. There were 187 deaths during the first week after our arrival.

I arranged to board in the house of Dr. Wartman, a person I knew from St. Augustine who had attended as medical officer at the hospital during Dr. Weightman's absence in the country. During meals he and Mr. Deane enjoyed their conversations that dealt in classical lore and literature.

During my stay I had a severe attack of intermittent fever, which made me very jaundiced. The sweating stage of the sickness continued so long that Dr. Deane grew impatient that he was unable to arrest it. At length he brought me a quart of brandy, part of which I asked him to sponge all over my body, and this eventually checked the sweating. Gradually I increased my strength so that I was able to walk about the city.

I took my papers to Colonel Hayne, who lived in a splendid residence in the suburbs. I was ushered upstairs into the most beautiful room I had ever seen in my life; marble staircase, marble floors, and marble tables. I found the colonel a most gentlemanly and agreeable person. After he had examined my papers, I was directed to a lawyer's office where I was paid my full arrears of clothing and pay as stated in the certificate.

I remained in Charleston for five weeks, paying $5 per week in board, for which I had a comfortable bedroom and excellent meals. The doctor's wife was a good manager and had two Negresses to do the cooking and kitchen work. It was a custom while we were dining that two or three little children, as black as ebony and quite nude, would be running around the table (whilst their mama waited upon us) and the white ladies would jump them upon their knees and kiss them. Other than my sickness, I spent a very pleasant time at the doctor's.

While sitting at table one day I made a sympathetic remark regarding slavery, when my neighbor, an Englishman from Woolwich, cautioned me, telling me that such statements were not safe. He said, "If one of the planters heard you, possibly you might be found tomorrow lying stabbed in the gutter." This made me realize that I was in the hotbed of slavery.

One day I strolled through the Negro Mart. It was a sickening sight to see human beings chained and ironed to the walls like dogs. One man looked so furious that I still see his glaring hatred in my mind's eye. He was a powerful young man, who I felt would be very dangerous if he had his liberty.

Charleston was populated by the most miserable poor and the immensely rich, the riches being the fruits of slavery. It was a port city, with considerable foreign trade, the main commodities being rice and cotton. There were some good streets, including King Street, where most of the trade was transacted. The suburbs were extremely quiet and the buildings were fine and spacious with verandahs. They were separated from each other by gardens and were evidently the homes of merchants and planters. The city was full of blacks, probably two to every white person. In the event of any disorder there was a standing city guard, centrally stationed at the Citadel. Charleston was generally unhealthy, particularly during the summer, when the upper class moved to Sullivan's Island, about seven miles out of the city and situated at the eastern side of the entrance of the harbor.

The whites were seldom seen to work. One day I purchased a trunk and was carrying it on my shoulders, when a young Negro stopped me saying, "Massa, me tote dat for you," and he was quite astounded at my refusal of his services, saying, "Ah, baccra man, Nigger only work here." He was right, for all soon learned the sad lessons from slavery of idleness, licentiousness, and uselessness. A gentleman on the wharf told me that the English and Scotch were no exceptions to the general custom. "If you look around," he said, "you will find our principal merchants are Scotch. They came here as lads with a conscience and would scoff at keeping a Negro. But finding that money was easily gained by keeping and renting out Negroes, they soon overcame their contempt of the prevailing customs." So, you see, you can scarcely live with the wicked unless you adopt their ways.

I booked my passage on the ship *Medira*, a fine vessel commanded by Captain Budd. He had captained the schooner *Wacchamaw* to St. Augustine with the Charleston volunteers aboard. At first he refused because of my jaundiced appearance, but I told him that the yellowness would disappear before the ship sailed. He asked me for $120 for my passage to England, but when I advised him that I did not drink, he accepted $60. We did not sail for three days after getting into the Bay, due to a severe gale, which luckily arrived before we were out on the ocean. The captain was an excellent seaman and gave every indication of being a brave, as well as courteous, gentleman. His son, a lad of twelve years, was aboard and, as an amusement, I taught him a little arithmetic and I kept a log with the 1st mate.

Being the only cabin passenger, I got on famously with the captain and crew and was made to feel very comfortable. We had a pleasant and quick voyage, arriving in Liverpool after five weeks. The *Medira* was the finest and quickest vessel I had sailed on and often managed sixteen knots. My first impressions upon arrival in Liverpool were not good. The streets were very muddy, and the poorer quarters looked squalid, with women working in the streets wheeling barrows. It did not say much for my country, and I felt like a stranger and one who would have difficulty living amongst such miserable surroundings. The quantity of beggars and continuous patrols of police seemed to imply that there was great poverty and distress. I stayed only two days in Liverpool before leaving for Manchester, where I remained for two weeks. It was equally dirty, but I preferred it to Liverpool. During my journey home the countryside became more pleasing and, as I neared Newark, old impressions of my native land returned. Everything seemed the way I had left it, except that the towns, villages, and rivers appeared smaller.

Upon arriving home, I began to reflect upon my adventures in America. How the Indians had been able to outmaneuver a standing modern army, not by any formal tactics, but through their native fighting abilities and customs. The forest was their home, their tracking ability defied understanding, and they used stealth to overcome their prey. Our soldiers were always at a disadvantage, constantly at risk of an ambush.

There was great difficulty keeping the army supplied during our campaign. Long distances between supply stations, forts, and points of engagement caused increased problems for the provision department. The generals were forced to restrict the length of sorties through the Indian Nation, which prevented them from concluding otherwise successful engagements. In addition, many soldiers fell sick while on the march, which decreased the fighting force and increased the workload of the healthy.

I still regard the three years that I spent in the city of St. Augustine to be my happiest time in America. When I worked in the hospital I was surrounded by many true friends and excellent companions. I was fortunate in selecting Scofield as my attendant, as we worked well together and enjoyed each other's company. In our free time we would often be together strolling through the city or around Fort Marion in the early evenings. He recalled later in a letter that the eleven months we served together were his happiest days. He eventually became an orderly sergeant, with the responsibilities of acting commissary and quartermaster sergeants and librarian combined, which earned him the handsome salary of about $22 per month. My positive attitude toward my duties made me lifelong friends, especially Dr. Weightman, whose name I gave to my first son.

Home in England

Upon my return to England, I travelled to London to try and find some worthwhile occupation. While there I met with Mrs. Lowth, but comparing notes, I realized that she did not know the reason of my leaving her employ and we both learned how badly we were deceived. She retained the porter for some time after my departure, but ultimately he was fired. We met by chance about twelve years later at Arlington Hall when I was on a day picnic. As I stood outside the inn, I saw a man that I recognized and called out to him by name. I asked if he knew me, then watched as he gradually turned pale. "Good God, it is Bemrose." He told me how he had degraded himself to become a wanderer, dependent upon strangers for employment. He regretted his own misfortunes as well as those he had inflicted upon others. He was anxious to escape my company and seized the first chance, probably hoping to avoid uncomfortable disclosures or questions. I remained three or four hours longer but we did not meet again, leaving me to reflect upon some expressions: "Guilt makes cowards of us all;" "God is not mocked;" and "The measure you mete out to others shall fall upon your own head."

Not long after arriving in London my health failed, forcing me to return home to convalesce. At that time, I received the following:

Oakham
June 24th, 1837.

Dear John,

Allow me, my young friend, to give you some motherly advice. We know that all must die, but we do not know when, except it may be when we least expect it. Should we not therefore be prepared for such a journey and should we also seek a friend to intercede for us. Such a friend should be powerful and willing. Jesus Christ came into the world in human form to seek and to save sinners. He died for us and he rejects none that go to him. He heals the brokenhearted, comforts the afflicted and soothes the distressed. This applies to all who are cast down and humbled, mourning for their sins. Those who feel that there is no good in them, that they are utterly unworthy of such a Savior. To those who seek refuge in his righteousness, having none of their own, he says: "Come unto me all ye that are weary and heavy laden and I will give you rest." Therefore blessed is the man, whoever he may be, whether Israelite or stranger, that joining himself to the Lord and taking hold of his everlasting covenant, the same that God has made with us through Christ. The new covenant of which Jesus is the mediator, I say, may this be your stronghold. May you be found in Christ for there is no condemnation to them who are in Christ Jesus. God is the justifier of him who believes in Christ, Romans, Chap. 8, verse 1.

Excuse me dear friend for pressing the subject of your eternal welfare upon you. It may be that you are already acquainted with the way of salvation. If not, believe now my motive for wishing you to become so, is from a true feeling of friendship. For how can I hope to possess heaven and happiness without wishing those I esteem especially, to partake of it. It would afford me unspeakable pleasure to receive a letter from you signifying you have given heed to my words of encouragement. At all events, I shall be glad to see you at any time and hope soon to hear how your health is, for I assure you, we shall be anxious about you.

  Mr. Wellington sends his kind regards and joins me in wishing you enjoy better health and believe me to remain.
DearBemrose,
Your sincere friend, Ann Elizabeth Lowth.

When I had first arrived in St. Augustine, I wrote Mrs. Lowth a nasty letter telling her how I escaped her tyranny, which I considered worse than what I observed of Negro slavery. How humbled I was to receive this noble response from this true Christian woman. This proved how the young and headstrong often do not know their true friends.

My ill health prevented me from accomplishing all my plans after returning to my homeland and delayed my visit to the mother of Ambrose Mackay. I then wrote to Sergeant Scofield requesting that he find Ambrose. The following was the letter I received in reply:

Stamford, August 12, 1838,

My Dear Friend,

  I received your letter of the 29th of May and was truly pleased to hear again from one for whom I feel almost a brotherly affection. I feel that I had three brothers in the army whose names were John. H. Potter, George W. Caull and John Bemrose. My youngest brother Entricken, although belonging to the same family, I can only class as one of my male cousins. But my dear friend, I was and am and shall be, greatly distressed on account of your continued ill health but I am sincerely in hopes that you may soon regain your health, at least in a tolerable degree. But I have doubts (excuse me for plainness) if you ever become perfectly hale and robust, for I believe that your constitution was materially injured during the Florida Campaigns. But you must still hope, for as one of your English poets has it "hope of all passions most befriends us here."

As it regards myself, I am still engaged in a school and enjoying a tolerable degree of good health, but I have suffered considerably this summer from a severe pain in my side and breast, with a heavy cough, but am much better at present. Now my dear Bemrose, in reply to your friendly and generous invitation, I have to answer that I cannot accept it. And as I scorn all prevarication, I will frankly state my reasons for declining. My Dear John, we have known each other as equals, for in the service, I considered all as equals who conducted themselves in a manner becoming men, or soldiers. But in civil life it is generally different for let us disguise it as we may, there is virtually an aristocracy either of family or wealth (I speak only of the enlisted portion) and there is nothing to prevent a pure, free, generous and disinterested friendship. Friends of this nature, I believe we were and I trust ever shall be. But let me embrace your generous offer and the scene instantly changes and I become in the strictest sense of the word a dependent, perhaps indeed a favored one, but a dependent still. I should become dependent upon your bounty and generosity in a great measure for my living, the equality would cease and my friendship let it be ever so pure, ever so disinterested, would probably be called worldly and selfish, if not by you, it might by others, which the proud soul of W.H.S. could not submit to.

My family, I believe are strictly honest, they are not what you call poor, but they are far from rich. They are worth probably some four or five thousand dollars and with industry, prudence and economy are enabled to live, but they could ill afford to supply me with sufficient cash to make a jaunt to England for pleasure, or to see a friend, for they do not know him and I myself, having nothing but my hands and an independent spirit. These are my reasons and I hope you will think them sufficient. But my dear Bemrose, I am not the less grateful for your kind offer and it was in my power, to visit you considerately with the duty which I owe myself, you may be assured, I should be most happy to comply. For I should be glad to visit England and doubly so to visit it, in company with an old friend, with whom I have spent five years of my life that we might talk of the present, the past and the future, without any embarrassing thoughts, but enough, enough. My dear John, if you should ever again cross the Atlantic, I shall expect that you would pay me a friendly visit, which, I should certainly do were I ever to come to Old England.

In answer to your letter respecting Mann or Grey (Ambrose Mackay) I have to state that having kept up no correspondence with the company since I left, I did not at first know how to commence to find him. But upon thinking a few moments upon his former character and disposition, I thought it more than probable that he had reenlisted, I accordingly wrote to the Adj. General of the U. States Army, respecting him and received an answer to the following purport. Private Andrew Mann of D. Company, 2nd Artillery, reenlisted in that Company on the 7th May 1837 to serve for three years. He was present for muster in the Company at Ross Landing, Cherokee Country, Tennessee, on the 30th of June 1838, the date of the last muster roll. The above abstract of the Adj. Gen.'s letter will inform you of his present situation. I wrote to him immediately upon the receipt of his address, but have received no answer. I will write again, with a request to the Post Master to forward the letter to the address of the Company, as it is probable that it may have removed. I believe the Seminole campaigns have closed. I saw Harris (an Englishman) in N. York this spring, I believe he is somewhere on Long Island. My paper is full so no more.

But to sincerely wish you may regain your health and enjoy a life of prosperity and happiness,

I am, Dear Bemrose,
Your sincere, grateful and lasting friend W. H. Scofield

You will notice in Scofield's letter that Ambrose Mackay, the real name of my friend, is given as Andrew Mann, or Gray, which requires an explanation. When Mackay enlisted at Fort Marion, St. Augustine, he called himself Robert Gray, but when the company reached Fort King, he was found out to have deserted from another artillery company and was entered on their muster roll as Andrew Mann. I suspected this was not his true name and confirmed the truth when I corresponded with his brother-in-law, the Reverend Laurent of Alford.

Those letters confirmed that he was estranged from his family, possibly the black sheep, but it was cruel of him not to answer the appeals of his aged mother and to remain estranged from his family. Once he told me that his mother was the proudest woman in England, but there was something deep that caused the chasm between this mother and son. One of the Reverend's letters from Ambrose actually stated that he died at the house of a Mr. James Harris of St. Augustine in 1832. This would have been about the time he reentered the Army at St. Augustine. It would seem that he inherited his portion of pride from his mother.

I Bequeath My Land

In the winter of 1873 I read an article in the *Pharmaceutical Journal* relating to a book, *The Resources of the Southern Fields and Forests* by Francis P. Porcher, M.D., of Charleston, South Carolina. Believing that he might be the son of Doctor P. Porcher of St. Augustine, I purchased the book and wrote to him. He was not a son but a cousin to the doctor and called upon Dr. Porcher the same evening he received my letter. The old man at once remembered me and was delighted to renew our ancient intimacy. Dr. Frank also answered my letter and remarked about the happiness my letter had brought to my old friend.

I kept these letters as mementos, though most of them told a sad story. After I left St. Augustine for Fort Drane, Doctor Porcher was appointed surgeon of the troops under General Hernandez, who was stationed south of the city. The doctor survived a few skirmishes with the Indians, but ultimately left the hardships of Indian warfare and settled with his wife and two sons, Charles and Frank, and a daughter in Charleston, South Carolina. He also told me about his tremendous misfortunes, such as the loss of his children, and that his wife had been thrown out of her carriage and lost her leg. The Civil War deprived him of his Florida estate, his slaves, his wealth, and position in society, reducing him to a very poor man, with only his profession to rely upon in his old age. The poverty was so great after the war he was barely able to make a living. Through this reversal of fortune, the distinguished, gentle-mannered doctor that I knew had become bitter and abusive toward the North. He saw in the Yankee the personification of all that was mean and despicable, and he especially hated General Sherman the most.

I had read a letter that General Sherman wrote to a Ms. Anna Gilman Bowen of Baltimore, a copy of which follows. He wrote: "If I know my own heart, it beats as warmly as ever towards those kind and generous families that greeted us with such warm hospitality in days long past. They remain in my memory. If today Frank and Mrs. Porcher, Eliza Gilman, Mary Lamb, Margaret Blake, the Barksdales, the Quashis, the Pryors, and indeed all of our cherished circle, including their children and grandchildren were to come to me as of old, the stern feelings of duty and conviction would melt as snow before the genial sun and I would strip my own children that they might be sheltered. Yet they call me barbarian, vandal and monster and all the epithets that language can invent, that are hateful and malignant."

Upon reading this, I wrote to General Sherman to solicit his aid towards the Porchers, telling him that I was entitled to a land grant of 160 acres, value of $200, for my services in the Florida War. At once I received the following reply:

Headquarters Army of the United States,
Washington, D. C.

April 17th, 1873.

John Bemrose,
Long Bennington,
Lincolnshire,
England.

Dear Sir,

Your long and interesting letter has been received and the names and facts recited prove certainly that you have all the claims on me that I recognize in every old and faithful Soldier of the American Army.

I remember Frank Porcher Junior very well, the same who married a Miss Gilman of Charleston, but I never knew the Father. Still I doubt not he is fully worthy of the gratitude you feel for him and I would be most happy to be the means of transmitting from you to him any act of recognition. I have placed your letter in the hands of an Officer of the War Office, who will look to the Muster Roll and if you state your services correctly I think you are entitled to a Land Warrant for 160 acres of Land, which warrant is assigning and would be worth about $200. I take it for granted you are paid in full to day of discharge, in which case there is no cash due you, and the Land Warrant would be all.

I will hold this letter till the Officer reports and will enclose his memorandum, with this and the necessary blanks necessary for you to execute, in applying for the Land Warrant.

All the Porchers were against us in the Civil War, and of course shared the fate of the unsuccessful and defeated but the moment that resistance ended, they received possession of their landed estates less Negroes, and now enjoy the same liberty of action that we do. I have not seen Frank Porcher since 1864, but can readily communicate with him by mail and would send him your letter; only it contains expressions that might hurt his feelings.

Truly yours,

W.J. Sherman
General

P.S. If you have not received a Land Warrant under the act of Congress, I mail to you a pamphlet, containing instructions for making out the application.

W. J. S.

I was able to obtain the proper affidavits to prove my identity to the United States War Office with considerable trouble and anxiety. Again, I transmitted the papers signed by Squire Neville and Reverend Oxley, the Vicar, and in due course received my Land Warrant after which I notified my old friend that I wished to give it to him in his great need. It was a long time before I received an answer from my poor old doctor friend and began to imagine that he could not receive it from the hands of General Sherman. In the end his great poverty overcame all scruples, and he wrote me a friendly letter stating that his needs were so great that he had to waive all ideas of pride and hate.

Consequently I was able to transmit the warrant to General Sherman and he forwarded the same to Charleston, South Carolina, to the commandant at the Citadel. In return I have enclosed Dr. Porcher's receipt and another of General Sherman's letters:

Charleston, S.C.

September 10th, 1873.

Received of General Sherman U.S.A. Land Warrant No.113412, for one hundred and sixty (160) acres of Land given and assigned to me by John Bemrose, late private in Capt. Drane's Company 2nd Regiment of U.S. Artillery. This Warrant was received through B.L. Brigadier. General. R. A. Jackson U.S.A. at the Citadel, Charleston, S.C.

Peter Porcher, M.D.

The following is the letter from General Sherman confirming the transfer of my land to Dr. Porcher.

Headquarters Army of the United States,
Washington, D. C.

September 15th, 1873.

John Bemrose,
England.

My dear Sir,

I now enclose you the receipt of Dr. Porcher for the Land warrant you presented him.

This concludes a transaction that I hope has afforded you a real pleasure.

Truly your Friend,
W. J. Sherman,
General.

As the General surmised, it was "a real pleasure" when I learned that my fondest wish to help one who was always kind and considerate to me in years gone by, was consummated. I now possess "God's Book of Nature," a gift of the doctor, and remember the kindness he showed towards me. The Seminole War found me another true friend in General Duncan D. Clinch and I often thought about his special kindness toward me on many occasions. I never understood why a commanding general would be so friendly to one so greatly inferior. I have now learned from Dr. Porcher's letters, that the general's wife was his cousin and the general made the doctor's house his home when in the city. I am now confident that Dr. Porcher had given a good recommendation of me to the general.

After presenting the Land Warrant to Dr. Porcher, General Sherman used his authority to ensure that both the doctor and his cousin, Doctor Frank Porcher, were elected visiting surgeons to the Charleston Hospital. Both received good salaries, more than they deserved, for all the bitterness and hatred they felt towards the North and the general.

Conclusion

My reason for writing this historical tale is to show how I, supposedly brought up to play a respectable role in society, failed through a lack of self-control, owing to improper discipline during my formative years. Shortage of funds and good sense quickly reduced my station to be a member of the lowest class in society. As a consequence I saw how my stupidity brought these circumstances upon myself. I not only degraded myself, but brought great anxiety to my ever kind and loving Father. My greatest punishment was to never see him again on this side of the grave. I suffered much, but not half of what I deserve. If I had fallen to the Indian savage or to disease, it would have been my just desserts for not obeying God's command to "Honor our parents."

Osceola, the Seminole war chief, once said, "Why multiply words?" It is because I am trying to make amends. I made copies of the sixty letters written to my son, Weightman, and distributed them among my other children so that all of them may derive some benefit. By looking at my faults they may become more cautious in their own lives. My hardships experienced as a common soldier, complete with all the bloody adventures, should dissuade my children from thoughtless behavior. My story does not support the concept of military glory for I merely played a small part in executing a government bureaucratic decision at the expense of aboriginal natives being forced off their own land.

We who live inland are apt to imagine that a home on the coast would be most desirable. I had nearly four years of such a life and certainly, at first, it was most agreeable. I delighted in the freshness and diversity of the new sights, but eventually the rippling tide and beautiful expanse of ocean began to fade from my senses as I longed for the quiet and shade of the woods, or the beautiful expanse of the prairie. Occasionally I wished to be a citizen of beautiful Philadelphia, or exciting New York, but eventually I longed for the peaceful country village life once more. The truth is that we are never fully satisfied, so we should be grateful to have the changing seasons, which in their diversity give us hope.

Solomon, the wisest of men, brought everything he touched to perfection. Yet surrounded in his glory, he told us truly that it was all vanity. Therefore, may we try to fill our lives with fidelity, strive to honor God in our duty, trust in Him for our lasting inheritance, to be content in this life and, by walking in His ways, we may look to his Son for eternal life.

John Bemrose
London, England
1866

Bits and Pieces

The Watermelon

These few verses, from a Canadian newspaper, were sent to me from my cousin, Joseph Bemrose, of Montreal in 1887 and refer to the Withlacoochee River. This reminded me of the time when I was acting as secretary to General Clinch, who had referred to this river in a dispatch that he wrote to General Call, who commanded the Florida Light Horse. The poem also names many places in Florida that I knew, but it was the Withlacoochee that General Call referred to as the Rubicon in the war against the Seminole Indians.

*From the banks of old St, Mary's, From the rolling Tybee River,
From the shores of the Oconee and the classic Withlacoochee.*

*The Ogeechee, the Ocmulgee, Brier Creek and Ochlochonee.
From the Flint and the Savannah, Beautiful Altamaha and sunny
Brunswick's breezy bay.*

*Shortly comes the watermelon. Comes the Georgia watermelon.
Laden with the sweets of Southland, with the Syndicate's permission
soon will come this luscious melon, Pride of every native Georgian.*

*It will come from Chattahoochee, Milledgeville and Hatcher's
Station, Buzzard Roost and Tallapoosa, Tuckahoe and Sugar Valley,
Double Branches, Coosawattee, Nankin, Nickajack, Jamaica,
Jimps, Geneva, Marietta, Hickory Flat and Okapilco, Gully Branch,
Mazeppa, Ophir, Hard Cash, Plains of Durra, Jasper, Long Pond,
Two Run, Hannahatchee, Huckleberry, Parkins Junction, Riddleville,
Persimmon, Trickum, Hardaway, McDade, Suwannee, and from
every little clearing from Atlanta to the seashore. Where there lives a
Georgia cracker in the pride of his half acre.*

*Let it come, this watermelon, This imperial Georgia melon. Stay it
not as north it cometh, though the crop will be two millions, yet there's
room for millions more.*

Translations

Indian

Aaufka	Boiled rancid Indian corn
Alewargus Iepus	Not a rascal
Amuppa	Topmost
Cha	Good
Mico	King
Iepus	Rascal
Inclemais cha	Good
Istalusty	Black Man
Isteradka	White Man
Istichatty	An Indian
Olewargus	Bad
Oochena	Pork
Tuggilaggi	Bread
Tustenuggee	Sub-Chief

Old English

Barouche	A four-wheeled carriage
Cognomen	A nickname
Conjoined	Brought together with
Crotchets	Highly individual and often eccentric preferences
Johnny Crappeau	A Frenchman
A Pat	An Irishman
Pelf	Money or riches

Latin

Nolens Volens	Willing or unwilling
Ad Libitum	As one wishes
Medius Res	In the middle of (whatever)
Non est	Nonexistent

Sutler	A person who followed an army and sold provisions to the soldiers

Medical Terms

Bistoury	A long narrow surgical knife
Good Cicatrix	Scar of a healed wound
Ecchymosis	A small blue or purplish hemorrhagic spot on the skin
Epistaxis	Nosebleed
Erythema	Redness of the skin
Eschar	Dry scab
Femoralis	Pertaining to the thigh
Latissimus Dorsi	A broad, flat muscle on each side of the midback
Linea Alba	Fibrous band on the abdominal muscle (Hunters Line)
Liniment	A liquid preparation that is applied to the skin as a counterirritant
Os Ileum	Illiac bone-the largest bone of the pelvis
Ossi (abrev)	To convert into or cause to harden like bone
Poultice	A material used to assist in reducing inflammation
Rectus Abdominis	Long flat abdominal muscles stretching from the center of the torso back to the spinal column and from the ribcage to the pubic region
Resina	Resinic acid or salt
Ricinine	Castor oil
Sartorius	Leg muscle of the thigh
Serratus Anterior	A thin muscular sheet of the thorax

Succus glycyrrhiza	Licorice juice
Summum	Main thing
Suppurate	Formation of pus
Teres Major	A back muscle joined to the rear shoulder blade and spine
Tertian Intermittants	Intermittent fever
Tincture	A solution of alcohol or of alcohol and water, containing vegetable, animal or chemical drugs
Ung	Unguent or ointment
Venesection	Bloodletting

Army Pay

The American Amy contained a variety of nationalities including Irish, and Germans being the most numerous. The officers were scientific men, being educated at West Point, upon the Hudson River in the State of New York. The pay of the officers was ample, so they could maintain themselves looking like gentlemen. The pay and allowances for the noncommissioned grades and privates was a fair remuneration, in comparison with the commissioned grade. This new pay schedule went into effect March 25th, 1835. The following is the new pay to officers of infantry and artillery, when serving with their companies and holding no staff appointments.

Colonel:	$2,510 per year
Lieutenant Colonel:	2,088
Major:	1,822
Captain:	1,567
1st Lieutenant:	1,259
2nd Lieutenant:	887
2nd by brevet:	$ 767 per year

The pay at some stations varied on account of fuel.

Medical Staff Pay

Surgeons of 10 yrs. service:	$1,822 per year
Assist. surgeons of 10 yrs.	1,431
Under 10 years	1,530
Under 5 years	1,139
Under 2 years	$1,019 per year

N.B. There may have been a slight difference between stations.

Non-Commissioned Officers' Pay

	Former Pay Per month	New Pay Per Month
Sergeant Major	12.00	18.00
Ordinance Sergeant	12.00	17.00
Quartermaster Sergeant	12.00	16.00
Commissary Sergeants,	12.00	16.00
2nd, 3rd, & 4th	8.00	12.00
Orderly Sergeant	9.00	15.00
Corporals, 1st, 2nd, 3rd & 4th	7.00	8.00

Ordnance Sergeants were promoted on the basis of their length of service. There were none of this grade before the new act. The act furthermore specified that the clothing of the U.S. Army was to be changed from the date of the order. The undress was to consist of sky blue cloth with facings as before. The forage caps were to be made of leather and in future shoes were not to be issued to the troops. Each man would receive boots in summer and in winter. The full dress coats were of superior cloth and made after the fashion of the French military dress codes. The cap also was to be made very similar to the French, consisting of beaver with patent leather covering the crown and coming down upon the sides about an inch, with a straight peak. The facing was a tulip with an opening to receive a plume of red and white feathers, with the number of regiment and crossed cannon in front. Each soldier enlisting under the new act was to receive a military greatcoat the color of sky blue and two blankets. The prices remained the same for all grades.

Table of Clothing Allowance for the Army
in the Old Contract

Old Act Regulations	Contract	Price
Grey Jackets	3 in 5 Yrs.	1.25
White Jackets	3 in 5 Yrs.	. 56
Grey Trousers	2 pr. p.a.	. 75
White Trousers	3 pr. p.a.	. 75
Uniform Coats	5 in 5 Yrs.	4.50
Uniform Caps	2 in 5 Yrs.	2.50
Great Coats	2 in 5 Yrs.	5.00
Blankets	3 in 5 Yrs.	3.00
Flannel Shirts	2 p.a.	1.50
Cotton Shirts	2 p.a.	. 56
Stocks	3 in 5 Yrs.	. 13
Forage Caps	3 in 5 Yrs.	1.25
Stockings, Long,	2 pr. p.a.	. 35
Stockings, Short	2 pr. p.a.	. 19
Vests	2 pr. p.a.	1.75
Shoes	2 pr. p.a.	1.25
Haversacks	3 in 5 Yrs.	.20
Haversacks	2 in 3 Yrs.	.20

Table of Clothing Allowance for the Army
in the New Contract

New Act Regulations	Contract	Price
Sergeants Uniform Coats	2 in 3 Yrs.	7.25
Sergeants Trousers	2 pr. p.a.	2.00
Corp. Uniform Coats	2 in 3 Yrs.	6.75
Pvt. Uniform Coats	2 in 3 Yrs.	6.25
Greatcoats	1 in 3 Yrs.	8.00
Blankets	2 in 3 Yrs.	3.00
Undress Jackets	2 in 3 Yrs.	2.25
Undress Jackets, White	2 in 3 Yrs.	.56
Blue Trousers	2 pr. p.a.	1.25
White Trousers	3 pr. p.a.	.50
Uniform Caps	2 in 3 Yrs.	2.75
Forage Caps	2 in 3 Yrs.	1.25
Flannel Shirts	2 p.a.	1.50
Cotton Shirts	2 p.a.	.56
Stocks	2 in 3 Yrs.	.13
Stockings, long	4 p.a.	.35
Boots	4 pr. p.a.	1.75

Seminole Chiefs of the Second Seminole War

Osceola, Asceola, Osini-ola, Assiniya-hola, Powell: These are the various names attributed to this man, who became famous during the Second Seminole War. The word Osceola is derived from Asse, the black psychic drink, which the Indians used to purify themselves prior to going into council or the corn dance festival. The drink acted as an emetic, but the Indians believed it had the moral effect of cleansing the body of all untruths. Ola is a cataract. The full translation means, The gurgling or noisy tea drinker. He was aptly named for that was how he drank the potion. When I knew him at Fort King he was a subchief, or Tustenuggee. Before he became Osceola or Rising Sun, he belonged to the Talcy tribe, but later joined with the Miccasukys, under Olate-Mico, or Blue King. He was one-fourth Indian, his mother having married a Scotchman. He was about thirty years old, light complexion, grey-green eyes, somewhat effeminate, five foot ten inches tall, slender, small feet, swelling nostrils, curling lips and an expressive countenance with piercing eyes. His profile was more striking than his full face. He had an easy grace, a stealthy step, and vibrant spring. He had two wives who were both young and pretty. I even had a portrait of one, Peoka and her child.

Osceola had a fair degree of sarcasm. On one occasion, while he was acting as guide to a party of horsemen, he found that they were moving too slow and inquired the reason, to find out that it was on his account. With one of those smiles he alone could give, he bade them proceed more rapidly. They put spurs to their steeds and he, afoot, kept up with them during the entire route, not showing any fatigue. At the end of the day he arrived at the appointed destination, with the same vigor as those who were mounted.

Hicts: He was the nephew of King Payne, who was killed in action in 1812. When hostilities began he was about eighty, and upon the death of Islapoopaya was chosen as the top chief, although he was neither the son of Payne, nor Bowlegs Stiarky, who was next in authority and also a nephew of Payne. Bowlegs stood up for his rights against Hicts for just two days before conceding. Hicts had two wives; one was a very pretty squaw and the other a half-breed Negress who was very ugly, so the old man delighted in extremes.

Micanopy: His name comes from Mico, meaning a king, and Amuppa, meaning topmost. Short, very fat with heavy dull eyes set in a bloated and carbuncled face. He was ignorant, unrefined, sluggish, and dirty, with a mind suited to his physique, unlike other chiefs who were fond of finery. His dress consisted of a loose check frock reaching to the middle of his thighs; a common worsted belt secured his waist; his head was wrapped in a cotton handkerchief; his legs were bare, but he wore moccasins. Micanopy had three wives, one Indian and two Negroes. The black ladies were his favorites. At Payne's Landing, after having double rations, he complained of being hungry. He owned nearly one hundred Negroes and a large stock of cattle and horses. When Hicts died, Micanopy became the great Pond Governor and wore a crown, which was given to Cow Keeper, uncle of the elder Payne, by the British government, for his aid in the American revolution. Micanopy harbored old prejudices that originated during the Jackson campaigns against the American Indians and said that he would not comply with the Treaty of Payne's Landing. He said that he would prefer to be shot upon his native soil, rather than be expatriated. In council he seldom spoke and sat with a vacant expression.

Jumper, or Otemathla: He was a Seminole, although he denied it and objected to being called one. He boasted that he was descended from a distinguished race, of which he was the sole survivor. He was tall, well proportioned, with a long narrow face, small keen eyes and a prominent nose. Overall he had a repulsive sinister countenance. Jumper was a brave warrior who became famous in the war with Jackson. He was a good speaker and first orator in council with a great deal of common sense.

Abraham, or Yobly: He was the chief interpreter and succeeded Jumper as "Sense Carrier" to Micanopy. Yobly was a Negro slave who ran away from his white masters while he was a boy in

Pensacola. Like most Negroes he dreaded going anywhere that would restore him as property. At forty-five years of age he had a large frame, square face, and thick full lips. He was plausible, pliant, but deceitful, for under an exterior of profound meekness he hid a persona bent on dark and bloody purposes. He displayed more sense than all the Indians and Negroes I saw at Camp King, and I believe that he was the prime mover behind the rebellion. I remember having an instinctive aversion to him and could not imagine any Indian that would be more cruel or implacable.

King Philip (Eamatla): He was a grey-headed chief with very fierce features, rendered more harsh by the age lines on his face. It was plain to see that he was an implacable foe.

Cloud: A great fighter and had an agreeable expression.

Coahadgo (She-Wolf): He always looked depressed. He was fond of his children and when caressing them, there seemed to be gleams of kindness upon his face.

Mackenzie: The chief of the bloody Miccasukys. He was a ferocious but good-looking warrior, although his mustache was going grey. He was a very self-willed and desperate looking Indian, who was responsible for the murder of Private Dalton, a mail carrier.

Charley Omathla: A genial, warmhearted Indian, full of fun and jokes and always a cheery smile to greet you with. His nature was not wholly Indian, for he gave one the impression of a comfortable and rather jovial farmer dressed in Indian clothes. He was very wealthy with a large herd of cattle and was a good friend to all. He was frequently seen at General Clinch's quarters. One of our artillery sergeants had serious thoughts of marrying one of Charley's daughters and becoming a cattle grazier in Florida, had not the war and Charley's murder frustrated his ambitions.

Black Dirt: As his name implied, he was an inane-looking person, yet he was a staunch supporter of the whites.

There were many other Indian chiefs whom I saw in conversation with General Clinch at Fort King, but I took little notice of them. They reminded me of gypsies who were commonly seen on English country roads. They were also athletic men of fine stature. General Clinch was a tall man but many chiefs towered over him. They were more lithe but not as strong as their comparable white man in a fair fight.

The following are the various Indian towns and sites of the Seminole Tribe, which were extracted during a talk held by General Jackson with the Chiefs Blount, Nea-thoe-o-Mathla and Mulatto King at Pensacola on 19th September 1821.

Editor's Note: Most of these names no longer exist, especially with the current spelling. I suspect that since they were not written down on any map they were phonetically transcribed during conversation. I have included current possible names in italics.

1. Red Town at Tampa Bay

2. Oc-back-o-nay-yake, above Tampa

3. O-po-nays. Town in the back of Tampa.

4. Tots-ta-la-houts-ka, or Watermelon Town, on the coast, west of Tampa Bay. The greater part of these inhabitants fled from the Upper Creeks.

5. A-ha-pok-ka (*Apopka*), situated back of the Mosquito.

6. Low-walta Village, composed of those who fled from Coosa and followed McQueen and Francis as their prophets.

7. McQueens Village on the east side of Tampa Bay.

8. A-lack-away-talofa, in the *Alachua* plains; populous. Took-o-sai-mothly was the chief.

9. Santa-fee-talofa (*Santafe*), at the east fork of the Suwana. Lock-taw-me-cookey was the chief.

10. Waw-ka-saw-su, on the east side of the Suwana's (*Suwanacoochee Spring*) mouth, on the seaboard. These were from the Coosa River and followers of McQueen and Francis.

11. Old Suwannee Town. Burnt in 1818, on the Suwannee River. These were from the Tallapoosa towns and the upper creeks.

12. Ala-pa-ha-tolafa (*Alapaha River*), West of the Suwannee and east of the Miccasuky (*Miccosukee*). The chief, Okmulgee, was lately dead.

13. Wa-cissa-talofa (*Wacissa*), near the head of St. Marks River. These were natives of Florida.

14. Tallahassee, on the waters of the Miccasuky Pond (*Miccosukee Lake*). The natives have lived there a long period. Had about 100 warriors.

15. Top-ke-gabga (*Topeka*), on the east side of the O-clock-ney (Ochlockonee) near Tallahassee.

16. We-thoe-cachy-talofa (*Withlacoochee*), between the St. Marks and O-clock-ney rivers, in the fork of the latter.

17. O-chuce-ulga (*Ocoee*), east of the *Apalachicola*, where Hambly and Blunt lived. About 250 souls. Cothum was the chief.

18. Choco-nickle Village. The chief was Nea-thoe-o-motla and the second chief was Mulatto King, They were raised here, had about 60 warriors. Located on the west side of the Apalachicola.

19. Top-hulgar. This village was joined to Choco-nickle. The warriors were raised in East Florida, and removed there.

20. Tock-to-oth-la. West of Fort Scott and *Chattahoochee*. Ten miles above the forks. 40 or 50 warriors were raised at the O-cun-oha-ta or red ground and moved down to this location.

21. O-chu-po-crasse (*Ochopee*) was another town in East Florida. These were moved down from the Upper Creeks with about 30 warriors and a great many women and children to settle

there.

Settlements in East Florida:

22. Pelacle-ca-ha. This was the residence of Micanopy; chief of the Seminoles situated about 120 miles south of Alachua.

23. Chu-ku-chatta (*Chukuemeka*).

25. Hich-a-pul-susse. Located about 20 miles southeast of Chu-ku-chatta, at the same distance from the head of Tampa.

26. Big Hammock settlement. The most numerous north of Tampa Bay and west of He-ca-pul-sussee.

27. Oo-la-wa-haw (*Ocklawaha*) on the river of that name, west of the St. Johns.

28. Mulatto Girl's Town, South of Caskawilla (*Tuscawilla*) Lake.

29. Bucker Woman's Town, near Long Swamp, east of Big Hammock.

30. King Heifahs south and Payne's Negro settlements in Alachua; those are belonging to the Seminoles, in all about 500.

31. John Hicts Town. West of Payne's Savannah, Miccasuky.

32. O-he-a-fenoke (*Okefenokee*) Swamp. South side, a number of Cow-otas.

33. Beech Creek. Settlement of Cheehaws.

34. Spring Garden. Above Lake George. Uchee Billy, their Chief, was killed by General Shelton.

35. South of Tampa, near Charlottes Bay, Choctaws.

At the time all the Indians in Florida were estimated to number about 5,000.

Bemrose Reflections

American Slavery and Civil War Reflections

To keep a Negro is the greatest roguery the World has produced.

"Mankind is disposed to deluding ourselves with wicked ideas that spring from a selfish love of power and oppression and we use this ability to deceive our consciences in order to subjugate others. The greatest example in our time is American Slavery. Murder, robbery, and lust take possession of its abettors, while the most liberal government substantiates the injustice in law, which must inevitably lead to destruction. How many times I met with Southerners who were most amiable, kind, and friendly. But such behavior was just a facade for the stranger, especially to an Englishman, for they valued us more than their Northern countrymen. But let an English visitor mention the heinousness of slavery, their attitude changed immediately. How many times I heard Negroes being taunted by white Americans, such as 'You damned nigger, stand out of my way.' Following the Dade Massacre I noted how Negroes joined their Indian brothers in killing the wounded and how they came upon the dying soldiers shouting, 'What have you got to sell?' The same insult that was so frequently used against them at the Tampa Bay slave market."

I wrote those words when I was a young man in America, without realizing that I would be vindicated in my lifetime, as I read about the carnage of the American Civil War I am reminded about what I witnessed and how I felt. I saw for myself how the system nourished the sins of murder, dishonesty, cruelty, drunkenness, idleness, and the debauchery of rape and incestuous intercourse and how it affected the whole community. Southern aristocracy deluded themselves into a macabre belief of superior genealogical origins and boasted about their idle dignity. These assumed rights manifested themselves not with kindness, compassion, and generosity upon a helpless subjected people, but with oppression and barbarity and disdain. The false ministers of religion who mitigated the offenses only listened to the oppressor, whose wealth and status blinded them to the plight of their black brethren and to the enormous sin of Slavery.

I was blind not to foresee that such a trade was doomed and yet I did not expect that twenty-seven years later the perpetrators would suffer the consequences of their sin. Now we witness the Judgment of the Lord, who has summoned the vultures to gloat over their battlefields. All foul birds are satiated by the horrid repast and brood amidst the desolation of the land. The oppressors reap as they have sown and receive a deserved punishment. Humanity now lies in heaps, all a result of the mad ambition of men who stirred up strife and set brother against brother and father against son. Who could have imagined these consequences? We English are sick of the bloodshed and horror of this war, believing Americans to be fools for engaging in such fratricidal strife.

I am ashamed to say that my own countrymen are hypocrites. These British Isles, who set their captives free many years ago, are strong adherents of the South; while professing to hate slavery they are lured by greed and profits and join in the trade by assisting with aid. Once we begin to tamper with our conscience we forfeit all principle and conscience.

This is easy to say, as men have always inflicted misery on the defenseless and motivated their impressionable and ignorant youth to fight their battles. We will continue to cut each other's throats until all our demons are satiated and put to rest. In the meantime America groans and mourns, wives are made widows and childless, while cities and towns are laid waste. The curse of sin is like a knife to one's own throat, which only the Almighty in his mercy can remove. Know your own sins and see how they increase until they become unbearable. Unless we repent, sin will carry us to infamy, destruction, and death.

Now let all men beware, these four million black slaves are equal to all men of whatever color, nation, or tongue. Since they are subjected by white men, they are the oppressed and we are the oppressors. We are the fallen, the persecutors, whilst they patiently wait for freedom. Shame upon shame should Christendom ever again use the scriptures to keep them in bondage. The ministers of God are sent to protect the poor and innocent, but when they neglect their vocation, they lose grace and eventually lose their souls. Such men deserve no sympathy, for even during the rebellion they exhibited extreme cruelty, especially after defeats when they murdered those with whom they did not agree.

Humanity is the same everywhere, becoming tyrannical and unjust when left to himself. God's judgments seem to come late, but come they surely do, for the time of reckoning must come to all of us. Our sojourn here is short, our lifespan of seventy years is but as gnats in the sunshine. If we perceived it that way, then maybe with His grace we would try more earnestly to do our duty fearlessly for good, casting aside sinful ways and living in peace and harmony as becomes a true Christian. Yet look at Christians of today and see how many sects there are of Christ's followers, each acting as if they were the chosen ones, divided up and preferring one or another due to some minor doctrinal point or method of practice.

Surely a new and better era is looming for the future as the whites should now begin to see the wrong heaped upon the blacks. They are God's people like you and I and have patiently waited for their freedom. With slavery dead and the hatred purged, I see all the peoples of Florida amalgamating, with all free men to come and go and each to use his own strength and energies that God has so equally bestowed to all. It is my hope that the poor white will seek useful pursuits where industrial rivalry supersedes his past life of listlessness and indiscipline. He should put aside his horse racing, raccoon baiting and bear hunting so that a drunken, reckless, and degraded heathen may give birth to future generations of enlightened Christian men, where people of all shades and politics would be viewed as one Christian brotherhood.

This is my hope for the future of Florida and the other Southern states. For I have a vision of teeming races of mankind amalgamating and loving each other as children of God, making the fair lands of the South one sea of wealth and plenty. It is my fondest wish that the eight million poor whites of the South shall be the instrument to free the four million blacks from bondage. For this honorable act, God in His mercy will raise them up to the highest dignity of man. Abraham Lincoln is worthy of such an honor and that should forever be enshrined in the hearts of future generations.

Death of a President

April 27, 1865: Yesterday evening I had just written about the murder of a United States soldier by Louisianans and as I lay down my pen the mail arrived, bringing news of the assassination of that good and great man, President Lincoln. The assassin was most probably a Southerner. I heard from Grantham and it was confirmed in the newspaper that with Lincoln dead Mr. Seward was also likely to die. I knew Southerners first-hand and they would, if wronged, spill the blood of their best friend. I was filled with apprehension all last night regarding the report.

I hoped against hope that this humane, blessed man, and staunch friend of the Negroes would live to see the results of his labors. It was a tragedy for him to be taken away at the very time his beneficial plans were about to be consummated, and to be denied, during his declining years, the comfort of seeing prosperity grow in the land he had redeemed. Future generations of blacks and whites will revere President Lincoln as a great and noble man and grant him equal prestige with the world-renowned George Washington. I long admired his great courage, his modesty, and his honesty of purpose and believe he departed this world a saint, destined for eternal glory, enshrined in the hearts of Americans, who will mourn him for many years.

Lincoln spoke prophetically about his own demise and was willing to die for his great cause. He said:"I feel that I cannot succeed without Divine aid, upon which I rely and always sustained me." More than once he told his audience:"Again, I bid you all an affectionate farewell." They prayed for him, but were unable to protect him and save him.

When I learned that the president was shot, I realized how the stigma of assassination reflected upon England. J. Wilkes Booth is a Southerner by birth, but his progeny is English. He is the son of Junius Brutus Booth, an actor at Covent Garden, and Mary Holmes. With a few facts and immature wisdom I have made a case, a tale of contrasts, which I will share with you.

Randal J. Agostini

Self-revealing truths and the acquisition of knowledge, under God, even by a poor man, may raise him to distinction and compare him equally with others born into a higher station. However, wisdom must be accompanied with training in self-control, a benefit that bestows a much greater chance for happiness. Lincoln was raised in a slave state. His father was a poor white, too poor to possess a slave. He had a Christian mother, whose ambition was that her son should learn to read well enough to study his Bible, a reason perhaps as to why he was named Abraham. His early training and family duties made him industrious, while his earnings from his manual labor were used to further his education to become a lawyer. His character, dedication, and reputation made him an attorney of some distinction. Later he became a senator and lastly the president of one of the greatest nations in the World.

This was the man whom Sir Alexander Beresford Hope, one of our English magnates, distastefully called "The Rail Splitter," which emphasizes how our foolish nobility and gentry degrade manual labor. Yet when adversity comes to any of them, they become poor and discontented and unable to provide for themselves. This seems to have been the case with Junius Brutus Booth, the murderer's father, who was the son of a respectable London attorney who moved in influential circles and led a genteel lifestyle in society. The Wilkes came from his mother's maiden name. Junius Booth entered the Navy, then tried the law, then printing, and eventually became an actor. It was said that he always complained about his bad luck, but it may have been his indifferent training that led him to be a dissatisfied young man. He was passionate, willful, and irresolute and never able to understand that it was his lack of self-control that created his own disappointments. He never followed the rules of his father's house, which estranged him from his family and caused him to leave home to become an actor. Then there was a quarrel with a fellow actor, whom he nearly murdered in a jealous rage, whereupon he fled to the United States. His son became the assassin of the president of the United States of America.

The backgrounds of Lincoln and Booth were starkly different, but one distinction between the two shows that Lincoln was raised in a God-loving family. Surely our existence is meaningless if we are not properly trained in our youth? I count myself as one of those wretched ancestors who should have behaved more wisely than selfishly. My unflagging attention to my business for the past twenty years has secured a little money, less the sense to use it properly. I should have been a better example. Wealth without Godliness is not gain, but just another vanity.

I hope that God and you, my son, and my other children forgive me this great wrong. Industry, together with a good example, with the love and fear of God, ought to go hand in hand. Through such example the children of our generation may become self-controlled, loving, and courteous, not only within the family, but also within society.

Major Gates

November 1868: I have just cut out of an American newspaper the following last memento of Major Gates.

"The first cadet ever entered at West Point, Colonel Gates, was buried from Trinity Church, New York, on Saturday last. After honorable service of more than half a century, he had reached only the pay of a Colonel and the brevet rank of Brigadier General. Colonel Gates was older than General Scott or General Jackson. He was a nephew of General Gates, of revolutionary memory. He had fought bravely in the last War with England and was present at the capture of York, now Toronto. He had served long and faithfully in the Indian wars and captured the great Indian chief Osceola in Florida. He had distinguished himself in the Mexican war."

I knew Major Gates during my service in Florida and frequently wrote about him in my letters. He was a most kind and human man, a great stickler for sobriety, most gentlemanly, and one whom I thought would become most successful. I remember when he was unfairly court-martialed and confirmed by General Scott, just before I left Florida. His brother, Captain Gates, died at Fort Drane. I see that the major had to wait half a century to obtain the rank of a brevet general, while hosts of younger men walked over his head.

This shows that promotion comes neither to the strong nor the gentle and deserving, but more often to those of a more adventurous spirit. It is probably better this way, for the major lived to a great old age and was probably happier in a more humble position than his peers.

The General Belknap Scandal

The *Daily Telegraph*'s correspondent wrote from New York on March 3, 1876. The week yielded two sensations. The first was a revival of the Emma Mine Scandal and the other referred to the Post Tradership corruption practiced by General William W. Belknap, the secretary of war, and his wife, for which he was eventually impeached. This time he was arraigned for the Fort Sill Tradership that was shown to be only part of a system which had prevailed since his appointment to the War Department. The general had friends in high places and was able to receive bribes and conceal his crime from the public eye year after year.

In 1874 a Captain George T. Robinson of Baltimore visited Washington, and gave the president the names of officers who were involved with the Tradership frauds. Captain Robinson had obtained an affidavit from one of the traders that stated the exorbitant charges were necessary to enable them to pay General Belknap a fee of $15,000 a year for the privilege they possessed. The president ignored the information and Belknap responded by bringing Captain Robinson before a military tribunal of junior officers and had him cashiered. Rank was no guarantee, for when General B. W. Hazen was in command of camp supply in the Indian Territory, he found out and reported that the post trader at the camp was also paying Secretary Belknap an annual fee. General Hazen was promptly removed to a more remote posting.

Upon reading this news I recalled those trying five weeks of November and December in 1831, when I was stationed upon Bedloe's Island. How I suffered terribly from the cold and insufficient rations so that the then Captain Belknap could line his pockets. One step invariably led to many more, and Mrs. Belknap also publicly acknowledged her extravagance during their Washington posting, which truly shows that the seductions of the world are often more than humanity can withstand. Though I did feel sorry for him in his current disgraced circumstances, I was not surprised that he had moved on to greater dishonest dealings.

I knew him as a handsome man favored by nature, who had a military band under his command. He used his authority to take the band to New York City to play dance music at assemblies where there were rich and powerful men. He was a welcome visitor, but such performances required great expense, which was beyond the pay of a captain. This was the beginning of a dishonest association with his noncommissioned officers, who helped him embezzle the necessary funds.

The American

After General Gaines's troops arrived at Fort Drane, we had to look after eighty of them who were driven crazy through famine. They were reduced to miserable creatures for whom I had to find shelter. It was then I witnessed the greatness of the American skill as a wood craftsmen. A large force of axe men immediately set to work, and within three days, they erected and covered in a large wooden building of two stories made entirely of pine, including the supports, rafters, shingling, and clapboards. It was a wonderful experience for this Englishman and other aliens to witness their extraordinary energy and ability in response to an emergency. The great power of the American woodsman to clear and create is scarcely credible.

We English are too eager to ridicule our American brothers who share our language. Our supercilious nature toward all countries springs from our isolation born of self-sufficiency. It is a consequence of ignorance. A perfect example occurred during a recent visit I made to Lord Duncannon's Woods and Forests Office in London. While waiting to see Mr. Phillips, the chief clerk, I was introduced to another clerk who had recently arrived from the United States. Upon hearing my accent he answered in a drawling self-sufficient tone, "Ah, a nation of hewers of wood and drawers of water." This poor inflated scribbler was obviously no witness to what I had seen, otherwise his own insignificance would have held his tongue and he would have learned a lesson not to speak despairingly of other nations. When a fool gets wrapped up in his own esteem, how can he come to learn about his own lack of knowledge?

John Bull is often depicted with ape's ears, which may suit him, for the majority of our people are willfully ignorant about America and Americans. I predict that before many generations pass, America will supersede England in education, knowledge, and skill. They already exceed us in shipbuilding, telegraphy, and photography because they are more energetic and hungry to learn. We restrict our knowledge to ten thousand of the upper class, for our main goal is to obtain wealth and independence and then keep it. Once we possess wealth we bask in pride and become aloof to all who have less prosperity. A rich Englishman is seldom open to criticism.

Americans believe that independence is the zenith of their existence. They do not give up easily and if misfortune strikes, buoyed up by their self-dependence, they will rise like a phoenix ready to soar from its ashes.

Throughout life we garner many misconceptions, especially if we do not go with the crowd. Some criticism is probably deserved, but there are times when someone that we love or trust strikes us down, almost crushing the life out of us. It is then that we poor mortals may recall the commendation of our superiors, teachers, pastors, and masters of former days. It is probably better to leave such things to God and to put our trust in Him, yet within our nature there is a longing for recognition and appreciation from those that we trust and love. When I am in need of such comfort my mind inevitably reverts to my American friends and comrades, many of whom were closer than a brother. They were true friends, cast in adverse circumstances. When I was sick they tended to me and when I was sorrowful they comforted me.

Afterword

Spiritual and Other Insights

Editor's Note: Throughout John's letters there was a constant thread of spiritual and other reflections which overlaid his experiences to form sermons for the benefit of his children. I removed them from the text to provide continuity to his story, but they are presented here because they form an integral part of his character. They are presented in alphabetical order.

Christianity: A true believer is not selfish, but loving, morally true in all his dealings, full of compassion, gracious, and patient under difficulties. A Christian man must not cause the world to judge him as a fool. A true follower of Christ should be wise, noble, and just.

Church: I had the opportunity to attend church weekly, but spent those leisure hours reading. I only remember one occasion when I went to a place of worship. Scripture says: "He that hath not the Son, hath not the Father," and I am a witness to this great truth. When I think of our past life, I wonder how Scofield, Potter, and I did not sink lower. I have to thank God for rescuing us from Florida so that we could find Him later, for our sake and that of his children.

Death: The death of my Father was like a dagger to my heart. I blame myself for the monstrosity of my heartless conduct and the guilt I feel in running away. Thoughtless youth should beware! Filial obedience brings a blessing. Those who do not seek the approval of their superiors, or value what is good, possess little that is praiseworthy and, as a consequence, do little for the benefit of others.

Disregard: It is wrong to ignore anyone. We display this cruel behavior through silence, a disdainful toss, an impertinent shrug, a foolish whistle, and even careless attention to duty. All of which emanates from the sin of pride and self-love.

Friendship: Though it is our duty as parents to choose our companions carefully, it is a family failing to seek the company of inferiors, if only to look better than others. We should recognize that there are wicked men to whom we ought to give a wide berth and seek associations with those who are discreet and just. I hope I have been a good example so my children do not become proud, but that they should possess sufficient self-respect to free them from mean and groveling companions. Neither do I wish them to shun the poor who may be God's humble children. I do wish them to be gentle men and women professing God as their father.

God's Grace: We receive God's grace every moment of every day, yet we are thankless creatures who seldom remember our most gracious Father. No wonder we so easily forget our earthly friends and benefactors. When placed in situations beyond our control, how readily we seek the help of the Almighty who is ever gracious. Only God can guide us and give us His love and affection when all earthly things fail us. We are incapable of doing good by ourselves, so we look to Him in prayer for He has promised His help to conquer our infirmities.

God permits poverty and misfortune to fall upon his children for a wise purpose. When we become intoxicated with our success, we forget the source of our bounty. Through our misfortune we receive the opportunity to renew our faith to thank "the Giver."

Gossip: Be careful who you choose as your associates and be discreet with all who are about you. Especially avoid those that gossip for they are not safe as companions or friends. People full of chatter must inevitably injure someone, and they waste time, which is not theirs to lose, and cause their listeners to do likewise. Time is worth money and lost time is more precious, for it is irretrievable. We must use our opportunities to the best of our ability, so that we may not repent when old age or sickness comes upon us, as it must come to all.

Greener Pastures: When I was a youth I read the novel *Robinson Crusoe*, in which a sailor's life was portrayed as being exciting and adventurous, which made me yearn to see the world. Some books may portray an author's lively imagination, for the life of a sailor is arduous and hazardous. Sea life may be tolerable for a short voyage, but the discomfort and filth soon make it unbearable. I learned that what often appeals to our imagination is not so in reality. The truth may be a life of hardship or danger.

Infidelity: When a man fosters unfaithful ideas, he leaves himself open to wickedness.

Impulsiveness: In whatever we do, may we do it thoughtfully and conscientiously, using our judgment with fear lest we come up short of what is expected of us as accountable beings.

Integrity: Guard yourself against those that want to use or compromise you with persuasive arguments. Evil can be attractive with temptations of wealth, position, or influence. God will not bless us with prosperity unless it is arrived at honestly. Give me a man who is thoughtful before he speaks, unafraid to admit his mistakes, ready to expose error, and unwilling to please a wicked person. I would rather my children suffer deprivation than resort to dishonorable work, or live meanly by the sweat of the oppressed. Though misfortune may come, we should stay the course, trust in God, and strive to do our best for industry provides comfort, if not competency.

Liquor: Almost all of Company D were spirit drinkers, with rum being the greatest negative influence in the lives of American servicemen. It was the chief cause of sickness amongst the troops. I wish that sugarcane had never been distilled, for alcoholic spirits create a thirst that is never quenched. Drunkenness leads a drinker to a temporary false sense of elation, which rapidly renders one incapable of proper thought and physical capability, sometimes leading to death. There were about five groggeries along the main street in St. Augustine and about the same number in my own village. Most of the accidents reported in our newspapers are the result of the use of liquor. I hope that God saves mankind from this destructive habit and shows us a way to close down liquor stores and drinking houses. If poverty is the natural consequence of drunken extravagance, then I say let it come, if it is the only means to effect a cure.

Love: Honorable and happy people live to overcome evil by good. Through the assistance of God, we can change our hearts and minds and subdue all envious feelings of others. With a keen sense of sympathy, let kindness be our daily motto, so that we may follow in the footsteps of the One who never told us a wrong, or created one.

Morality: When foolish men forsake the decrees of our Creator and make laws to suit themselves, then we must eventually fail and fall, for society cannot successfully war against itself. Our choice is between good and evil. Choose good and the Almighty is at our side, choose evil and the propensities of man's nature lead us to perdition. Prospects on earth will wither, life wasted, lost to good intentions and purposes. We become a burden to ourselves, our friends, and family and eventually lose all hope, with nothing to show for our existence.

Purpose: *Quid futurum sit, necessimus.* "It is necessary to live for something." The best way for us to live is to acknowledge our daily mercies and to strive to live in the fear and love of God. The truest bravery of all springs from Christian principles. A godly man does not pursue personal desire, but the unselfish welfare of his neighbor. He believes in and tries to live by the rule of doing to others as he would would have them do unto him. When he fails, he is sorry, admits his faults, and tries again until he succeeds. With God's grace he fights evil every day, but when he does wrong, he goes to those that have suffered because of him and seeks their forgiveness, or he makes amends, then he goes to his heavenly parent to be healed.

Salvation: The first wish of any man is the well-being of his children, who are daily exposed to the evil forces of the world. If children learn the benefits of a pure and enriching Christian life they will grow in the love of God, whose grace will become an everlasting gift. Too often faith is regarded as foolishness and despised by intellectual men. Yet if those with a superior intellect put their hearts toward the honest study of it, they would most assuredly succumb to its gracious and abundant influence. Putting our faith in the work of man damages our influence for doing good and endangers our eternal joy.

Sin: We inhabit a fallen world, causing strife in the workplace, the alehouse, and at home. When sin contaminates a household in selfishness toward one another, it destroys relationships and cultivates suspicion and hate, instead of clinging one to another for mutual protection. I daily read the sordid details of failed family life and believe this human misery must be so to bring us nearer to our Maker.

Smoking: Cigars were manufactured in St Augustine and were commonly used by both men and women. It was normal while taking a stroll in the city to come across a group of ladies puffing cigars. They were a cheap but harmful narcotic stimulant that promoted idleness. Cigar and tobacco smoking is now becoming a popular habit in England, even with the heavy duty, and I fear that it will become the root cause for smokers to neglect their responsibilities.

Suffering: We have to suffer trials every day, but what poor creatures we would be without them. Our problems help us to develop patience and strength to overcome them. How selfish and thoughtless we would be without our own suffering. It is selfish to destroy our own happiness by harboring insult in our hearts, for malicious feelings are so deceitful that many have destroyed their own lives by constantly hating others as well as themselves. The world would be a dismal place if our hearts dwelled in malice.

"My Lord, you have preserved me in much suffering and danger. Your hand has protected me through it all and I give you all my thanks. Blessed be thy Holy Name."

Teachers: The schoolmaster would stand preeminent before the public if he would, by example, make his profession more Godlike through his teaching and daily routine. The young mind is ever ready to be impressed with whatever is set before him, whether for good or evil. Unfortunately as independence and money grow in importance, teachers barter their knowledge, which has an ill effect upon the generations to come.

Tipping: We English find fault with the American habit of tipping. Should not workers have a stated salary, so they know what finance they have to live on? Would it not mean that they would become more thoughtful and self controlled? During the old coach days I witnessed disgraceful behavior when honorable men, modest ladies, and the timid have been taken advantage of by a dishonest driver. I have also seen rich scoundrels walk away free following a disgraceful war of words. How insensitive it is to go and eat a meal and then feel obliged to the service, to avoid suffering, or to receive special service on your next visit. The custom of tipping leaves all to the mercy and possible abuse of a servant. What else but tips could have degraded our fellow humans to a class, to be known as and insulted by the title, Lackey! What an abominable name for an otherwise honorable person. It is not the servitude that is degrading, but the associated habits, of which tipping is the worst.

Vanity: When I recall my written exploits in Florida, I notice how the pages are filled with vanity borne of self-complacency. I used to consider that Scofield, Potter, and I were superior to the majority of other soldiers, but now see that I judged from a very low standard. We certainly received the respect, approval, and praise from our superior officers for sobriety and strict attention to our duties. But I now realize in my heart how I was not conscious of my many infirmities and immature ignorance. If only I had known God, what a different example I could have been. Instead we formed a clique and held ourselves aloof from the drunkard, the swearer, and the thief. In my position as steward, I had the opportunity of viewing many sides of human nature and found the drunkard was often the most tender-hearted, the swearer hated a lie, and the thief and whoremonger abhorred themselves. If we had focused on our own deficiencies, we would have become aware of the goodness of God even amongst our most wretched comrades.

Veracity: Lying is Satan's great strategy. White lies, exaggerations, or even those in jest darken our soul and prepare the way for greater error. Lie upon lie leads us to where we find we cannot avoid them, for they become the first option at every difficulty or danger. We deceive ourselves to protect our vanity, pride, and false self-righteousness. Keep us humble, Lord, and free our hearts to harbor truth in all circumstances. For truth will always maintain our self-respect and dignity. None of us are safe without our Maker's influence, for left to ourselves we are adrift without a rudder or compass.

Work: No calling, however menial, can degrade a true Christian for, like Paul, they feel it is better to gain Christ through honest industry. Be humble and content to secure a decent living, for enough is as good as a feast. Labor is honorable, and Christians' desire is to assist their fellow man through honest labor in their respective callings rather than to seek the world's esteem through position. Such a man was Lincoln who, from splitting rails, raised himself to be the president of a great nation. We should not malign such men. In England we also have noblemen and merchants who delight in work. Many men of higher class have learned that labor has ennobled their position. Surely labor should have the respect of all and idleness the reprobation of all.